The Lalita-Vistara: Or Memoirs Of The Early Life Of Sakya Sinha

Rajendralala Mitra

BIBLIOTHECA INDICA;

A

COLLECTION OF ORIENTAL WORKS

PUBLISHED BY THE

ASIATIC SOCIETY OF BENGAL.

New Series, No. 455.

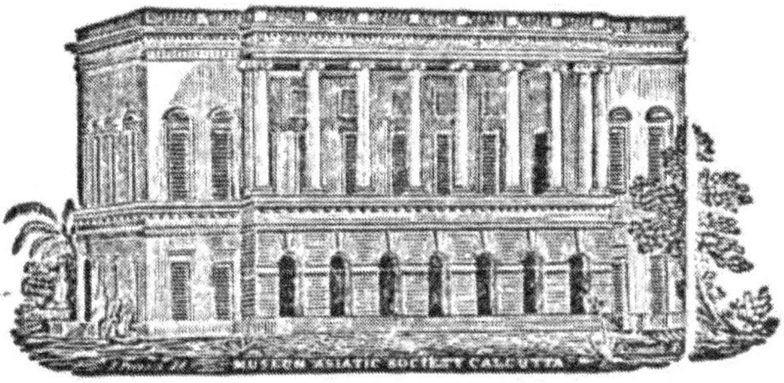

THE

LALITA-VISTARA,

OR

MEMOIRS OF THE EARLY LIFE OF S'A'KYA SIÑHA.

TRANSLATED FROM THE ORIGINAL SANSKRIT.

BY

RA'JENDRALA'LA MITRA, LL. D., C. I. E.,

FASCICULUS I.

CALCUTTA:

PRINTED BY J. W. THOMAS, BAPTIST MISSION PRESS,

AND PUBLISHED BY THE

ASIATIC SOCIETY, 57, PARK STREET.

1881.

LALITA-VISTARA.

CHAPTER I.

INTRODUCTORY DISCOURSE.

INTRODUCTION.—Bhagaván at S'rávastí—his followers—is absorbed in Samádhi—Devaputras request him to recite the Lalita-Vistara—its contents—Bodhisattvas and S'rávakas solicit Bhagaván to recite the same—Bhagaván vouchsafes their request.

Om ![1] Salutation to all Buddhas,[2] Bodhisattvas, Áryas, S'rávakas and Pratyeka Buddhas[3] of all times, past, present and future; who are adored throughout the farthest limitless boundary of the ten quarters of the globe (*Lokadhátu*).[4]

It has thus been heard by me,[5] that once on a time Bhagaván[6] sojourned in the garden of ANÁTHAPIṆḌADA at Jetavana in S'rávastí[7], accompanied by a venerable body of twelve thousand Bhikshukas[8] who had the following for their foremost; namely ;—Jṇána-kauṇḍilya,[9] As'vajit, Váshpa, Mahánámá, Bhadrika, Yas'odeva, Vimala, Subáhu, Púrṇa,[10] Gavámpati, Uruvilla-kás yapa, Nadí-kás'yapa, Gayá-kás'yapa, S'áriputra,[11] Mahá-maudgalyáyana, Mahá-kás'yapa, Mahá-kátyáyana, Kaphila, Kauṇḍilya, Chunanda, Maitráyaníputra, Aniruddha, Nandika, Kasphila, Subhúti, Reveta, Khadiravaṇika, Amogharája, Mahápáraṇika, Kakkula, Nanda, Ráhula,[12] Svágata, and Ánanda.[13] There likewise accompanied him thirty-two thousand Bodhisattvas,[14] all linked together by unity of caste,[15] and perfect in the virtues of Bodhisattva *Páramitá*;[16] who had made their command over Bodhisattva knowledge a pastime, were illumined with the light of Bodhisattva *Dháraṇís*,[17] and were masters of the Dháraṇís themselves; who were profound in their Bodhisattva meditations, all-submissive to the lord of Bodhisattvas, and possessed of absolute control over *Samádhi*;[18]—great in self-command, refulgent in Bodhisattva forbearance, and replete with the Bodhisattva element of perfection.[19] Among these the following were the principal; namely,—the most excellent Bodhisattva (*Bodhisattva mahásattva*) MAITREYA; the most excellent Bodhisattva DHARAṆÍS'VARARÁJA, the most excellent Bodhisattva SIÑHAKETU, the most excellent Bodhisattva SIDDHÁRTHAMATI, the most excellent Bodhisattva PRAS'ÁNTA-CHARITRAMATI, the most excellent Bodhisattva PRATISAÑVITPRÁPTA, the most excellent Bodhisattva NITYA-YUKTA, and the most excellent Bodhisattva MAHÁKARUṆÁ-CHANDRÍ.

Now then, Bhagaván, arriving at the great city of S'rávastí, sojourned therein, respected, venerated, revered and adored by the fourfold congregation[20];—by kings, princes, their counsellors, prime ministers and followers;—by retinues of Kshatríyas, Bráhmaṇas, householders, and ministers;—by citizens, Tírthikas, S'ramaṇas, Bráhmaṇas, recluses, (*charakas*,) and ascetics (*parivrájakas*). Although regaled with all sorts of edibles and sauces, *the best that could be prepared* by purveyors, and supplied with cleanly mendicant apparel (*chívara*), alms-bowls (*piṇḍa-pátra*), couches, and pain-assuaging medicaments, the benevolent lord, on whom had been showered the prime of gifts and applauses, remained unattached to them all, like water on a lotus leaf; and the report of his greatness *as* the venerable (arhat),[21] the all-knowing (samyak-sambuddha,) the learned, the well-behaved, the god of happy exit,[22] the great knower of worlds, the valiant, the all-controlling charioteer, the teacher of gods and men, the quinocular[23] Lord Buddha fully manifest, spread far and wide in the world. And Bhagaván, having, by his own power, acquired all knowledge regarding this world and the next, comprising Devas, Máras,[24] Bráhmyas, (followers of Brahmá) S'ramaṇas and Bráhmaṇas as subjects, that is both gods and men,—sojourned here, imparting instruction in the true religion, and expounding the principles of a Brahmacharya,[25] full and complete in its nature, holy in its import, pure and immaculate in its character, —auspicious is its beginning, auspicious its middle, auspicious its end.

Once about the middle watch of night was Bhagaván absorbed in the meditation (*samádhi*) called the 'Ornament of Buddhas' (*Buddhálaṅkára-vyúha*). While he was thus lost in contemplation forth issued from the crown of his head, through the interstices of his turban,[26] a flame of light called the *Púrva-buddhánupasmrityasaṅghájnánálokálaṅkára,* (the light which dispels the ignorance and forgetfulness regarding former Buddhas and their congregations—*saṅgha*[27]). The flame illuminated the residences of gods, and thus commanded Maheśvara and the rest of an innumerable host of Devaputras[28] of auspicious homes; and from it burst forth these didactic verses (Gáthás) :—

"O ye! embrace the great sage S'ákya Siñha, the light of knowledge, the dispeller of darkness, and the dispenser of blessings. His splendour is all-brilliant and stainless; his body is tranquil; his mind benignly serene. Betake to the support of him who is an ocean of learning, the holy and magnanimous, the lord of sages and religion, and the knower of all things;—who is the god of gods, the adored of men and gods, the self-taught (*lit.* created) in religion, and the controller of all. Him, who hath subdued to his will the intractable mind, and whose heart owns not the snares of Mára; who is an enemy to all thievish propensities, and to whom *even* the life of a serpent is sacred; —him, who is elevated and qualified for the calmness of beatitude;—O ye, approach him with absolute faith: he is all-resplendent in the inestimable religion, and is the annihilator of gloom. He is perfect in morality, tranquil in his actions, and unfathomable in his understanding. He is the prince of physicians, and the dispenser of the draught of immortality. He is the hero of disputants, the suppressor of the wicked, and the friend of the truly religious. He is the knower of absolute good, and the divine marshaller to the way of salvation."

The tranquil Devaputras of auspicious homes and persons, touched by the divine light, "the dispeller of the ignorance and forgetfulness regarding former Buddhas and their congregations," and impelled by the verses, sprang up from their meditations, and were absorbed in the thought of a numberless immensity of Buddhas in reflecting on the great Buddha,—of their places *of advent*, their meritorious career, their congregations, as also their moral ordinances.

About the end of that night Ísvara, Maheśvara, Nanda, Sunanda, Praśánta, Mahita, Praśánta-viniteśvara, and several other Devaputras of auspicious homes and exalted dignity, proceeded towards Jetavana, refulgent with the holy flame, decorating it by their surpassing beauty. There, approaching Bhagaván, they made him obeisance, laying their heads at his feet; then sitting apart, addressed him thus: "There exists, O Lord, an amplified[29] treatise on religion, the noblest of Sútras,[30] called the Lalita-Vistara.[31] It expounds the source of Bodhisattva blessings; discloses the light of Tushita,[32] the consultation,[33] advent, career, birth-place, and the greatness of the birth-place *of Buddha*; it narrates the special excellencies of his boyhood; his proficiency in all worldly occupations,—in writing, arithmetic, and numeration, in mechanical arts, in the practice of the sword, bow and arrow, and in all sorts of gymnastics; it unfolds his conjugal enjoyments; recites the method of acquiring the final and immutable reward of all Bodhisattva discipline; displays the career of Tathágata[34] triumphing over the legions of Mára, and his might and majesty in all their eighteen declensions; points out the heresies of the Buddha religion, and, in short, constitutes the whole of what was imparted by former venerable and absolute Tathágata Buddhas, such as Padmottara and others.[35] Thou, O Lord, relate the same unto us."

Bhagaván, for the good and gratification of the many, in mercy to mankind, for the prosperity of all worldly actions, for the satisfaction of men and gods, and the mortification of heretics for the diffusion of the Maháyána,[36] for encouraging Bodhisattvas and promoting the majesty of those who betake to the Yánas, for the suppression of all evil passions, as well as in mercy to the true religion, and to the family of the three precious ones,[37] in order to perpetuate its memory, and for better exposition of Buddhism,—yea, in great compassion towards men and gods, benignly vouchsafed their request. The Devaputras, Maheśvara and others (as named above), elated by the reception they met with, their hearts overflowed with joy, love and goodness, saluted his feet with their heads, and thrice circumambulating his person, disappeared, strewing around powdered sandal, aloe wood, and mandára flowers.[38]

At the close of that night Bhagaván proceeded towards a bamboo grove, and, arriving there, at the request of the Bodhisattvas and S'rávakas, seated himself among them, and conversed with the Bhikshukas.[39] The Bodhisattvas and venerable S'rávakas, then saluting Bhagaván with closed hands, thus addressed him; "O Lord, for the good and gratification of the many, in mercy to mankind, for the well-being of worldly actions, and for the prosperity and satisfaction of men and gods, relate thou unto us that excellent treatise on religion known as the Lalita-Vistara." Bhagaván, in mercy to gods, men and demons, and the all-truthful Bodhisattvas and noble S'rávakas, silently vouchsafed the request of his audience.

Regarding this it may be said :

"This night, O Bhikshukas, when I was comfortably seated, free from female company, with my mind intent and unagitated, and absorbed in auspicious recreation, there came unto me Mahes'vara, Chandana, Ís'a,[40] Nanda, Praśántachitta,[41] Mahita, Sunanda, S'ánta,[42] and a myriad of other such Devaputras,—sages bright with immaculate splendour, illuminating the grove of Jetas by their beauty. Approaching, they saluted my feet, circumambulated my person, and seated themselves around me. Then folding their hands *by way of supplication*, they thus reverentially beseeched me: 'O Sage, relate unto us that auspicious and amplified Sútra, the prime source *of religion*, and antidote to evil passions, which was propounded by former Tathágatas, for the good of generations past.' Thus addressed, the sage benignly listened to their entreaty, and, for the removal of the sins of Bodhisattvas, recited the excellent discourses of the Maháyána, to the utter overthrow of the demon of love—Namuchi. They, overwhelmed with delight and joy, rained flowers in their ecstasy. Listen ye now, O Bhikshukas, to the same amplified Sútra, the prime source of religion, which former Tathágatas propounded for the benefit of generations past."

NOTES.

1. *Om.*—It is scarcely necessary to observe that this symbol of the Deity is an importation from the Bráhmaṇic writings. The Jains have not only adopted it, but coined a new word (EM) to denote the female energy or efficient cause of the universe, Om being, according to them, a representative of God as quiescent and unconnected with the world. For the changes which Om has undergone in Bráhmaṇic writings, see my paper on the subject in the Journal of the Asiatic Society of Bengal, XXIV, p. 324.

2. *Buddha.*—Buddhists believe that from time to time and after intervals of immeasurably long and distant periods (kalpas) men of superior intellect, by persevering virtue and unceasing meditation, attain perfect knowledge of universal truth, and proclaim it for the spiritual welfare of the world; but that after a period their instructions are neglected and lie dormant until revived by succeeding individuals. Numberless Buddhas have thus appeared, each undergoing the usual routine of devotion, attaining Buddhahood, and proclaiming the principles of the faith, which have always remained the same; for (say the Buddhists) as truth remains unchangeably the same, and each of these holy and wise men perceives the whole truth, the doctrines of each successive Buddha must necessarily be identical with those of his predecessors. The last Buddha is accordingly made to preach (p. 4) only what his predecessors had already imparted to the world; and in this

respect he holds the same relation to the Buddhist scripture as Vyása does to the Bráhmaṇic. It is, however, very doubtful if S'ákya himself adopted this cloak to invest his religion with authority. The word Buddha signifies 'one possessed of wisdom,' 'a follower of reason,' a 'rationalist,' a 'gnostic,' and it is natural to suppose that he, having adopted this title, should go forward preaching his doctrines as founded on truth and reason, and working on the self-love of man, without seeking the aid of antiquity to shew the superiority of his religion over that of his opponents, who relied on faith, and on the antiquity of their written records—the Vedas: although it is possible that he might quote ancient antivedic philosophers, as Kapila and others, in support of his opinions:—and to this fact, perhaps, is to be traced the origin of his Buddha predecessors, if the natural veneration of mankind for antiquity, and in particular the anxiety of Buddhists who compiled the Saugata Canon, to trace its origin to the earliest times, be not sufficient to account for it.

3. *Bodhisattvas, Bodhisatto*, Páli, *Pu ti sa to, Pua-sa* vel *Phusa* Chinese. *A'ryas, &c.*—Beings of high rank in the scale of Bauddha perfection. I have elsewhere noticed the distinguishing characteristics of these worthies.

4. *Lokadhátu.*—For a critical examination as to the exact import of this word see Burnouf's *Histoire du Buddhisme indien*, tom. I, p. 594.

5. *It has thus been heard, &c. evam mayá s'ratam*, Sanskrit.—This style of opening a discourse is peculiar to the Sútra division of the Buddhist Canon, and tradition ascribes this form to Buddha's own direction to his disciples. (Burnouf's *Histoire du Buddhisme*, p. 45.) The *Riksha-bhagavatí*, in common with other works of this class, begins in this way, and its commentator, naturally enough, identifies the "me" of his text with the author of that work, who, he says, was ARYÁNANDA.* It is a pity that we have not a commentary to point out who was the author of the Lalita-Vistara.

6. *Bhagaván*, nominative singular of the crude form *Bhagavat.*—*Bhagavá*, Páli, *Btchom· ldandasa*, Tibetan. The technology of the Buddhists is to a great extent borrowed from the literature of the Bráhmaṇs. The *Víja-mantra* of Buddha begins with Om,†

* MS. No. 813, Liby. As. Soc. f. 4.

† *Memoires concernant l'Histoire, des Chinois*, tome V, p. 59.

their metaphysical terms are exclusively Hindu, and the names of most of their divinities are taken from the Hindu pantheon. The word Bhagaván, which, according to the *Abhidharma-kosha-vyákhyá*, a Bauddha work of great repute, "is not an arbitrary or superfluous, but the most appropriate title of Buddha," has been, by the Vedas, used to designate the Deity's self. It is said in the Vishṇu Puráṇa, in accordance with the interpretation of Yáska, that, "the essence of the Supreme is defined by the term Bhagaván: the word Bhagaván is the denomination of the primeval and eternal god: and he who fully understands the meaning of that expression, is possessed of holy wisdom, the sum and substance of the three Vedas. The word Bhagaván is a convenient form to be used in the adoration of that Supreme Being, to whom no term is applicable, and therefore Bhagaván expresses that supreme spirit, which is individual, almighty, and the cause of causes of all things." * * * "The dissyllable *Bhaga* indicates the six properties, dominion, might, glory, splendour, wisdom, and dispassion. The purport of the *va* is that elemental spirit in which all beings exist, and which exists in all beings." (The usual etymon of the word, however, is *Bhaga* with the possessive affix मतुप्.) "This word, therefore, which is the general denomination of an adorable object, is not used in reference to the Supreme in a general, but a special, signification. When applied to any other (person) it is used in its customary or general import. In the latter case, it may purport one who knows the origin and end and revolutions of beings, and what is wisdom, what ignorance. In the former it denotes wisdom, energy, dominion, might glory, without end, and without defect."* All the Sútras invest S'ákya Siñha with this title, and, next to Tathágata, it is perhaps the most common appellation of Buddha. M. Burnouf, citing the *Abhidharma-kosha-vgákhyá*,† observes that the epithet is primarily applicable to absolute Buddhas, and secondarily to Bodhisattvas, who have discharged all their religious obligations and are ready to become Buddhas; but not to Pratyeka Buddhas.

7. *S'rávastí*,—(*Sávasti*, Bhagavat Puráṇa;‡ *Sawatthipura*, Pali;§

* Wilson's *Vishṇu Puráṇa*, p. 643.

† *Historie du Buddhisme indien*, p. 72.

‡ *Vishṇu Puráṇa*, p. 361.

§ Turnour's *Mahávanso*, p. 240.

Shewei, and *Shy-lo-fa-syte*, Chinese ;* *Mnyan-yod*, Tibetan,†) the ancient capital of Kośala, placed by the Chinese travellers Fa Hian and Hiouan Thsang nearly on the site of Fyzábád in Oude. General Cunningham has since identified the locality with great precision. (*Arch. Survey Reports.*) The place was celebrated for being the site of a large religious establishment dedicated to S'ákya by a rich householder of the place, a minister of Prasenájit, named Sudatta. The man was noted for great liberality which had earned for him the title of "Almoner of Orphans," *Anáthapiṇḍada*.

8. *Bhikshukas*,—(*Bhikshuṇí ;* Fem. *Gelong* Tib.—*Pi-khieau*, Chinese,) literally, mendicants or those who have renounced home, and embraced monasticism. They bear the same relation to Upásakas (householders) as the friars of the Christian Church do to the laity, with this exception that, while the latter are eligible to clerical duties, the former are bound to devote their whole life to the study of the doctrines of their faith, to meditation, and to the acquirement of those excellencies which characterise a perfect Buddha, without ever being allowed to engage themselves in any priestly occupation. They are called *Sramaṇas*, from their great sanctity (the Sármanes of the Greeks) ; and for having constituted the audience of S'akya (*Srávakas* hearers) : their elders are styled *Sthaviras*, and the more distinguished among them *Mahá Sra'vakas*—great hearers. For a lucid account of the ceremony of initiation into this order, the reader is referred to Mr. Hodgson's work on Buddhism, p. 212 ; and for the religious and social observances appropriate to it, including asceticism, mendicity, &c., to Professor Newmann's "Catechism of the Shamans." M. Spiegel's *Liber de officiis Sacerdotum Buddhicorum* is a brief summary of the ceremony of initiation in Páli, which may likewise be consulted.

9. Jñánakauṇḍilya.—Every one of these names is preceded by the epithet *Áyushmat*, "life-possessing," "immortal," (in Páli, *Áwusso*), which I have not deemed necessary to repeat. According to Cingalese etiquette this epithet, expressive of affection and tenderness, is applicable to equals and inferiors but not to superiors.‡

* *The Pilgrimage of Fa Hian*, p. 169.

† *Asiatic Researches*, XX, p. 86.

‡ Clough's *Páli Grammar*, p. 70.

10. PÚRṆA.—A merchant of Surpárika (Σιππάρα, *Sippára* of Ptolemy; modern Sipeler), a sea-port near the mouth of Kṛishṇá. He was converted by S'ákya himself at the recommendation of Anáthapiṇḍada, and was ever afterwards one of the most faithful and renowned disciples of the great Teacher. The Vinaya legends abound in anecdotes of his great goodness and imperturbable patience, and even S'ákya himself is often made to apostrophise at his excellencies.

11. S'ÁRIPUTRA,—one of the first disciples of S'ákya Siñha. The first volume of the Dulva gives a long account of his life. It is said that he was the son of Tishya (*Skar-rgyal*, Tib.), a learned Bráhman of Nálandá, a village near Rájagriha, and early evinced great proficiency in Bráhmaṇic learning. His real name was Upatishya, (*Nye rgyal*, Tib.), but was commonly called S'áriputra, in commemoration of the wisdom of his mother S'áriká. He had, in company with his friend and neighbour Maudgalyáyana (called in the text Mahá-Maudgalyáyana) travelled over all central India in search of true wisdom, and at last betook to the asylum of S'ákya, whose religion they adorned and upheld. S'áriputra was noted for intelligence, and his friend for great proficiency in performing miracles.*

12. NANDA, RÁHULA.—NANDA, (*Gávo*, Tib.) brother of S'ákya: —RA'HULA, sometimes called LÁHULA, (Tib. S'GRA-G'CHAN H'DSIN) the son of S'ákya by YAŚODHARÁ.

13. ÁNANDA.—(Kun-gávo, Tib.) son of Dotodana, brother of Suddhodana. For further particulars regarding Ánanda see Note,—Chap. XXVI.

14. *Bodhisattva,—Bodhisatto*, Páli; *Phousa*, Chinese. He who possesses the essence of Bodhi, or, of the intelligence of Buddha; a title originally applied to those disciples of S'ákya, who stood next to himself in the order of perfection. But the theistic speculations of later times, which even apotheosized metaphysical abstractions, devised a very intricate system of Buddhas and Bodhisattvas wholly superhuman, and we may add,—ideal. "According to this system," says Mr. Hodgson, "from an eternal, infinite and immaterial Ádi Buddha proceeded divinely and not generatively, five lesser Buddhas, who are

* *Asiatic Researches*, Vol. XX, p. 48, et seq. My Sanskrit Buddhist Literature of Nepal, p. 45.

considered the immediate sources (A'di Buddha being the ultimate source) of the five elements of matter, and of the five organs, and five faculties of sensation. The moulding of these materials into the shape of an actual world is not, however, the business of the five Buddhas, but is devolved by them upon lesser emanations from themselves, denominated Bodhisattvas, who are thus the tertiary and active agents of the creation and government of the world, by virtue of powers derived immediately from the five Buddhas, ultimately from the one supreme Buddha. This system of five Buddhas provides for the origin of the material world, and for that of immaterial existences, a sixth Buddha is declared to have emanated divinely from A'di Buddha, and to this sixth Buddha, Vajrasattva by name, is assigned the immediate organization of mind, and its powers of thought and feeling."* The number of universally admitted divinely-descended Bodhisattvas are five, namely, Ratnapáṇi, Vajrapáṇi, Samantabhadra, Padmapáṇi, and Viśvapáṇi. They act by turns each serving as the creator and governor of the universe for a certain number of ages, the fourth or Padmapáṇi, being the ruler of the present Kalpa.

Human Bodhisattavas "are distinguished during life by their extreme goodness, by universal benevolence, and by a self-abandonment, which impels them to sacrifice themselves for the benefit of all other creatures."† S'ákya in his anterior existences, is accordingly said to have, at different times, offered himself a willing victim to the rapacity of tigers and hawks in lieu of doves and other defenceless creatures.

15. *All linked together by unity of caste.*—Lit. "by all bound in one caste." *Sarvairekajáti-pratiboddhah*, i. e., all had merged into one caste, or had lost all caste distinctions.

16. *Páramitá.*—Ten Páramitás are enumerated, namely, *Dána* "charity," *S'ila*, "goodness," *S'ánti*, "tranquillity," *Virya*, "fortitude," *Dhyána*, "meditation," *Prajṇá*, "understanding," *Upáya*, "expediency," *Bala*, "power," *Praṇidhi*, "circumspection," and *Jṇána*, "knowledge of universal truth."‡

* *Journal As. Soc.* Vol. XII, p. 400.

† *Fa Hian's Pilgrimage*, p. 63.

‡ Hodgson's *Illustrations of the Literature and Religion of the Buddhists*, p. 31.

17. *Dháraṇís.*—"Short significant forms of prayers, similar to the *mantras* of the Bráhmaṇs."* They are, like their prototypes, the Bráhmaṇical mantras, declared highly efficacious antidotes to worldly evils. Some are said to overcome devils, some assuage pain, others make their wearers invisible, some facilitate victory, others again are said to ensure the love of truant fairs.† The author of the *Aparimitá Dháraṇí*‡ (Transcendental Formula), observes, that they were promulgated by S'ákya himself, when in S'rávastí, to save mankind from untimely deaths, and promote prosperity. M. Burnouf, however, after a careful examination of the Nepalese collection of Buddha works collected by Mr. Hodgson, is of opinion that it is of a modern origin, and formed no part of the religion promulgated by S'ákya; for while the Tantras of modern times abound with these mystical charms and magical formulas, the simple Sútras, which he has reason to believe are the most ancient, shew no trace of their existence or of the belief in their efficacy.

18. *Samádhi*, Ecstacy.—"Deep and devout meditation restraining the senses, and confining the mind to contemplation on the true nature of spirit." WILSON.§ Hemachandra‖, a celebrated Bauddha lexicographer, defines it to be "meditation causing a manifestation of the object meditated upon;" and the *Garuḍa Puráṇa*,¶ describes it to be an "intense application of the mind to some particular object, which identifies the meditator with the object meditated upon." Many supernatural phenomena attend this act of Bauddha-Bráhmaṇic devotion, of which we shall have ample instances as we proceed.

19. *Element of perfection; Bhúmi;* Sans.—The Bauddha disclosure of a future state, in accordance with its belief in transmigration, treats of several states or stages of existence, through which an adept in Buddhism must pass before he obtains his final reward, the perfection in any one state of existence being denominated, the attainment

* Hodgson's 'Illustrations' &c., p. 27.

† My Sanskrit Buddhist Literature of Nopal, p. 41.

‡ Sanskrita MS. No. 816. Libry. As. Soc. f. 2.

§ Sansk. Dic., p. 896.

‖ *Abhidhána-chintámaṇí*, Chap. 1, Verse 85.

¶ Rádhákánta's *S'abda-kalpadruma*, Vol. VI, p. 5917.

of the element *(Bhúmi)* of that state. The commentator of the Riksha-bhagavatí enumerates ten Bhúmis, appropriate to the priesthood, the last being Buddha Bhúmi.*

20. *Fourfold congregation,—i. e.*, ecclesiastics of all the four different orders: "1st, those who accomplish justice, that is the Buddhas, the Lokajyesṭhas, (honorables of the age,) the Bodhisattvas, the Pratyeka Buddhas, the S'rávakas, &c., whose virtue transcends the law itself, and who surmounting every obstacle accomplish their own deliverance (Mukti). 2nd, The *ordinary Sañghas of the age*: that is, men who shave their beards and heads, and dress themselves with the *kia-sha* (a kind of cap worn by Buddhist priests), who embrace monastic life and its obligations, and observe the precepts and the prohibitions of Buddha. 3rd, The *dumb sheep Sañghas*, (*Ya yang seng*, Chinese,) those dull and stupid characters who are unable to comprehend the distiction betwixt the commission and the non-commission of the fundamental sins, (murder, theft, fornication, lying,) and who, when guilty of crimes of less enormity, make no show of repentance. 4th and last, The *shameless Sañghas*, who, having embraced monastic life, unscrupulously infringe the precepts and observances enjoined upon them, and, devoid of all shame and chastity, are indifferent even to the bitter fruits of their wickedness in ages to come.†"

21. *Arhat,*—Nom. Sing. *Arhan*: (*Alohan*, Chinese; *Noshrta*, Tib.) "The Arhat or Venerable," says M. Burnouf,‡ "has, with relation to knowledge, reached the most elevated rank among sages, and the *Sútras*, as well as the *Avadánas*, attribute to him supernatural faculties, that is to say, the five *Abhijṇánas* or superior faculties, namely, the power of assuming any form one desires; the faculty of hearing sounds however feeble they may be; the power of knowing the thoughts of others, and the anterior existences of animated nature; and lastly the power of seeing objects at a great distance. The note of M. Remusat, quoted above, (Fou Kou Kie, p. 95,) teaches us that an *Arhat* has to traverse twenty thousand Kalpas

* Sanskrita MS. No. 813, Libry. As. Soc. f. 42. My Sanskrit Buddhist Literature of Nepal, p. 81.

† *Fa Hian's Pilgrimage*, p. 8.

‡ *Hist. du Buddhisme*, p. 294.

before he obtains the supreme science. Other beings, according to the text of Nepal followed by Chinese authors, obtain the rank of an Arhat on the annihilation of the corruption of sin ; and it is probably in this circumstance, that we may find the cause of the false etymology of the name of *Arhat*, which the Buddhists of all schools, North as well as South, propose, and which consists in regarding *Arhat*, as synonymous with *Arinám hattá*, (Páli) "the vanquisher of enemies." We have already (M. Lassen and myself) pointed out this erroneous interpretation (Essai sur le Páli, p. 203) ; and I add here, that its presence amongst Buddhists of all countries proves that it comes from an unique, and most certainly, ancient source. The Jains, who are in India the true descendants of the Buddhists, do not appear to have fallen into the same error if we may rely on the testimony of the Vishṇu Puráṇa, which well derives the word Arhat from *arh* to "merit," "to be worthy."' (Wilson's *Vishṇu Puráṇa*, p. 339.) (Orientalists are now unanimously of opinion that the Jains date from before the Buddhists, and some are disposed to think that Buddhism is an off-shoot of Jainism.)

"Bohlen has ingeniously approximated the word *Arhat* to the Aritoniens quoted by Nicholes of Damas. (*Das alte Indien*, t. I. p. 920). As to the value of this approximation we may admit with Lassen that the Arhats were known to the Greeks. The Σεμνοί (*Simnoi*) or venerable who, according to Clement of Alexandria, rendered worship to a pyramid raised originally to the relics of a god, are the Arhats whose name has been thus translated by the Greeks. We may add that Clement mentions likewise of Σεμναί or venerable females, who are very probably the Bhikshuṇis of our text." I think, however, M. Burnouf is mistaken in believing the *Simnoi* to have been Arhats ; etymological similitude would lead one to believe they were the *Sramaṇas*, in those days popularly called *Samaṇas*, whence Simnoi is an easy transition.

"The Arhan is one," says Remusat, "who has himself arrived at perfection and knows how to direct others to it, he is ten million times superior to the Anágámi, and a million times inferior to a Praytyeka Buddha, according to the scale of merit applied to the different classes of saints, a scale attributed to S'ákya Muni himself."*

* *Pilgrimage of Fa Hian*, p. 33.

22. *Sugata*,—from *su*, "well," and *gata*, "gone." Homboldt explains it in much the same way; according to him it means, "that which is so well gone as to have attained perfection." The word is no doubt another version of Tathágata, and the meaning must necessarily bear a strong similitude to the sense of that word.

23. *Quinocular; Pancha-chakshu*, Sans.—He who has five eyes, or rather fivefold vision, or five powers of perception. Mr. Hodgson, to whose invaluable papers, published in the Transactions of the Asiatic Societies of Bengal and Great Britain, we are indebted for much of our knowledge of Buddhism, innumerates the fivefold faculty of vision thus: 1st, *Mánsa-chakshu*, or the carnal eye; 2nd, *Dharma-chakshu*, the eye of religion, or the faculty of seeing through religion; 3rd, *Prajnána-chakshu*, or the power of seeing by the intellect: 4th, *Divya-chakshu*, (divine eye), or the faculty of seeing what is invisible to the naked eye; 5th, *Buddha-chakshu*, the eye of Buddha, or the power of seeing all things past, present, and future.*

24. *Mára*,—in Chinese *Mo*; in Tibetan *Dhoud*; in Mongol *Simnou*; in Mandchu *Ari*, (obviously from the Sanskrit *Ari* "an enemy"). The god or demon of love, wrath, mischief, and death; he is the great enemy of Buddha and his religion, and plays a conspicuous part in the Bauddha legends. The reader will have ample instances of Mára's enmity to S'ákya as he proceeds, particularly in Chapter XXI, which is entirely devoted to the exploits of S'ákya against the legions of Mára.

25. *Brahmacharya*.—This is another instance in support of what I have advanced, respecting the technology of the Buddhists, (Note 6). "It appears to me," says Burnouf, "one of the most indubitable proofs of the priority of Bráhmans in regard to Buddhists. All the Sanskrita texts of Nepal, and principally the Sútras (that is to say, those which I have reason to believe are the most ancient) make use of this term to describe in a general manner the monastic duties of a Buddhist, and in particular chastity. If this term had been rarely employed, still it would not be easy to explain its presence in the Buddhist texts, in which 'Buddha charya' ought to take its place: an expression which equally exists, but exactly signifies Buddhism, and is nearly synonymous with *Buddha-márga*, 'the way of Buddha.'

* Journal As. Soc. Vol. V, p. 93.

But either term is equally common in the Sútras; it appears even in the most important formulas, in the phrase by which he who desires to become a Buddhist, makes his vow before S'ákya or one of his disciples, on entering a religious life: 'Strengthen us, O Bhagaván, under the discipline of the very renowned law, to enter into religious life, to receive investiture, and to become an ecclesiastic. Strengthen us, O Lord, to accomplish under Bhagaván, the duties of the *Brahmacharya.*' Bhagaván replied with the voice of Brahmá; 'Come, children, accomplish the duties of the *Brahmacharya.*' This term receives undoubted preference to some extent in such phrases as the following: 'They spread my religious law *(Brahmacharya),*' says Buddha; to which his adversary Sin, replies in the same form, 'Thy religious law *(Brahmacharya)* is spread; it is admitted by many nations, it is become immense.' *Vaistárikám te Brahmacharyam bahujangam prithubútam.* (*Mándhátri* in the *Divya Avadán*, f. 996.) Again: 'the manner in which the religious law *(Brahmacharya)* may continue long.' (M. in the D. A) In all these passages and many other similar ones that I could cite here, it is evident that the term Brahmacharya is used in a special sense, in that of 'life,' or 'religious law;'—a sense which does not exclude, I confess, that of chastity, but is much more comprehensive. Now to be admitted in this sense by the Buddhists, it must be that this term had lost its original signification, which it has in Bráhmaṇical writings, *i. e.*, the state of *Brahmacharya* or 'the Bráhmaṇ in his noviciate,' and it must follow that the Buddhists had forgótten the value of the title of Brahmachárin, which signifies and cannot signify more than 'that which proceeds from the Veda.' That a Bráhmaṇ designates by it his son or his pupil—that the law of Manu sanctions this denomination, and points out in detail the duties of the noviciate of which the first and most difficult, in truth, is a life of chastity,—is not difficult to comprehend. But that the founders of Buddhism should adopt this term, it must be that they had not paid more attention to its primary signification, that of a Bráhmaṇ novice, and that the word can be employed with impunity in the sense of 'one who undertakes a religious noviciate;' and lastly it must be that it was pretty popular in this sense before the advent of S'ákya Muni, in order that he might without fear of confounding his law with that of the Bráhmans, extend the very remarkable usage I have adverted to."*

26. *Turban.*—The word in the Sanskrit text is *Ushṇisha,* "a turban." But I am not aware that the primitive Buddha mendicants had such an article of dress. In the Vinaya legends the cloak or mantle (*Chívara*) is constantly mentioned, but the turban, seldom, or never. Among the Buddhists the word indicates the curled hair with which a Buddha is born; it also indicates the knot into which the unkempt matted hair of a hermit is tied, but in chapter V. the material of the turban is described to be *paṭṭa,* "silk," and it is to be understood, therefore, that the Bodhisattva at Tushita is assumed to have used a turban.

27. *Sañgha*—"Community."—The body politic of the Buddhist priesthood is so called; the word *Bauddha Sañgha* being exactly equivalent to "Bauddha church." It also implies a congregation of ecclesiastics, or the clerical community of any particular district or monastery. In philosophical works this word has, however, a very different signification. According to them it is the name of the third member of the Buddhist triad, and represents actual creative power, or an *active* creator and ruler, deriving his origin from the union of the essence of Buddha and Dharma.†

28. *Devaputras*—lit. sons of gods.

29. *Amplified,* Sans. *Vaipulya.*—A sub-division of the Sútra class of Bauddha writings. Mr. Hodgson says, that this order of books "treats of several sorts of Dharma and Artha, that is, of the several means of acquiring the goods of this world (*Artha*) and of the world to come (*Dharma*).‡" According to Chinese authors quoted by Landresse, this order includes most of the works of the *Great Translation,* "of which the doctrine and sense are as ample as vacant space."§ For further particulars, *vide* note 30.

30. *Sútra.*—It does not appear that the last human Buddha, or rather the first founder of Buddhism, ever reduced any of his doctrines to writing. His disciples, however, on his death, at a council held at Rájagraha under the auspices of Ajátaśatru, king of Maga-

* *Histoire du Buddhisme,* t. I, p. 141.
† Hodgson, in the Transac. Roy. As. Soc. Vol. II, p. 247.
‡ As. Researches, XVI, p. 427.
§ Landresse. *Fou Kou Kie,* p. 328.

dha, in the year 542 B. C., arranged and classified the whole of the discourses and doctrines of their master under three different heads, collectively called the *Tripiṭhaka*, or the three repositories; and severally, the Sútra, the Vinaya, and the Abhidharma.

Of these the first or Sútra division comprehends all the fundamental maxims of the religion (*Múla-grantha*), and as such, is held in the highest veneration. It was compiled by Ánanda, a cousin of S'ákya, and is said to be made up principally of the very words of the founder, (*Buddha-vachana*). The title of Sútra is not applicable to the form of the compositions included under this head; they consist of dialogues relative to ethics and philosophy, and, instead of the almost enigmatic sententiousness peculiar to Brahmaṇical Sútras, are remarkable for their endless tautology and fatiguing verbosity. They are called Sútras merely on account of their containing maxims which in the Bráhmaṇical writings are expressed in the concise manner denoted by that term.* They all begin by naming some particular scene of S'ákya's ministry and his audience in the set form alluded to in note 5, (*ante*, p. 7,) and terminate with a sentence to this effect: "When Bhagaván had finished his discourse, all present were greatly delighted, and approved his doctrine." Some of them are simple in style, and free from all mythological machinery, while others are amplified versions of some simple original, and bring into the scene of action supernatural beings of various grades. Although all of them are attributed to Ánanda, there is every reason to believe, they were composed at various times between the first and the third convocation, and perhaps long after. The amplified (*vaipulya*) Sútras are written in a mechanical style, mingling prose and verse in regular alternation, the poetical portion being an abstract of the circumstances detailed in the prose, and generally introduced (as if) for their corroboration. They allude to individuals who lived long after the days of their alleged author, and claim a degree of elabora-

* अल्पाक्षरमसन्दिग्धं सारवद्विश्वतोमुखं ।
अस्तोभमनवद्यञ्च सूत्रं सूत्रविदो विदुः ॥

"Those who are versed in sútras best, explain a sútra to be a short, succinct, unerring and apt definition, without fault and redundance."

tion and finish, which leave no doubt as to their having been compiled at a much later period.

31. *Lalita-vistara*—Or the Exposition of Recreations: in Tibetan *Gya cher rolpa* (རྒྱ་ཆེར་རོལ་པ).

32. *Tushita*—literally, the abode of Joy, the highest mansion in the world of desires (*Kámávachara*), and the heaven where S'ákya resided as a Buddhisattva previous to his advent in this world to become a Buddha: it is one of the minor heavens (*bhuvanas*) of the Hindus. For an excellent account of Bauddha heavens, see Hodgson's sketch of Buddhism in the Trans. of the Roy. As. Soc. Vol. II, p. 233, *et seq.*

33. See Chapter III.

34. *Tathágata.*—"The title of Tathágata is one of the most dignified of those which are given to a Buddha; the unanimous testimony of the Sútras and the legends proves that S'ákya Muni had assumed it during the course of his instructions. One may see the expositions which the learned, chiefly M. Schmidt (Mem. Acad. des Sciences de S. Pétersbourg, I, p. 108,) and M. Remusat, (Foe Koue Ki, p. 191,) who are engaged in the study of Mungol and Chinese Buddhism, have proposed. According to my plan, which is to consult the Indian sources first, the interpretations which we ought to place in the first rank are those which are found in the books of Nepal, or what we learn from Mr. Hodgson, and those which Mr. Turnour has extracted from the books of Ceylon. The expositions which we owe to the two authors, whom I have just named, are tolerably numerous, and I think it sufficient to refer the reader to them. He will there see by what processes, more or less subtle, the Buddhists have endeavoured to find in this title the ideal of perfection which they suppose *to belong* to a Buddha. (Hodgson's *Europ. Spec.* in the *Journal As. Soc. of Beng.* Vol. III, p. 384, Turnour, *Mahávanso*, p. 401,) Csoma de Cörös, after the Tibetan works, is of opinion that *Tathágata* signifies, 'he who has finished (run through) his religious career in the same manner as his predecessors.' (Csoma, As. Res. XX, p. 424.) This meaning is as satisfactory with regard to the subject as with the form; it shows us in the term *Tathágata* a title by which S'ákya wished to authorize his innovations by the example of ancient sages whose conduct he pretended to imitate."* Mr.

* Burnouf's *Histoire du Buddhisme*, p. 75.

Hodgson's Nepalese authorities, which are always remarkable for much metaphysical nicety, explain this word in three different ways. "1st, it means *thus gone*, which means gone in such a manner, that he (the *Tathágata*) will never appear again; births having been closed by the attainment of perfection. 2nd, *thus got* or obtained, that is to say (cessation of births) obtained, degree by degree, in the manner described in the Buddha scriptures, and by observance of the precept therein laid down. 3rd, *thus gone*, that is gone, as it (birth) came—the pyrrhonic interpretation of those who hold that doubt is the end, as well as the beginning, of wisdom; and that *that* which causes births, causes likewise the alternate cessation of them, whether that 'final close' be conscious immortality or virtual nothingness."*

35. In the Sanskrit text a list of fifty-five names follows the word *Tathágata*. I have not thought fit to break the thread of the narrative by inserting this list in my text, for reasons which, I believe, the reader can easily conceive. "Truly for mine own part," says honest Dogberry, "I could find it in my heart to bestow all my tediousness on your worship."

List of Tathágatas who had expounded the principles inculcated in the Lalita-Vistara previous to the advent of Sákya.

1 Padmottara.	15 Vararúpa.
2 Dharmaketu.	16 Sulochana.
3 Dipañkara.	17 Ṛishigupta.
4 Guṇaketu.	18 Jinavaktra.
5 Mahákara.	19 Unnata.
6 Ṛishideva.	20 Pushpita.
7 S'rítejas.	21 U'nitejas.
8 Satyaketu.	22 Pushkara.
9 Vajrasañhata.	23 Surasmí.
10 Sarvábhibhú.	24 Mañgala.
11 Hemavarṇa.	25 Sudarsaṇa.
12 Atyuchchagámi.	26 Mahásiñhatejas.
13 Pravátaságara.	27 Sthitabuddhidatta.
14 Pushpaketu.	28 Vasantagandhin.

* *Journal, A. S. B.* Vol. III, p. 384.

29 Satyadhermavipulakírtti.	43 Meghaśvara.
30 Tishya.	44 Sundaravarṇa.
31 Pushya.	45 Áyustejas.
32 Lokasundara.	46 Salílagajagámí.
33 Vistirṇabheda.	47 Lokábhilásita.
34 Ratnakírtti.	48 Jitaśatru.
35 Ugratejas.	49 Sampújita.
36 Brahmatejas.	50 Vipaschit.
37 Sughosha.	51 S'ikhi.
38 Supushya.	52 Viśvabhú.
39 Sumanojṉaghosha.	53 Krakuchchhanda.
40 Sucheshṭarúpa.	54 Kaṇakamuṇi.
41 Prahasitanetra.	55 Káśyapa.
42 Guṇaráśi.	

36. *Maháyána.*—The three-fold division of the Buddha scriptures mentioned above (note 30, p. 17) has reference to the nature of the subjects they treat of. With regard to the reward they hold forth to their followers they are classed into various *Yánas* or *media of transport-translations*,—the Bauddha dispensation of reward and punishment, in accordance with its belief in transmigration, treating of different states or stages of existence through which an adept in Buddhism must pass ere he obtains his final recompense. This adaptation of the religion for different grades of intellect is a counterpart of the Brahmaṇic dispensation which has its ceremonials (*Karmakáṇḍa*) for the ignorant, and its intellectual adoration (*Jṉánakáṇḍa*) for the learned.

According to the most approved authorities there are *three translations*, the *less*, the *mean*, and the *great*,—the first leading successively to birth among men, demons and gods; the second, to deliverance from pain and bodily existence; and the third, to final emancipation, and the power to emancipate others from pain. For a lucid account of the different translations I must refer the reader to the work I have already so often quoted. All the information hitherto possessed on the main points of Buddha history, (and a great deal more,) has been collected in it in so complete a shape that it would be an unpardonable affectation in me, to mar its value by partial quotation in a work which has no pretension to original research. I of course allude to Mr. Laidlay's edition of the "Pilgrimage of Fa Hian," which is by far the most valuable work that has yet been published on the subject. I have made no hesitation in using it, together with Hodgson's "Illustrations" and Burnouf's *Histoire du Buddhisme*, as my standard references.

37. *The three Precious ones: Triratna*; Sans.—This phrase evidently alludes to S'ákya Siñha, his son Ráhula and cousin Ánanda. The triad, *Buddha*, *Dharma* and *Sangha*, is likewise denominated the *triratna*; but the allusion to a family and the contents of the book distinctly indicates the sense in which the expression is used here.

38. *Mandara flowers*,—a flower common in the gardens of Indra's heaven.

39. *Conversed with the Bhikshukas*.—Although I do not think myself at liberty to alter any part of the Sanskrit text against the concurrent testimony of five different Mss., I am of opinion that the subjoined sentence, which follows the word Bhikshukas in the Sanskrit original, belongs to the preceding paragraph, but has been dislocated by some blundering scribe; and that the expression "as before" (*púrvavat*) is an interpolation introduced afterwards to preserve consistency. The sentence alluded to, runs thus:—

"Thus, O Bhikshukas, when the night was over, the Devaputras of stainless tenements and persons, namely, Iśvara, Maheśvara, Nanda, Sunanda, Chandana, Mahita, Praśánta, Viníteśvara and others, disappeared as before."

40 *I'śa*,—not named in the prose portion, p. 4.

41. *Praśántachitta*,—changed to Praśántaviniteśvara in the prose portion.

42. *S'ánta*,—not named in the prose portion.

CHAPTER II.

THE EXHORTATION.

O Bhikshukas, on the subject of what this amplified work on religion, the noblest of Sútras, called the Lalita-Vistara, is, the following verses were signalized at the commencement of the great convocation[1] from out of eighty-four thousand[2] harmoniously resounding hymns which were poured forth, as with the voice of a clarion, on the virtues of the honorable and adored Bodhisattva,[3] when dwelling in the noble mansion[4] of Tushita, in all the glory of the place and his own godliness, praised, eulogized, extolled and glorified by a hundred thousand devas.

"Remember him,—the storehouse of virtue, the asylum of mind and memory, and the illuminator of infinite wisdom;—him, who excels the unrivalled might and vigour even of Dipañkara.[5]

"Remember him whose noble and transparent heart knows no stain from the workings of the three passions[6] and from dirt generally; who is free from the effects of pride and all vicious propensities; whose mind is immaculate and auspicious; who is full of benevolence and wisdom.

"Remember, O ye of noble birth, the great in civility and quietness,—his forgiveness, and his austerity,—his vigour, might, meditation and wisdom adored from ages without number.

"Think, O thou of notable deeds, think of the numberless Buddhas adored of yore who were merciful to all: neglect not, the favorable time has *now* arrived.

"Many are the Devas and Asuras—many Nágas, Yakshas, and Gandharvas[7] who anticipate thy auspicious advent,—that which will proclaim the immaculate law, and annihilate pain, decay and death. Therefore descend! O Lord, descend!

"Enjoyment with thee for even a thousand Kalpas produces not satiety, as pouring their contents into the ocean satisfies not rivers; come thou, therefore, O contented in wisdom, and allay the desire of this longing world.

"Thou art of untarnished fame, dallying with virtue and not with vice;—cast thy benign eye of grace on men and gods.

"The rehearsal of religious discourse satiates not the godly; —even deign to turn thine eyes on those who have been for the rescue of mortals.

"Thou beholdest Buddhas over the ten quarters of the globe, and hearest of the great religion;—O pure-eyed, dispense the same unto mankind!

"The beauty of thy righteousness, oh thou prosperous, irradiates the mansion of Tushita; shower thou, O kind-hearted, thy favours on Jambudvípa.

"The Dévas, who overstepping the limits of the region of desire *(Kámadhátu)*, have attained that of semblance *(Rúpadhátu,[7])* long to come in contact with the Bodhi of perfect devotion.

"O Lord! thou destroyer of the works of Mára;—thou hast overcome heretics[8]:—O knower of the trinity, why dost thou tarry? the time is come; neglect it not.

"O mighty, enveloping, as with a cloud, the earth burning with the fire of misery, pour on it the showers of immortality, and assuage the sufferings of perishing mankind.

"Thou proficient and truthful Physician of the eternally sick, hasten to place them in the felicity of extinction *(nirváṇa[10])*, with the panacea of triple emancipation.

"Unaware of thy lion's roar, jackals howl undismayed; resound thou thy voice of Buddha Siñha to confound all vulpine heretics. (*Tírthikas.*)

"Holding forth the lamp of intelligence, and with thy benign might and vigour, descend on the face of the earth, and destroy Jina and Mára with the palm of thy hands.

"Cast thy eyes on the regents of the four quarters who long to present thee with a dish, and on the S'akras and Bráhmaṇs who will accept thy advent.

"Reflect, O intelligent, on the great and far-famed races, nobly descended, abiding among whom thou shalt reveal the duties of Bhodhisattva.

"O thou of immaculate intellect, wherever in Jambudvípa,[11] it behoves jewels to abide, shower ye there the inestimable jewel."

Thus did these and many such verses, in mellifluous numbers, beseech the kind-hearted, saying, "the time is come, tarry thou not."

NOTES.

1. *Great convocation.*—It is generally believed that, in obedience to an injunction of S'ákya Siñha, and with a view to determine what should be regarded as the true Law in opposition to misconceptions which threatened to destroy the identity of the faith, the Buddhist clergy, at four different times, met in council, and compiled the canons of their religion. The first council was held under the auspices of Ajátaśatru, king of Magadha, immediately after the death of S'ákya, B. C. 543; the second, a century after, under Káláśoka; the third, under Aśoka, in the year 247 B. C.; and the fourth, under Kanishka, king of Káshmir, B. C. 143. It is difficult to determine with precision which is the convocation here meant, though the first is the one most likely to be thus noticed. For further details regarding the convocations, the enquiring reader is referred to the 'Journal of the Asiatic Society of Bengal,' Vol. VI, pp. 501 *et seq.* Both the dates and the number of the convocations have lately been questioned by competent scholars.

2. *Eighty-four thousand harmoniously resounding hymns.*—It is believed that the instructions imparted by S'ákya were comprised in eighty-two thousand verses—or rather divisions or distinct topics of discourse, to which were added two thousand more by his disciple and cousin A'nanda, at the time of the first convocation, when he expounded the *Dharma;* and these together constitute the Buddha scriptures. But it is doubtful if there be any other ground for the

4

foundation of this statement than the partiality which the Indians generally, and the Jains and the Buddhists in particular, evince for the mystical number 84. The distinguished scholar and archæologist, Sir Henry Elliot, has collected many examples of the preference shewn to this number in India, and advanced some very plausible conjectures as to the cause of this preference. See *Supplemental Glossary* v. *Chourási.*

8. The word "Boddhisattva" is preceded by one hundred and sixteen epithets remarkable only for their extreme imaginativeness, but in no way important as elucidatory of any notable deed of the party to whom they are applied, or of his doctrines, though they sadly break the continuity of the narrative. I have, therefore, taken the liberty to remove them from their right place to this note. The epithets are:—(1) the dweller in the noble mansion of Tushita, (2) the adored of the adored, (3) the anointed, (4) the bepraised, belauded and described of a hundred thousand Devas, (5) the inaugurated, (6) the accomplished in meditation *(Praṇidhána)*, (7) the eye of the full and pure knowledge of all Buddha religion derived from past Buddhas, (8) who had his full knowledge enlivened by memory, mind, motion and retentiveness, (9) who had attained the Páramitás, through the mighty means of charity, civility, forgiveness, vigour, meditation, and knowledge, (10) who knew the friendly and benevolent way to Brahmá, (11) who was facing the sight of the great wisdom-overpowering knowledge, (*mahábhijṉásańgávaraṇajṉána*), (12) who had acquired the full ten-million (topics of) knowledge of the religion of all Buddhas through memory, proximity, complete union, wealth, feet, organs, power, intellect, body, and conduct, (13) whose body was adorned by all the emblems of unmeasured virtue, (14) the great follower of reform, (15) who did what he said, and kept correspondence in his speech and actions, (16) who followed the straight, uncrooked, unbent path, (17) who had exceeded all arrogance, haughtiness, pride, fear and dejection, (18) who was equally attached to all created beings, (19) who was devoutly adored by numberless millions of millions of Buddhas, (20) whose face was looked upon by many hundreds of thousands of millions of tens of millions of Boddhisattvas, (21) whose glory was bepraised of S'akras, Brahmás, Maheśvaras, Lokapálas, Devas, Nágas, Yakshas, Gandharvas, Asuras,

Garuḍas, Kinnaras, Mahoragas, and Rákshasas, (22) who had perfect knowledge of all distinctions of rank, (23) who knows the Dháraṇís revealed by former Buddhas, and remembers them and their uses, (24) who is the master of the pearl of virtue to be acquired by the great boat of religion, through memory, proximity, complete union, wealth, feet, organs, strength, intellect, body, road, and Páramitá, (25) who has determined to cross the fourfold passage, (26) the enemy of pride, (27) the oppressor of heterodox sects, (28) the inaugurated master of battles, (29) the destroyer of the enemies which inflict pain, (30), the fierce striker with the thunderbolt of knowledge, (31) who had acquired the penalty of the great kindness, which is the root of Buddha inclination, (32) who had been bathed in the water of gravity, (33) the steersman of the easy means of salvation, (34) the proficient in the meditation of Boddhyanga; (35) the filament of Samádhi, (36) the lotus in the lake of merits, (37) the stainless large lotus divested of vanity, arrogance, on the moon of a stream, (38) the aroma which spread over the ten sides of the earth with civility and mercy, (39) the eldest in knowledge, (40) who is untainted by the eightfold worldly actions, (41) the lotus of great men, (42) who is redolent with the widespread aroma of virtue and knowledge, (43) the sun of the stainless hundred-petalled lotus, blown by the rays of the sun of the knowledge of Prajná, (44) who has recounted the great mountain of the fourfold wealth, (45) whose nails and teeth had been sharpened by the fourfold A'ryas, (46) whose appearance bespeaks his having enjoyed the fourfold Brahmá, (47) whose head had collected the fourfold collection of things, (48) whose body had attained mastery over the knowledge of the twelve members, (49) who was quite full of the thirty-seven Boddhi virtues, (50) the lion of the learning resulting from many sciences, (51) the yawner at the face of the threefold salvation (*moksha*), (52) whose pure eyes were able to see everything, (53) the dweller in the cave of the mountain of the attainment of meditation, salvation, and Samádhi, (54) the well grown tree in the forest which marks the fragrance in it, (55) who possessed the might resulting from the practice of the ten powers, (56) the horipilated form, having overcome the fears attendant on worldly wealth, (57) whose power was never contracted, (58) the destroyer of the Tirthas who were like a host of rabbits and deer, (59) who had resounded the lion's roar of no (supreme) soul, (60) the lion among men, (61) who had destroyed the light of the principles of Tírthikas, with the light of the knowledge of the meditations of salvation, (62) the enlightener of the dense darkness of profound ignorance, (63) of fierce might and vigour, (64) who had spread the majesty of virtue among gods and men, (65) the sun among great men, (66) who was above the dark moon, (67) who was the fullness of the waxing moon, (68) who was never unbecoming in appearance, (69) of invincible eyesight, (70) who was surrounded by hundreds of thousands of refulgent Devas, (71) who was the circle of the knowledge which had been purified by meditation, (72) who was the moonlight of the light of Bodhi felicity, (73) the blower of the worldly lily of Bodhi knowledge, (74) the moon among great men, (75) who was above the light of the fourfold congregation, (76) who was endowed with the sevenfold jewel relating to Bodhi, (77) who applied his mind equally to all created beings, (78) who was of invincible wisdom, (79) who had performed the penances of the ten salutary works, (80) who had resolved to tread the salutary path full of beneficent wealth, (81) who was the turner of the wheel of invincible and nobly virtuous religious wealth, (82) who was nobly born in the family of an imperial *(Chakravarti)* race, (83) who was full of the deep, unfathomable, invincible jewel of religion, (84) who had crossed the ocean of unsatiating, unheard of, wide-expanding knowledge and civility, (85) whose eyes were directed towards the great lotus, (86) whose understanding was as expansive as the noblest ocean, (87) whose mind was as (vast as) the earth, water, heat, and wind, (88) who was firm in his might as a kalpa (many millions) of Meru mountains, (89) who was proficient in civility, (90) whose understanding was as stainless and vast as the lower surface of the sky, (91) whose object was thoroughly pure, (92) who had nobly bestowed great charities, (93) who had duly performed all preceding Yogas, (94) whose possessions were well-earned, (95) the root of all happiness, (96) who had attained all his wishes, (97) the root of all happiness, like final beatitude, (98) the root of all the happiness collected in course of seven kalpas, (99) who had bestowed the seven kinds of charity, (100) who had been served with the things of the five kinds of religious deeds, (101) who had performed good deeds with his body in three ways, with his speech in four ways, and with his mind in three ways, (102) who had traversed the paths of the tenfold auspicious works, (103) who had fully accomplished the duties performable by the application of the body in forty different ways, (104) who had meditated the forty kinds of bodily meditations (*praṇidhánas*), (105) who had achieved the forty bodily seats (*adhyásaya*), (106) who was full of the purification achievable by the fortyfold application of his body, (107) who had made straight the final emancipation (*adhimukti*) by the fortyfold application of his body, (108) who had followed the path of the forty times hundreds of thousands of millions of tens of millions of Buddhas, (109) who had given gifts to fifty-five times hundreds of thousands of millions of tens of millions of Buddhas, (110) who had acquired the fourfold merits of hundred-fold tens of millions of Pratyeka Buddhas, (111) who had established the road to heaven and salvation for an innumerable number of mankind, (112) who longed to attain the thorough knowledge (*samyak sambodhi*), which is liable to no extinction, (113) who was bound to unity of caste, (admitted no distinction of caste,) (114) ascending from here who dwelt in the noble mansion of Tushita, (115) the noblest among the Devaputras of the name of S'vetaketu, (116) the adored of all classes of Devas.

4. *Mansion*, Sans. *Vimána.*—This word has the following epithets to qualify it, (1) it was placed on thirty-two thousand Bhúmis, (2) it was ornamented with covered terraces, doors, gates, windows, chambers, and pavilions, (3) it was set off with uplifted umbrellas, flags, penons, and awnings of network decorated with jewels and bells, (4) it was furnished with beds covered with Mándárava and Mahámándárava flowers, (5) it was enlivened by hundreds of thousands of millions of tens of millions of hymns sung by Apsarasas; (6) it was beautified by valuable trees of *Dalbergia oujeiniensis*, *Michalia champaka*, *Bignonea suaveolens*, *Bauhenia variegata*, *Pterospermum salicifolium*, a large variety of ditto, *Jonesea asoka*, *Ficus Indica*, *Jesmenea pubescens*, yellow *Pterospermum*, *Mesua ferrea*, and mangoes, (7) it was spread over with golden networks, (8) it was decorated with large well-filled vases, (9) it was provided with level

courts, (10) it was refreshed with the delightful breeze blowing over new blown jasemines (11) it was being beheld by hundreds of thousands of millions of tens of millions of Devas, (12) it was divested of desires, longings, anxiety and pain by the recitation of the great and widespread hymn of religion, (13) it was freed from all feelings of anger, enmity, arrogance, vanity, and pride, (14) it excited love, delight, and exhilaration, and enlivened the memory.

5. *Dipaṅkara.*—" The last Buddha of the twelfth proceeding, or 'Sáramanda,' Kalpa, in which four Buddhas appeared. He was born at Ramyavatínagara.* His parents were Sudeva Rájá and Sumedhyá Deví. He, as well as all other Buddhas of this Kalpa, attained Buddhahood at Uruvelaya, now called Buddha-Gayá. His 'bo' tree was the 'pippala.' Gautama was then a member of an illustrious Bráhmaṇ family in Amrávatinagara."†

6. *Three passions.*—Lit. "threefold dirt," and may mean dirt resulting from the body, speech and mind.

7. *Nágas, &c.*—The Nágas were a race of Dragons, who are said to have inhabited Ceylon before the advent of the last Buddha, who converted them during his miraculous visit to that island. They are supposed to have been a race of beings superior to man, and had constant access to the heaven of Indra.

Yakshas.—" Demons, attendants especially of Kuvera, the god of wealth, and employed in the care of his gardens and treasures." The *Brahmavaivarta Puráṇa* describes them as having peculiarly ugly countenances, with tawny brown eyes, large bellies, and long necks. The colour of their body is white (" crystal-coloured ;") and they dress in red clothes. I do not know if the Yakshas of the text are different from these Pauránic demigods, but think not.

Gandharvas, celestial musicians, the Glendoveers of Sonnerat,—

" The loveliest race of all of heavenly birth."

(*Curse of Kehama.*)

They have a region of their own under the heaven of Indra, and constitute the orchestra at all celestial concerts.

* According to the rules of Sanskrit grammar this word ought to be written *Ramyavannagara*, or *Ramyavatí Nagarí* : the same remark applies to *Amarávatinagara.*

† Turnour's *Mahávanso*, p. xxxii.

8. According to the *Abhidhamma Sangaha*, a Páli work on Bauddha metaphysics, celestial regions are divided, with reference to the predominant characteristics of their inhabitants, into 4 classes; 1st, *Arúpyávachara* (world of semblance), which includes three regions: 2nd, *Kámávachara* (world of desire), comprehending six regions: 3rd, *Rúpávachara* (world of form), comprehending eighteen regions: and 4th, *Lokottara*, including eleven regions, of which ten are appropriate to Bodhisattvas, and the last is the abode of A'di Buddha.

9. *Heretics*. Sans. *Kutírthikas*, lit. wicked Tírthikas. From the circumstance of the Tírthikas having been described as followers of the Vedas I take them to be Hindus. Burnouf also did so; but some European scholars are of opinion that they were Jains. See Proceedings of the A. S. B. for 1878, and Journal R. A. S. Vol. X.

10. *Nirváṇa.*—This is perhaps the most important word in the annals of Indian metaphysics, and fully to explain the various senses in which the different schools of Philosophy, whether Bauddha or Bráhmaṇic, have defined it, would amount to nothing short of a summary of all that has been written by the Indians regarding the ultimate end of man. Leaving aside the heretics, one finds that even the orthodox Buddhas are divided into four different sects according to the meaning they attach to this term. I had made long extracts in illustration of how it is at one time made equivalent to eternal matter—a *primordia cœca*, or the abode of eternal bliss, or exemption from transmigration; and at another time a *positive nothing* or *nihility;* but as I find I would be, after all, in the same predicament as honest Cicero, when he said, "though I have translated the Timæus of Plato, I do not understand it," I have suppressed them altogether, and will only state that it is invariably used to indicate the ultimate reward which the various Indian systems of religion hold forth to their votaries,—be that absolute nihility, eternal repose, or enjoyment in higher spheres.

11. *Jambudvípa.*—According to the united testimony of the eighteen Puráṇas, this word indicates the whole of Asia, but the Buddhist works confine it within the natural boundary of India.

CHAPTER III.

THE DYNASTY.

Bodhisattva at Tushita—his audience. The prophecy. Characteristics of a Chakravartí Rájá—the seven precious things, *viz.* the wheel, the elephant, the horse, the wife, the jewel, the master of the household, and the commander. Pratyeka Buddhas disappear at the report of Bodhisattva's descent. Bodhisattva reflects on four different things, and why? Dévaputras discourse about the tribe wherein and the woman of whom Bodhisattva should be born. The merits and demerits of the Vaideha dynasty—of the Kauśala dynasty—of the Vañsarája dynasty—of the dynasty of Vaishalí—of the Pradyota dynasty—of the Kañsa dynasty—of the Páṇdu dynasty—of the Sumitra dynasty. Devaputras consult Bodhisattva on the subject. Sixty-four qualities appertain to the dynasty wherein Bodhisattva is to appear. Thirty-two characteristics peculiar to the woman of whom Bodhisattva should be born. Verses regarding the same.

Thus, O Bhikshukas, at the exhortation of Time and Religion Bodhisattva[1] repaired to the noble temple of *Dharmochchaya,* where seated, he had of *yore* preached about religion to the Devas of Tushita; and, entering it, seated himself on the lion throne *Sudharmá.* Those Devaputras who held their places around him, and belonged to the same order *(Yána)* with himself, also entered the temple. Several Devaputras and Bodhisattvas who had flocked from the ten quarters of the globe, and had attained places equal to himself, who were free from the company *even* of Apsarasas,[2] and of all newly created Devaputras, who claimed equal precedence for all, and comprised a retinue of sixty-eight thousand koṭis (six hundred and eighty billions), entered the temple likewise, and betook to their respective seats.

Twelve years hence,[3] *O Bhikshukas, will the Bodhisattva be conceived in his mother's womb.*

Now the Devaputras of untainted tenement and persons, relinquishing their divine forms, appeared in Jambudvípa, and assuming the shape of Bráhmaṇs imparted to Bráhmaṇs[4] instruction in the Vedas.

Whoever enters the womb of a woman in the manner prescribed, attains thirty-two characteristics of greatness, and whoever possesses these characteristics, necessarily obtains one of two states of existence.

1st. If a householder, he becomes a universal sovereign *(Chakravartí rájá)*[5], the lord of a four-fold army, a conqueror, a virtuous king, the lord of religion, and the owner of seven jewels[6]; namely, a wheel *(Chakra-ratna)*, an elephant *(Hasti-ratna)*, a horse *(As'va-ratna)*, a wife *(Strí-ratna)*, a jewel *(Maṇi-ratna)*, a steward *(Grahapati-ratna)*, and a commander *(Pariṇáyaka-ratna)*.

How does a universal monarch attain unto the jewel of a wheel? For that anointed Kshatriya king, who is inaugurated, fasting, on the fifteenth day of the moon, seated in the highest apartment of his palace, surrounded by female apartments;—for him does the mighty and auspicious wheel appear in the east;—a wheel comprising a thousand spokes, complete with tire and nave, ornamented with gold works, of the height of seven palm trees, visible from the recesses of the gynecium, and worthy of a Chakravartí rájá. I, who now describe the Chakra-ratna, have been a Chakravartí rájá, and have heard that the anointed Kshatriya king, who is inaugurated, fasting, on the fifteenth day of the moon, seated in the highest apartment of his palace, surrounded by female apartments, and for whom appears the mighty and elegant wheel towards the east, becomes a Chakravartí king.

Now, when the mighty wheel does appear, an anointed Kshatriya king, kneeling on his right knee, and lowering one of his shoulders, should hold forth his right hand, and thus offer his prayer to the Chakra-ratna,—"Conduct, O lord, this precious wheel through virtue, and not through vice."

When the majestic wheel, on being thus addressed by an anointed Kshatriya king, proceeds in its aërial course towards the east for the promotion of prosperity, the Chakravartí rájá follows it with all his army, and wherever it halts, there does he likewise halt with all his forces. Thereupon all the provincial rájás of the east receive him with offerings of silver-dust in golden vessels, or of gold-dust in vessels of silver, saying, "Hail, O Deva! thou art welcome; all this is thine —this rich, extensive, prosperous, flourishing, beautiful and populous kingdom: thou hast, conquering, earned it; may it ever continue thine." The anointed Kshatriya king and lord should then thus address the provincial chiefs: "Virtuously rule ye these provinces, destroy not life, nor resume what has been given. Act not fraudulently through temptation; nor utter what is false. It is sinful to conquer him who sues for mercy, therefore do it not; nor do ye approve of the vicious." Thus when an anointed Kshatriya king has conquered the east, bathing in the eastern sea, he crosses the same. When the wheel, having crossed the eastern sea, proceeds southwards through the atmosphere, he follows it with his army, and like unto the east conquers the south; and as the south, so does he conquer the west and the north; then, bathing in the northern sea, returns through the atmosphere to his metropolis, and sits an invincible monarch in the inner recesses of his palace. Thus does a Chakravartí rájá acquire the *Chakra-ratna* or the jewel of a wheel.

How does a Çhakravartí rájá attain unto the *Hasti-ratna* or the most precious elephant? For the anointed Kshatriya king described above, the precious elephant appears like unto the wheel:—a white elephant, sound in wind and limb, of docile temper, capable of travelling through the atmosphere, bedecked with golden crests, banners and ornaments, and housed in golden networks;—Bodhi by name, the noblest of elephants. When the king desires to try such an elephant, let him, at early dawn, mount it, and, travelling over the great earth to the brink of the ocean, return to his metropolis, intent on justice, and then will he be able to appreciate its value.

How does a Chakravartí rájá attain unto the *Aśva-ratna* or the most precious horse? In the same way as the elephant: —a horse of a docile temper, having a dark blue head, a noble face, and silvery mane;[7] decked with golden banners and ornaments, housed in networks of gold, capable of travelling through the atmosphere, and named BÁLÁHAKA,[8] the noblest steed. Its merit may be tried in the same way as that of the elephant.

How does a Chakravartí rájá attain unto the most precious jewel? In the same way as the horse and the rest. The jewel is of the purest dark blue colour, having elegantly cut eight facets[9]; its brilliancy dazzling the interior of the palace. Should the king desire to test the value of this jewel, let him, at midnight, when all things are involved in darkness, proceed to observe the beauty of his garden, with the jewel raised on the top of a pole, when the whole of his fourfold army, the defenders of his people, will all become manifest, and the whole neighbourhood within four miles of the jewel, glowing in the light, will, rejoicing, say to each other, "Arise, O ye good men, open your shops—attend to your works—the sun has risen, and the daylight does appear."

How does a Chakravartí rájá obtain the most precious wife? In the same way as the jewel and the rest:—a woman of an equal Kshatriya race, neither very tall, nor short, neither corpulent nor lean, neither very fair nor dark; but exquisitely beautiful and delightfully handsome; every pore of her body emits the odour of sandal-wood, and her mouth is redolent with the aroma of the lotus: her body is soft as the down on the pod of the *Kuchinchika* (Abrus precatorious), and feels warm during the winter, and cold during the summer months. Such a woman never can have affection for any other than a Chakravartí rájá.

How does a Chakravartí rájá obtain a precious steward? In the same way as the wheel and the rest:—a steward, intelligent, learned and wise, and possessed of great penetration, whereby he can ascertain within four miles of the place wherever he may be, the existence of claimed treasures. These soon become ownerless, and he appropriates them to the use of his master.

How does a Chakravartí rájá obtain the most precious general? In the same way as the wheel and the rest. The general is wise and intelligent, and able to equip an army for action, whenever required by a Chakravartí rájá.

A Chakravartí rájá, having thus acquired the seven jewels, becomes the father of a thousand mighty, valiant and beautiful sons, subduers of their enemies. He likewise acquires and exercises sovereign power over the whole of this wide-extended earth to the shore of the ocean, undisputed, and without war —nay even without arms.

2nd.—Should he, however, relinquishing home, adopt the life of a houseless ascetic, he would become free from all carnal passions—a law-giver—an unrivalled divinity—a ruler of men and gods.

About this time many Devaputras appeared in Jambudvípa, and adored Pratyeka Buddhas.

Disperse, venerable Sirs, for twelve years hence will the Bodhisattva appear incarnate on the earth.

At this time there lived on the Galigula mount, in the great metropolis of Rájagriha, a Pratyeka Buddha named Mátañga.[10] On hearing this report, he fell like a clod against a stone, and then rose to the height of seven palm trees, when his fiery parts, like meteors, disappeared. His flesh, bones and humours (bile, &c.) were consumed by his fiery parts, and the relics which fell on the earth, are to this day called Rishipadání.

There, likewise, lived about this time, O Bhikshukas, in the Deer-park (Mriga-dáva) at Rishipaṭṭana, in Báráṇasí, five hundred Pratyeka Buddhas.[11] On hearing this report, they too ascended to the height of seven palm trees, where their fiery parts disappeared like meteors, consuming all their bones, flesh, and humours, and cast relics on the ground, whence the place is named Rishipaṭṭana (the town of the sages). Formerly this place was called Mriga-dáva,[12] from having been a park where deer grazed unmolested.

Now, when Bodhisattva was seated in the palace of Tushita, four different subjects worthy of consideration, engaged his attention. What were they? They were time, continent, district, and tribe.

Why did the Bodhisattva reflect on time?[13]

Because when, at the beginning of the world after a change of creation, a Bodisattva enters his mother's womb, he selects that time when the manifest world is in peace, when men know what is birth, what is decay, what is disease and what is death. Then does he enter his mother's womb.

Why did the Bodhisattva reflect on continent?[14]

Because Boddhisattvas do not take birth on an outlying continent (or the continent of savages), nor in Púrva Videha,[15] nor in Apara Godániya,[16] nor in Uttara Kuru,[17] the fact being that they are born in Jambudvípa.

Why did the Bodhisattva reflect on countries?

Because Bodhisattvas are not born in an outlying country (or the country of savages) where men are born blind, dumb, uncivilised, or ignorant of the distinction between good and bad speech. It follows that Bodhisattvas are born in the middle country *(Madhyamadesa)*.[18]

Why did the Bodhisattva reflect on families?

Because Bodhisattvas are not born in a low family, such as that of a Chaṇḍála or of a basket-maker, or of a chariot-maker, or of a Pukkasa (one born of a Nishádha by a S'údra female). It follows that they are born in one of two families, either in that of a Bráhmaṇa, or that of a Kshatriya. When the Bráhmaṇs are the most respected on the earth Bodhisattvas are born in Bráhmaṇ families, but when Kshatriyas are the most respected, they take their birth in Kshatriya families. Since now, O Bhikshukas, the Kshatriyas are in the ascendant, the Bodhisattva will be born in a Kshatriya family.

For these reasons the Bodhisattva, while dwelling in the noble mansion of Tushita, reflected on the four great objects. Having reflected on these he became silent.

Now, O Bhikshukas, the Devaputras discussed[19] among themselves about the noble family in which, and the kind of mother, in whose womb, the Bodhisattva would take his birth. Thereupon some said, "Here in the Magadha country the Vaideha dynasty[20] is wealthy, prosperous, amiable and generous: it is the most appropriate for the birth of the Bodhisattva."

"Not so," remarked others.

"Why so?"

"Because it has no children of pure parentage; it is unsteady and fickle; its virtues have dried up; it seems moved by virtue, but it is not immersed in profound virtue; it is but a semblance of a good family; it owns no profusion of gardens, tanks, and lakes. It exists like a torn rag in a corner, and is unfit for the purpose."

Others said; "the many-membered Kośala dynasty,[21] rich in wealth and equipages, is well becoming the Bodhisattva."

"Not even so," replied others.

"And why?"

"Because, it dates its rise from the downfall of the Mátañgas; it is neither pure on the mother's nor on the father's side; it is lost to all claim to salvation; and is neither illustrious, nor remarkably rich in treasures and precious stones: it is, therefore, unworthy of the Bodhisattva."

Some suggested, "the rich, thriving, kind and generous Vañsarája dynasty[22] was worthy of the Bodhisattva."

"Even that is unbecoming," said others.

"Wherefore?"

"Because it is a modern dynasty, passionate and inglorious; illegitimate by birth, and unadorned by ancestral or self-acquired greatness; its ruling head is no suppressor of evils. It is utterly unfit for the Bodhisattva."

Some said, "the rich, good, generous and happy city of Vaiśali,[23] inhabited by numbers and adorned by covered court-yards, gates, trumphal arches, windows, palaces, towers, lofty mansions, gardens and groves over-stocked with flowers, rivalling the domains of the immortals in beauty, is certainly a worthy place for the birth, of the Bodhisattva."

"That too is unworthy," responded some.

"And for what reasons ?"

"Because its inhabitants are irrational in their opinions; unmindful of religion; and regardless of the respect due to rank, superiors, elders and the aged; each proclaims, "I am the king, I am the king," and none condescends to become a disciple or study religion. It is therefore unworthy of the Bodhisattva."

"The Pradyotana dynasty,"[24] said others, "mighty, well-mounted, and victorious over foreign armies, is well suited for the birth of the Bodhisattva."

Others remarked, "that too is not suited."

"Why ?"

"Because it is passionate, fickle, irascible, cruel, timorous, without experience, and necessarily unbecoming the Bodhisattva."

"The rich, flourishing, kind, generous and populous city of Mathurá,"[25] observed some, "the metropolis of king Subáhu of the race of the valiant Kañśa, is a becoming place for the birth of the Bodhisattva."

"Not even so," objected others.

"And why ?"

"Because the king is a tyrant, and his race that of atheists. It is not becoming that the next-coming Bodhisattva should be born in such a race."

"But here is a king in the city of Hastinápura"[26] remarked some, "descended from the Páṇḍava race, valiant, and the most beautiful and glorious among conquerors; his family is certainly becoming for the Bodhisattva."

"Even that is not worthy," replied others.

"Why ?"

"Because the descendants of Páṇḍu tyrannized over their relatives the Kurus. Besides of that race Yudhisṭhira is said to have been the son of Dharma (god of the nether regions), Bhímasena of

Váyu, Arjuna of Indra, and Nakula and Sahadeva of the two Aśvins. It is, therefore, unbecoming of the Bodhisattva."

Others observed, "Here is the very charming city of Mithilá,[27] the home of the royal Sumitra. The king has a mighty army of elephants, horses, chariots, and foot soldiers; he is rich in gold both in ingots and in coins, precious stones, pearls, lapis-lazuli, conch-shells (*sañkha*), marbles, corals, silver, native and wrought, and all other objects of wealth; he himself is of undaunted might and vigour, well-allied and virtuous; his family is surely well worthy of the Bodhisattva."

"Not so," answered others. "The king, it is true, is well-allied and meritorious; but he is very old, unable to govern well his kingdom, and the parent of many children; his family, therefore, is not a fit birthplace of the Bodhisattva."

Thus, O Bhikshukas, did the Devaputras and the Bodhisattvas examine all the sixteen great dynasties[28] who reigned in the different countries of Jambudvípa, and proved them all defective. While thus perplexed, one of them of undeviating conduct, Jṇánaketudhvaja, by name, determined to ascertain the truth regarding the great translation (Maháyána), thus addressed the godly assembly of the Bodhisattvas: "Let us proceed, venerable sirs, to enquire of the Bodhisattva how qualified is the race in which the next-coming Bodhisattva will be born."

"Well said," they exclaimed, and, approaching the Bodhisattva, with joined hands thus addressed: "How qualified is that family of noble beings wherein the next-coming Bodhisattva should take his birth?"

The Bodhisattva, having observed the noble host of the Bodhisattvas and the Devas (who appeared before him), thus replied—"Sixty-four qualities[29] appertain to the family, venerable sirs, in which the next-coming Bodhisattva will make his appearance."

"What are the sixty-four qualities?"

(1) "Such a family is highly intelligent, (2) neither mean nor tyrannical, (3) of a high caste, (4) remarkable for having two

generations (living at the same time). (5) It is unsubmissive. (6) It has two predecessors, as well as (7) two successors (living at the same time). (8) It has two special generations living, (9) and having a member of the name of Maheśa in two successive generations, (10) as also many women, (11) and many men. (12) It is preëminent, (13) not poor, nor submissive, (14) nor covetous; (15) but courteous, (16) devoted to good actions, (17) unnoticed by the mean, (18) and productive of artistic ingenuity. (19) The members of such a family have enjoyed all objects of desire, (20) and are staunch friends. (21) They are not addicted to destroy animal life; (22) they are grateful; (23) they can go wherever they wish; (24) but they never go wrong, (25) nor in an infatuated way. (26) Such a family is brave, (27) and faultlessly fearless. (28) It enjoys (pleasure) without infatuation; (29) it bestows large benefactions; (30) it is freed from mental pain by religious rites, (31) by religiously forsaking objects of desire, (32) by charity. (33) It is (noted for) unflinching valour, (34) for might and valour, (35) for surpassing valour. (36) It is devoted to worship sages (Rishis), (37) gods (Devatás,) (38) Chaityas, (39) and the manes. (40) It bears prolonged enmity to no one, (41) and is renowned over the ten quarters of the globe. (42) It is many-membered; (43) its members are not divided by family disputes; (44) its members are endless. (45) It is the eldest of its race; (46) it is the noblest of its race; (47) it has acquired the submission of all the branches of its race; (48) it has the title of Maheśa (the great lord). (49) It knows its mother, (50) and its father. (51) It is preëminent. (52) It has the quality of Bráhmanhood in it. (53) It is rich in wealth, corn and treasuries; (54) it is affluent in gold, suvarṇa, (golden coin) jewels, pearls, native silver, wrought silver, (or coined silver, *rajata*) lands and resources; (55) it is possessed of multitudes of elephants, horses, chariots, camels, cattle, and sheep; (56) it is the master of numerous slaves, male and female, and domestics of various kinds. (57) It is uncontrollable. (58) All its objects are satisfied. (59) It is an imperial *(chakravartí)* family, (60) endowed with help of the root of former good works. (61) It is glorified by the appearance in it of a Bodhisattva. (62) It is irreproachable of all caste defects. Thus, sirs, among Devas, among regions, among Máras, among Brahmás and among Sramána and Bráhmaṇa populations, is the family endowed with the 64 qualities.

Venerable sirs, the lady in whose womb the next-coming Bodhisattva will descend will be endowed with thirty-two noble qualities.

What are the thirty-two qualities which appertain to the lady in whose womb the next-coming Bodhisattva will descend?

She should be (1) well known, (2) lovely, (3) free from defect, (4) of good birth, (5) of good lineage, (6) of great beauty, (7) of good name, (8) of good length and breadth, (9) childless, (10) of good behaviour, (11) charitable, (12) of smiling face, (13) clever,[30] (14) frank, (15) gentle, (16) proficient, (17) well-informed, (18) learned, (19) unintriguing, (20) deceitless, (21) unirascible, (22) unenvious, (23) uncovetous, (24) steady, (25) unwavering, (26) unscurrilous, (27) full of the aroma of patience, (28) modest, (29) free from passion, envy and folly, (30) inheriting no defect from the mother's side, (31) faithful to her marriage vow, and (32) well-endowed with noble qualities in every part of her person.* It is into the womb of such a lady that the next-coming Bodhisattva will descend. These, venerable sirs, are the thirty-two qualities with which the lady should be endowed, in whose womb the next-coming Bodhisattva shall descend. Nor, venerable sirs, does the Bodhisattva descend into his mother's womb during the fortnight of the wane; it is on the 15th of the waxing moon, when the moon is full, and in conjunction with the constellation Pushya, that the next-coming Bodhisattva will enter the womb of his purified mother.

The Bodhisattvas and Devaputras, having thus heard of the purity of the race and of the mother of the Bodhisattva, became thoughtful as to which could be the only race so endowed which

* The footnote on page 27 of my edition of the Sanskrit text is wrong.

had been referred to by the noble being? And thinking so, this occurred to them. Here verily is the S'ákya race, wealthy, prosperous, patient, generous, delightful, full of people; its king S'uddhodana is pure both by the mother's and the father's side, as also of that of his wife; he is of a slender make, well-formed, an able instructor, radiant with the glory of righteousness, born in a noble family, and the glory of an imperial race; he owns measureless wealth, jewels, and gems; he has thorough knowledge of work, and is free from vicious propensities. In the S'ákya country he is the sole king, worshipped and respected, as the chief by all householders, ministers, and dependants. He is contented, auspicious, looking neither very old nor very young, endowed with all good qualities, well acquainted with all the arts, divisions of time, the soul, religion, the ultimate principles and countersigns. He is a virtuous king, regulated in his actions by the mandates of religion; who has planted the root of all prosperity for created beings, and dwells in the noble metropolis of Kapilavastu. Whoever dwells in this city attains its qualities. Of this king, S'uddhodana, Máyádeví is the wife. She is the daughter of Suprabuddha the sovereign of the S'ákyas. She is of tender years, endowed with beauty and youth, yet childless, having neither son nor daughter, of great beauty, handsome as a picture, adorned with all sorts of ornaments like a celestial nymph, devoid of defects arising from the mother's side, truthful, not harsh, uncontumelious, unscurrilous, irreproachable, having a voice sweet as that of the cuckoo, unincoherent. She speaks sweetly and kindly. She is divested of all anger, pride, vanity, enmity. She is unenvious. She speaks in due time. She is charitable, well-behaved, fully-contented, faithful to her marriage vow, free from all thought of men other than her husband. She has well-adjusted head, ears, and nose. Her hair is as black as the large black bee. With well-formed forehead, of excellent eye-brows, without any frown, of smiling face, she is mindful of the past;* gentle, of mellifluous speech, clever, straightforward, uncrooked, frank, and unintriguing. She

* *Púrvábhilashiṇí*, a doubtful epithet.

has a well-born husband. She is not harsh, nor fickle, nor scurrilous. She is of clear speech. She has the aroma of no passion, envy, or folly, and is full of patience. She has her sight and mind directed to the guidance of her hands, feet and eyes. She has soft tender hands and feet, delicate to the touch as the down on the pod of the *Abrus precatorius*; with eyes pure as the new-blown blue lotus, nose prominent like the fruit of the *Flacourtea cataphracta*; well-proportionate body; and arms tapering like the bow of Indra. She is well-behaved; of well-proportioned body and members; of faultless body. She has lips like the bimba fruit; is of lovely look and tapering neck; well-adorned with ornaments; of pure mind; thriving; of charming appearance, of beautifully low shoulders, of well-fitted, well-formed arms; of arched abdomen; of undepressed sides; of deep navel pit; of rounded, large, smooth, hard gluteals; of body of adamantine firmness; of thighs tapering like the trunk of the elephant; of hands and feet like that of the gazelle; of eyes the most lovely on earth; of piercing sight. She is beautiful beyond conception; having the beauty of the noblest of the womankind; a picture of fancy (*máyá*) bearing the name of Máyá; learned in all the arts; manifest as a nymph from the Nandana garden of Indra; dwelling in the gynecium of the Mahárájá S'uddhodana. She alone is worthy of becoming the mother of the Bodhisattva. All the qualities of race which the Bodhisattva has referred to, can be seen only in the S'ákya race.

On this subject this is said:

1. That pure being and sage, seated on the lion-throne of Sudharmá, in the palace of Dharmochchaya, and surrounded by his following of Devas of equal rank with himself and of Bodhisattvas of great renown, was joyful.

2. The thought then struck the seater, in what family of pure and virtuous members, should the Bodhisattva take his birth, and where were the mother and the father of pure nature fit for him?

3. He surveyed all the Kshatriya royal dynasties in the con-

tinent named Jambu, and found all of them tainted, except the S'ákya race, which was devoid of all defect.

4. S'uddhodana was the noblest among all the royal personages; he was of imperial family, and absolutely pure in his body. He was rich, thriving, calm, august, good, and virtuous.

5. All other men in the city of Kapila were well-disposed, and possessed of virtue. Abounding in gardens and groves and pleasure-grounds, the birthplace was resplendent in the city of Kapila.

6. All the men were of unmasked might, of long arms, possessed of the nine treasures, and proficient in archery. They destroyed not life for their own living.

7. The chief favourite of S'uddhodana had obtained pre-eminence over a thousand ladies; she was as delightful as a picture of enchantment, (Máyá) and was called by the name of Máyádeví, the goddess of enchantment.

8. Beautiful as a heavenly daughter, of well-proportioned body and untainted and auspicious person; there was no mortal nor a celestial being who could be satiated by beholding her.

9. Neither tinged by passion, nor tainted by fault, she was placid, soft, frank and pleasing in her speech. There was no harshness in her, nor roughness; she was placid and smiling and guileless.

10. Modest and bashful, virtuous and decorous, neither dull nor fidgety, unenvious and unintriguing, trickless and benevolent, she was devoted to her friends.

11. Always attached to religion, avoiding all untruth, abiding in truth, she had her mind and body entirely under her control. In her existed not any of the numerous faults which beset womankind on earth.

12. There existed not in the region of the mortals, nor in that of the Gandharvas, nor even in that of the Devas, a lady who could be compared to Máyádeví. Verily, she alone was worthy of becoming the mother of the great saint.

13. For five hundred generations, she had become the mother

of the Bodhisattva, and so did S'uddhodana become the father on those occasions, therefore was that well-endowed lady worthy of becoming the mother.

14. She abided in penances like a hermit, always performing penances along with her consort. Having obtained the sanction of the king, she had not entertained carnal wishes for thirty-two months.

15. In whatever place she sat (whether) covered with bones (or not) there she slept and walked, and even there dazzled her celestial nature, resplendent by her attachment to virtuous actions.

16. There was not a god, nor a demon, nor a mortal, who could cast his glance on her with a carnal desire. All of them, throwing aside all evil motive, and endowed with honorable sentiments, looked on her as a mother, or a daughter.

17. Through the influence of the good actions of Máyádeví the large royal family was everywhere thriving, nay even territorial chiefs were thriving through the noble deeds and renown of the king.

18. Like unto her, there was none to be seen worthy of the venerable being, or one more fully endowed with good qualities, or compassion,—that mother is Máyá.

19. In the whole circuit of Jambu, there was not another woman who could bear the weight of the noblest of mortals; she was a goddess of the highest merit, endowed with the might of a thousand times ten elephants.

20. Thus did those sons of Devas, noble possessors of Sambodhi, and of profound knowledge, describe the excellent Máyá, as worthy of becoming the mother of the S'ákya prince.

NOTES.

1. *Bodhisattva* (p. 32). Here a particular individual who was to descend on earth and acquire Buddhahood, is intended. Besides him there were around him, according to the legend, numerous Bodhisattvas whose period of spiritual trial and moral refinement had not advanced sufficiently, to entitle them to look for the highest prize of Buddhahood within an early date. They are assumed to be of different classes, and the person under notice is supposed to have belonged to the class named S'vetaketu.

According to the Burmese version he had obtained his Bodhisattva-hood after his mundane existence as a prince under the name of Wethandra, during which, among other acts of beneficence, he gave "away his wife, the princess Madi, and his two children, Dzali and Gahna." As Bodhisattva in Tushita his specific name was Saytakaytoo, which the Sanskrit text takes to be his class name. Bigandet, I, p. 10. The Chinese version gives him the name of Hou-ming = Prabhápála, and assigns him a period of 4,000 years' sojourn in Tushita, after which five signs became apparent, namely, the chaplet of flowers on his head began to fade, his armpits exuded perspiration, his garments became less beautiful, his body lost its splendour and his seat or throne evinced signs of unsteadiness. These indicated that he was to hold his place no longer, but to descend on earth for his final trial. Beal, p. 24.

2. *Apsarasas* (p. 32). *i. e.*, they had no females in their company—not even celestial nymphs (Apsarasas), who have constant access to all the regions of desire, including the heaven of Indra.

3. *Twelve years hence* (p. 32). The Tibetan version gives the prophecy in the same words, but in the Burmese version of Bishop Bigandet, the following is substituted: "During his sojourn in that happy place, enjoying the fullness of pleasure allotted to the fortunate inhabitants of those blissful regions, a sudden and uncommon rumour, accompanied with an extraordinary commotion, proclaimed the gladdening tidings that a Phra was soon to make his appearance in this world." I, p. 19. In the Chinese version, (p. 25)

it is said that when the Devaputras perceived from certain infallible signs of decaying glory that the Bodhisattva was about to descend from Tushita "to be born in Jambudvípa, together uttered the cry, calling to the people who inhabit the earth, 'ye mortals! adorn your earth! for Bodhisattva, the great Mahásattva, not long hence shall descend from Tushita to be born amongst you! make ready and prepare! Buddha is about to descend and to be born!'" Here the time is not mentioned.

4. *Imparted to Bráhmaṇs, &c.*, (p. 33). The Tibetan version, according to M. Foucaux's rendering, is "parcouraient les Vedas et les Bráhmaṇas." This is, however, not correct. The verb *Adhyápayantisma* has two objectives, exactly as in the corresponding English sentence "they taught the Bráhmaṇs the Vedas." The Bráhmaṇas are parts of the Vedas, and it is not at all likely that those particular parts were named first, and the whole afterwards. Herr Lefmann, translating from the Sanskrit, has "unterrichteten sie die Bráhmaṇa in den Veda."

5. *Chakravartí rájá*, (p. 33). "One in whom the Chakra, the discus of Vishṇu, abides (*vartitate*); such a figure being delineated by the lines of the hand. The grammatical etymology is, he who abides in, or rules over, an extensive territory called a Chakra!" WILSON's *Vishṇu Puráṇa*, p. 101. Theoretically a Chakravartí rájá is he who rules over the whole earth, or an entire Dvípa; practically it means an emperor. M. Sennart, in his Essai, has discussed the subject at great length, and brought all the details to a focus, pp. 10f. The legend of the Chakra-ratna is no doubt an after-contrivance intended to adapt the title for a Buddha prince. The mark on the palm is invariably shown in all images of Buddha, and also on the images of Bodhisattvas.

6. *Seven jewels*, (p. 33). Much interesting information regarding them occurs in M. Sennart's Essai, pp. 21f.

7. *Munja-keśa*, (p. 35). Literally of the colour of the munja fibre—*Saccarum munja*, Rox.

8. *Báláhaka*, (p. 35). This epithet, or its variant *Váláhaka*, has often been used in Sanskrit writings to denominate a horse. The word Valáhaka means a mountain, or a dark cloud, whence Váláhaka would be an apt designation for a grey or an alpine steed, and the

estimation in which the grey breed is held by mankind, would easily account for its being often used to name a favourite animal. I am induced to think it has some relation to Báhlika, (modern Balkh), a place not undeservedly noted for its superior horses, even though the rules of Sanskrit grammar stand in my way—Báláhaka is not a regular derivative of Báhlika.

Whatever the origin the term, Bálábaka or Valáhaka implying a horse of a much-prized breed, was current from very ancient times in India, both among the Hindus and the Buddhists, and the Mahábhárata applies it to the horse of Indra, thus: *Tvam vajram atulam ghoram ghoshavána tvam Valáhakah* (I, 1289). The famous horse Uchchaḥśravá, produced from the churning of the ocean and appropriated to Vishṇu, was of an iron-grey colour and probably the type of the Valáhaka. The horse recommended for the Aśvamedha sacrifice was also an iron-grey one. In the Ṛig Veda, too, Indra in one place is described to be the owner of an iron-grey horse. This was quite in keeping with Indra's character as the lord of the clouds, though in some places he is assigned mastership of chestnut horses. In the case of the rising sun the chestnut was poetically the most appropriate. The word *maniratna* also occurs in the Mahábhárata (I, 1095). For further details, *vide* Sennart's *Essai sur la légende du Buddha*, pp. 27 f.

9. *Eight facets*, (p. 35). There is a vague impression that the art of cutting precious stones was first brought to India by the Dutch. In the Mrichchhakaṭí mention is made of artists engaged in boring pearls, but no mention is anywhere made of cutting or grinding precious stones to produce facets on them, and improve their brilliancy; but the reference here to the eight facets of the sapphire leaves no doubt that the art was known and practised in ancient India. No stone in a natural state could have had eight facets which could enhance its beauty, and be worthy of special note.

10. *Mátaṅga*, (p. 36). No reference is made to this sage in the Burmese and the Chinese versions.

11. *Five hundred Pratyeka Buddhas*, (p. 36). The Burmese version is silent about these, and the Chinese one modifies the story to some extent. According to it, "At this time, there were dwelling in Jambudvípa, five hundred Pratyeka Buddhas, in the

midst of a forest, practising their religious exercises; these five hundred Pratyeka Buddhas, having heard this cry, immediately rose up into the air and went together to Benares; having arrived there, they began to exhibit their supernatural powers; causing their bodies to ascend into space, and emit all sorts of brilliant appearances; and then having uttered a Gáthá, one after another, they ended their term of days and entered Nirvána."—Beal's *Romantic History of Buddha*, pp. 25, 26.

12. *Mrigadáva*, (p. 36). The place is of course the Sáranátha of the present day. The word Sáranátha, means "lord of antelopes," from *sára* "an antelope" and *nátha* "a lord" or "master," and typifies the affection which Buddha always evinced for those animals.

13. *Time*, (p. 37). The Burmese version makes the Nats *alias* Devaputras ask the Bodhisattva direct for the reasons which induced him to reflect on the four important subjects, and his replies are more amplified than in the Sanskrit. Thus as regards time, he is made to say—

"Phralaong observed that the apparition of Buddha could not have taken place during the previous periods of 100,000 years and more that had just elapsed, because during that period the life of men was on the increase. The instructions on birth and death, as well as on the miseries of life, which form the true characteristics of Buddha's law, would not then be received with sufficient interest and attention. Had any attempt been made at that time to preach on these three great topics, the men of those days to whom those great events would have appeared so distant, could not have been induced to look upon them with sufficient attention; the four great truths would have made no impression on their minds; vain and fruitless would have been the efforts to disentangle them from the ties of passions then encompassing all beings, and to make them sigh after the deliverance from the miseries entailed upon mankind by birth, life, and death. The period when human life is under a hundred years' duration cannot at all be the proper period for such an important event, as the passions of men are then so many and so deeply rooted, that Buddha would in vain attempt to preach his law. As the characters which a man traces over the smooth surface of unruffled water instantly disappear without leaving any mark behind, so the law and instructions that one should attempt to spread on the hardened hearts of men would make no lasting impression upon them. Hence he concluded that the present period, when the life of men was of about a hundred years' duration, was the proper one for the apparition of Buddha."—Bigandet I, p. 22.

The Chinese version does not refer to time, as that is settled by the five prognostics to which the other works do not refer.

14. *Continent*, (p. 37). On this subject, too, the Burmese version is more amplified. The following is its account:

"His regards glanced over the four great islands, and the 2000 small ones. He saw that the island of Dzaboudiba, the southern one, had always been the favourite place selected by all former Buddhas; he fixed upon it, too, for himself. That island, however, is a most extensive one, measuring in length 300 youdzanas, in breadth 252, and in circumference 900. He knew that on that island former Buddhas, and semi-Buddhas, the two great Rehandas, or disciples of the right and left, the prince whose sway is universal, &c., had all of them invariably fixed upon and selected that island, and, amidst the various countries on the island, that of Mitzima, the central one, where is to be found the district of Kapilawot. 'Thither,' said he, 'shall I resort, and become a Buddha'" (I, p. 25).

The decision about Kapilawot having been at once arrived at no occasion is left for a survey of the countries. On the subject of the family the following are the remarks of the Burmese version. "Having determined the place which he was to select for his terrestrial seat, Phralaong examined the race or caste from which he was to be born. The caste of the people and that of merchants appeared too low, and much wanting in respectability, and, moreover, no Buddha had ever come out therefrom. That of the Pounhas was in former times the most illustrious and respected, but that of princes, in those days, far surpassed it in power and consideration. He therefore fixed his choice upon the caste of princes, as most becoming his future high calling. 'I choose,' said he, 'prince Thoodaudana for my father. As to the princess who is to become my mother, she must be distinguished by a modest deportment and chaste manners, and must never have tasted any intoxicating drink. During the duration of 100,000 worlds she must have lived in the practice of virtue, performing with a scrupulous exactitude all the rules and observances prescribed by the law. The great and glorious Princess Maia is the only person in whom all these conditions are to be found. Moreover, the period of her life shall be at an end ten months and seven days hence ; she shall be my mother.' "—Bigandet I, p. 26.

15. *Púrva Videha*, (p. 37). Videha is Mithilá, modern Tirhut, and Púrva Videha must necessarily be the country to the east of the Mahánandá, including Dinájpur and Rangpur, or parts of them.

16. *Apara Godániya*, (p. 37). I cannot make out this place. M. Foucaux takes it to be western Gauḍa, but in my text, the letter used is *d* = द and not *ḍ* = ड.

17. *Uttara Kuru*, (p. 37). It is the country to the north of the Himálaya, extending as far as the North Pole. As the people had no knowledge of the North Pole, what they meant was the plateau beyond the Himálaya, with some of the barbarous tribes of which they were more or less acquainted. Perhaps they included the hill-tribes also by the term.

18. *Madhyamadeśa*, (p. 37). Lit. "middle country", the 'Mitzima' of the Burmese, which is intended to imply the whole tract of India proper, from the Vindhya range to the Himálayan mountains, and from Behar to the Punjab.

19. *The Devaputras discussed*, (p. 38). According to the Sanskrit text the discussion took place among the audience, which, failing to arrive at a satisfactory conclusion, ultimately repaired to the Bodhisattva for the solution of their difficulty. In the Burmese the survey of the different ruling dynasties is altogether omitted. In the Chinese version the Bodhisattva, being himself doubtful as to which family to select, consults one of the Devas, Kin-t'hwán by name, who for many years had, " over and over again, gone down to Jambudvipa" and knew all about it. " Devaputra," said he, " you have often gone down to Jambudvipa ; doubtless, therefore, you know the cities, towns, and villages, and the various lineages of their kings ; and in what family Bodhisattva, for his one birth more, ought to be born." The Devaputra then recounts the merits of the several families, and the Bodhisattva rejects them, one by one, for the reasons assigned.

20. *Vaidehí dynasty*, (p. 38). Videha is modern Tirhoot, and

the derivative Vaidehí must mean the dynasty relating to that province, but the province named is Magadha ; it must follow, therefore. that either ancient Magadha included Tirhut, or a scion of the Vaidehí dynasty reigned in Magadha. The last is the most probable.

21. *Kos'ala*, (p. 38). Ayodhyá, modern Oudh, of which S'rávastí, modern Fyzabad, was the capital. Brahmadatta, a heretic, was its king, and he is therefore denounced as the descendant of a Chaṇḍála.

22. *Vañśarája dynasty*, (p. 38). In the Tibetan the name is Vadsa, a country of which Kausámbi or Vatsapaṭṭana was the capital. General Cunningham has identified the site of Kausámbi in the Doab of the Ganges.

23. *Vais'ali*, (p. 38) more correctly spelt Vaiśálí. General Cunningham has identified this town with modern Besaḍḥ near Patna. (*Ancient Geography of India*, p. 443). It was of great renown in former times, and is frequently referred to in the Puráṇas and in Buddhist legends. Its most remarkable peculiarity appears to have been its republican institutions. The people were "regardless of the respect due to rank, superiors, elders and the aged," *i. e.*, they all held themselves to be equal, and each proclaimed "I am the king, I am the king." This was evidently an autonomous city somewhat like those of which Arrian makes mention on the west of the Hyphasis. Thus "Alexander had, moreover heard that the country beyond the Hyphasis was rich, and the inhabitants thereof good husbandmen and excellent soldiers, that they were governed by the nobility, and lived peaceably, their rulers imposing nothing harsh nor unjust upon them." Rooke's Arrian v. 25, II, p. 54. The words of Arrian are *πρὸς γαρ τῶν ἄριστον ἄρχεσθαι τοὺς πολλοὺς, τοὺς δὲ οὐδὲν ἔξω τοῦ ἐπιεικοῦς ἐξηγεῖσθαι.* Diodorus Siculus has something to the same effect, II, Cap. XXXIX. These suggest an oligarchical form of government, but the words of the text imply more. That it was a development of the village system so graphically described by Sir Henry Maine is evident. It is to be much regretted that fuller information on the subject is not available in ancient Indian works. Sir Henry Elliot, in his Muhammadan Historians, was of opinion that the idea of freedom among the Hindus was "the offscouring of college declamation :" the text of the Lalita-Vistara and the testimony of Arrian contradict that entirely.

24. *Pradyotana dynasty*, (p. 39). This dynasty reigned in Ujjayiní,

in Malwa. The Chinese version gives the name Mávanti, apparently a corruption of Avanti.

25. *Mathurá*, (p. 39). The city is celebrated in the Hindu annals as the capital of king Kañśa, the Herod of India, who immolated all the infants which were born on the birthday of Kṛishṇa, and was ultimately killed by Kṛishṇa.

26. *Hastinápura*, (p. 39). The account of the illegitimate birth of the Páṇḍavas shows clearly that the story, if not the Mahábhárata itself, was current from long before the date of the Lalita-Vistara. In the Chinese version Hastinápura is translated into "the city of the white elephant." According to the Hindus the city owes its name to king Hastin, who built it.

27. *Mithilá*, (p. 46). Sumitra lived at a very remote period of antiquity. His name is here not intended to be that of a king living at the time of Buddha's birth.

28. *Sixteen great dynasties*, (p. 40). None of the texts supplies the names of all the sixteen dynasties. The Sanskrit version has eight names, which are repeated in the Tibetan. The Chinese adds thereto three, *viz.*, those of Káśí, Pindu and S'ákya. In the Sanskrit the last is noticed separately. The Burmese is entirely silent about the rejected families.

29. *Sixty-four qualities*, (p. 40). My MSS. give details of only 62 qualities. The Chinese version limits them to sixty.

30. *Clever* (p. 42). The Sanskrit is *Pradakshiṇá-grahíní*, which means "she who accepts that which has been circumambulated," *i. e.* the choicest of gifts, or knowledge, and therefore clever. I am, however, not at all satisfied with the rendering. It might mean "she had selected her own husband" in svayañvará.

CHAPTER IV.

INITIATORY LIGHTS OF RELIGION.

Bodhisattva gives audience in the pavilion of Uchchadhvaja. He invites Devaputras. He takes his seat on a throne. The throne described. His address to the congregation. One hundred and eight subjects on which Bodhisattva lectured before his descent from Tushita. Effect of the announcement on the congregation. Gáthás in support of this narrative.

Thus, Bhikshus, the Bodhisattva, having surveyed the family wherein he would appear, ascended the great Tushita pavilion of Uchchadhvaja, measuring 64 yojanas in extent, wherein seated he had of yore instructed the gods of Tushita in religion. Having ascended the pavilion, he invited all the Devaputras of the class Tushitakáyika.[1] "Approach, O ye, and hear from him, who is about to cease to be a Boddhisattva, maxims of religion cognate to the descent."

On hearing these words all the Tushitakáyika Devaputras, along with Apsarasas, assembled in the pavilion. There the Bodhisattva remained in the centre of a congregation of the extent of the earth with its four continents. He appeared in beautiful colours, very showy, well-adorned, and very pleasing, while all the Devas, gods of the region of desire, (Kámávachara) and Devaputras of the region of semblance, (Rúpávachara,) made their abodes assume the name of cremation ground (*smasána, i. e.*, they deserted them to be present before him). Then did he ascend on a throne, refulgent with the lustre of his noble deeds. Its feet were set with innumerable jewels. It was spread over with layers of flowers. It was redolent with varied perfumes and burning incenses. It was steeped in the aroma of beautiful flowers of various colours. It was emblazoned with the light of a thousand jewels. It was spread over with nets of costly texture wherein innumerable little bells tinkled in the breeze, and hundreds of thousands of larger ones, ornamented with precious stones, resounded in the air. It was spread over with costly jewels. It was refulgent in the light of innumerable jewelled networks. Around it flowed costly tissue in exquisite profusion, and Apsarasas played, danced, and sang in ecstacy. Many were the panegyrics sung in its praise, and innumerable were the sovereigns who found asylum in its safety. Many were the Brahmás who paid obeisance to this throne, and countless were the salutations offered to its greatness. Thousands of Bodhisattvas surrounded it, and millions of millions were the Buddhas who were invited within its precincts from the ten quarters of the globe. It was a throne where was centred the collected virtues of the Páramitás, and morality of ages without number. Seated on this throne, the Bodhisattva addressed this crowded godly assembly, saying, "Observe, venerable sirs, the body of the Bodhisattva adorned with a hundred emblems of virtue! Behold, countless myriads of Bodhisattvas coming from everywhere, from all parts of the earth, north and south, east and west, above and below, to the noble mansion to meet the Boddhisattva of Tushita, surrounded by Devas, and now, ready for another transition, expounding the light of religion at the time of descent."

Beholding the Bodhisattvas in the presence of the Bodhisattva, the assembly saluted him with joined hands, and, five times circumambulating his person, thus burst forth in amazement: "Amen. Inconceivably wonderful is the presence of the Bodhisattva, by whose fiat we have just beholden these Bodhisattvas."

The Bodhisattva now invited the crowded godly assembly, and thus addressed them: "Listen, venerable sirs, to the initiatory lights of religion of the period of descent, which cause horripilation even in gods, and which have been expounded by these Boddhisattvas." One hundred and eight are the initiatory lights of religion which were expounded by the Bodhisattva at the time of his descent.

"What are they?"

"They are 1st, the light of Faith, *(śraddhá)* which upholds unswerving attachment; 2nd, the light of approbation, *(prásáda)*,[2]

3rd, the light of joy, (*prámodya,*) which embellishes it. 4th, the light of attachment, (*príti,*) which purifies the mind. 5th, the light of controlling the body, (*káyasamvara*),[3] which cleanses the body in its triple phases. 6th, the light of controlling speech, (*Vákṣamvara,*) which removes the fourfold defects of speech. 7th, the light of controlling the mind, (*manahsamvara,*) which overcomes all tendency to falsehood, murder and injury. 8th, the light of the memory of Buddha, (*Buddhánusmṛiti,*) which purifies vision. 9th, the light of the memory of Dharma, (*Dharmánusmṛiti,*) which maintains the immaculacy of the precepts of religion. 10th, the light of the memory of congregations, (*sanghánusmṛiti,*) which reduces every thing to propriety. 11th, the light of the memory of charity, (*tyágánusmṛiti,*) which destroys attachment to physical objects. 12th, the light of the memory of good behaviour, (*śilánusmṛiti,*) which exists for the promotion of meditation. 13th, the light of the memory of the Devas, (*Devánusmṛiti,*) which increases liberality of the mind. 14th, the light of friendship, (*maitri,*) which exists for attachment to ritual work. 15th, the light of mercy, (*karuṇá,*) which abides as an antidote to envy. 16th, the light of cheerfulness, (*muditá,*) which exists for the prevention of anxiety. 17th, the light of indifference, (*upekshá,*) which exists to the abasement of desires. 18th, the light of the abandonment of the transient, (*anitya-pratyavekshá,*) which exists to overcome desires and longings and earnestness. 19th, the light of contempt for pain, (*duksha-pratyavekshá,*) which exists for suppression of enterprise. 20th, the light of contempt for unspiritual objects, (*anátma-pratyavekshá*) which exists to retract the soul from unreality. 21st, the light of the sense of meekness, (*śánta-pratavekshá,*) which exists for the destruction of seduction. 22nd, the light of modesty, (*hri,*) which exists for the suppression of nature. 23rd, the light of bashfulness, (*apatrápya,*) as a restraint over worldly actions. 24th, the light of truth, (*satya,*) which exists for the suppression of discord among gods and men. 25th, the light of matter, (*bhúta,*) which exists for the suppression of all disputes regarding the soul. 26th, the light of the practice of virtue, (*dharmacharaṇa,*) which exists for the following of virtue. 27th, the light of threefold protection, (*triśaraṇa-gamana,*)[4] which abides for overcoming the threefold destruction. 28th, the light of gratitude, (*kṛitajṇatá,*) which upholds the acknowledgment of benefits received. 29th, the light of thankfulness, (*kṛitaveditá,*) which upholds the memory of others. 30th, the light of the knowledge of self, (*átmajṇatá,*) which produces a knowledge of self. 31st, the light of the knowledge of beings, (*sattvajṇánatá,*) which suppresses misfortune for others. 32nd, the light of the knowledge of religion, (*Dharmajṇatá,*) which displays the nature of primary and secondary religious duties. 33rd, the light of the knowledge of time, (*kálajṇatá,*) which promotes unfailing preception. 34th, the light of suppressing pride, (*nihatamánatá,*) which promotes knowledge. 35th, the light of unruffled mind, (*apratihata-chittatá,*) which supports one's powers. 36th, the light of avoidance of anger, (*anupanáha,*) which prevents improper acts. 37th, the light of final liberation, (*adhimukti,*) which upholds absolute certainty. 38th, the light of considering into evils, (*aśubha-pratyavekshá,*) which dispels the sophistry of desire. 39th, the light of unwickedness, (*avyápáda,*) which dispels sophistry of malice prepense. 40th, the light of freedom from delusion, (*amoha,*) which overcomes all worldly ignorance. 41st, the light of devotion to religion, (*dharmárthikatá,*) which investigates the real objects of desire. 42nd, the light of love for religion, (*Dharmakámatá,*) which secures ascent to higher spheres. 43rd, the light of investigating traditions (*śrutoparyeshṭi,*) which exposes the nature of religion and improves human nature. 44th, the light of application, (*samyak-prayoga,*) which promotes success. 45th, the light of the knowledge of name and nature (of things), (*námarúpa-parijṇána,*) which deserves all foreign connections. 46th, the light of destruction of the desire to enquire into causation, (*hetudṛishṭi-samudghâṭa,*) which exists for the attainment of worship and salvation. 47th, the light of the relinquishment of servility, (*anunaya-pratigha-prahâṇa,*) which maintains equal position, neither high nor low. 48th, the light of proficiency in the categories, (*skandha-kauśalya,*) which exists for a perfect knowledge of pain. 49th, the light of the confirmity of the elements, (*dhátusamatá,*) which exists for the relinquishment of created objects. 50th, the light of the controul of the senses, (*áyatanápakarshaṇa,*) which exists for the safe passage. 51st, the light of unaffected forbearance, (*anutpádakshánti,*) which exists for the visual cognition of final stoppage (of transmigration). 52nd, the light of the corporeal memory, (*káyagatasmṛiti,*)[5] which exists for corporeal recognition (of things). 53rd, the light of the memory of pain, (*vedanágatasmṛiti,*) which exists for sympathy for others. 54th, the light of the memory of the thinking principle, (*chittagatánusmṛiti,*) which exists for the consideration of the results of delusion. 55th, the light of the memory of duty, (*dharmagatánusmṛiti,*) which exists for the attainment of cloudless knowledge. 56th, the light of the four complete abandonments, (*chatvári-samyak-prahánáni,*) which exists for the destruction of all injurious works and the enhancement of salutary ones. 57th, the light of the four supernatural powers, (*chatváro-ṛiddhipádáh,*) which exists for the lightness of the mind and the body. 58th, the light of the faculty of purity, (*śuddhendriya,*) which exists for non-submission to others. 59th, the light of the faculty of vigour, (*víryendriya,*) which exists for the advancement of well-balanced understanding. 60th, the light of the faculty of memory, (*smṛitíndriya,*) which exists for the advancement of good actions. 61st, the light of the faculty of Samádhi, (*samádhíndriya,*) which exists for the salvation of the thinking principle. 62nd, the light of the faculty of Prajná, (*Prajnendriya,*) which exists for the advancement of the power of discrimination. 63rd, the light of the power of faith, (*śraddhábala,*) which exists for the overthrow of the powers of Mára. 64th, the light of the power of vigour, (*víryabala,*) which exists for steadiness in the right path. 65th, the light of the power of memory, (*smṛitibala,*) which exists for indestructiveness. 66th, the light of the power of Samádhi (*samádhibala*) which exists for the destruction of all casuistry. 67th, the light of the power of understanding, (*Prajṇábala,*) which exists for the prevention of intellectual weakness. 68th, the light of the memory of the body of Sambodhi, (*smṛitisambodhyañga,*) which exists for the acquisition of a knowledge of Dharma. 69th, the light of the waves of religion of the body of Sambodhi, (*dharmapravichayasambodhyañga,*) which exists for the advancement of all religion. 70th, the light of the power of the body of Sambodhi, (*víryasambodhyañga,*) which exists for superior intelligence. 71st, the light of affection for the body of Sambodhi, (*prítisambodhyañga,*) which exists for the promotion of Samádhi. 72nd, the light of trust in the body of Sambodhi, (*praśrabdhyasambodhyañga,*) which exists for promoting the performance of duty. 73rd, the light of profound meditation of the body of Sambodhi, (*samádhisambodyañga,*) which exists for the reconciliation of diverse doctrines. 74th, the light of indifference which forms a part of the body of Sambodhi, (*upekshásambodhyañga,*) which destroys all possible births. 75th, the light of thorough insight, (*samyagdṛishṭi,*) which exists for passage by the uncrooked path. 76th, the light of thorough resolve, (*samyaksañkalpa,*) which exists for the overthrow of all doubts, double thoughts, and indecisions. 77th, the light of all speech, (*samyakvák,*) which exists for the reconciliation of all letters, murmurs, sounds, loud sounds, speech and hearing. 78th, the light of the end of all work, (*samyak-karmánta,*) which exists for the perfection of one's work. 79th, the light of full existence, (*samyagájíva,*) which exists for the enhancement of all gratifications. 80th, the light of full exercise, (*samyag-vyáyáma,*) which exists for the attainment of the opposite shore. 81st, the light of full memory, (*samyak-smṛiti,*) which exists for the attainment of transcendental memory and super-humanity. 82nd, the light of thorough meditation, (*samyak-samádhi,*) which exists for the attainment of passionless, unsentient Samádhi. 83rd, the light of Bodhi thought, (*Bodhi-chitta,*) which exists for the severance of all bonds with the three families (those of father, mother and wife). 84th, the light of desire, (*ásaya,*)[6] which exists for preventing the contact of lower vehicles, (*hinayána*). 85th, the light of the Yoga of Adhyása,[7] (*adhyása-yoga,*) which renders the liberal Buddha religion manifest. 86th, the light of application, (*prayoga,*) which exists for the advancement of all salutary religion. 87th, the light of the duty of charity, (*dána-páramitá,*[8]) which exists for the purification of the characteristics and marks of the field of Buddhism, and the reformation of vain persons. 88th, the light of the duty of good behaviour, (*śíla-páramitá,*) which overcomes vicious conduct, and wins wicked people to good manners. 89th, the light of the duty of forbearance, (*kshánti-páramitá,*) which exists for the overthrow of all evils, all faults, vanity, pride, ostentation, and for the subdual of men with troubled minds. 90th, the light of the duty of vigour, (*vírya-paramitá,*) which exists for advancement beyond the initiatory religious light of the root of all good, and for the reclamation of usurers. 91st, the light of the duty of meditation, (*dhyána-páramitá,*) which exists for the generation of all knowledge and understanding, and for the subdual of men of distracted mind. 92nd, the light of the duty of understanding, (*prajṇá-páramitá,*) which exists for the destruction of ignorance, delusion, cloudiness, darkness, and false perception, and for the subdual of men of wicked understanding. 93rd, the light of aptitude of means, (*upáya-kauśala,*) which exists to reveal the course of emancipated people, and for the glory of the religion of all Buddhas. 94th, the light of the four collected things[9], (*chatvárí-sañgraha-vastuni,*) which exists for the congregation of men for the attainment of Sambodhi, and for the review of religion. 95th, the light of the maturity of being, (*sattva-paripáka,*) produces the decay of all unspiritual enjoyment, and the translation of beings without pain. 96th, the light of the acceptance of the true religion, (*sad-dharma-parigraha,*) which exists for the overthrow of the suffering of created beings. 97th, the light of trading-stock, (*paṇya-sambhára,*) which exists for affording sustenance to living beings. 98th, the light of wisdom-stock, (*jṇána-sambhára,*) which exists for the advancement of the ten (supernatural) powers[10]. 99th, the light of the stock of capacity (*samartha-sambhára,*) which exists for the attainment of the Samádhi of Tathágata. 100th, the light of the stock of acute vision, (*vidarsaná-sambhára,*) which exists for the attainment of the vision of knowledge. 101st, the light of arrival at knowledge, (*prati-samvidavatára,*) which exists for the attainment of the vision of religion. 102nd, the light of approaching the asylum, (*parisaraṇávatára,*) which exists for the improvement of Buddha vision. 103rd, the light of the attainment of retentiveness, (*dháraṇá-pritilambha,*) which exists for the retention of the sayings of all Buddhas. 104th, the light of the attainment of courage, (*pratibhána-pratilambha,*) which exists for the gratification of all beings by sweet speech. 105th, the light of the non-cessation of the sequence of religion, (*ánulomika-dharmákshánti,*) which exists for the following in due sequence the teachings of all Buddhas. 106th, the light of cessation from unrevealed religion, (*anutpattika-dharma-kshánti,*) which exists for the preservation of traditions or works called *vyákaraṇas* (which contain ancient legends). 107th, the light of undeviating fixity, (*avaivartika,*) which exists for the advancement of the religion of all Buddhas. 108th, the light of the knowledge of the relation with each other of the different stages, (*bhúmerbhúmi-sankránti-jṉána,*) for the consecration of the knowledge of those who know the subject. 109th,[11] the light of the consecration stage, (*abhisheka-bhúmi*), which exists for the exposition of the descent, birth, departure from home, penance, ascent on the Bodhimaṇḍala, overthrow of Mára, setting in motion of the wheel of religion, and the great final emancipation. These are, venerable sirs, the hundred and eight initiatory lights of religion which were for certain disclosed to the godly congregation by the Bodhisattva at the time of his descent.

Thus, Bhikshus, the initiatory religious lights having been disclosed by the Bodhisattva to the godly assembly, the hearts of eighty-four thousand Devaputras were interested in the sequenceless Sambodhi knowledge. In the hearts of thirty-two thousand Devaputras, who had performed the duties of all the previous stages, a feeling of satisfaction arose about the uncreate religion. Of thirty-six thousand Devaputras and of Devas by millions, the eye of religion was made dirtless, dustless and pure. The whole of the noble mansion of Tushita was covered knee-deep with excellent flowers.

On that occasion, Bhikshus, the Bodhisattva addressed these highly exhilarating Gáthás to the godly assembly :—

1. "When the noble being and leader descends from the excellent mansion of Tushita, casting aside all errors, he invites all the Devas.

2. All ye, who have the fullness of good inclination, and are thoughtful, listen to the fruit of work, the result of all former good actions.

3. Be not ungrateful, by casting away the accumulated store of unprecedented works. Go not again there where exist destruction, and unsurmountable trouble and pain.

4. Having heard this exposition of the true religion from me, with due respect, devote yourselves to it, and thereby attain constant, endless bliss.

5. All (worldly objects) are impermanent, undesirable, inconstant; there is nothing permanent or fixed in them; they are delusive like the mirage, and transient as the lightning, or froth.

6. Nor are our desires gratified by them, even as (thirst is not satisfied) by the drinking of salt water. Do you gratify yourselves by this noble, everlasting, stainless knowledge.

7. It cannot be rivalled by music, innumerable like the waves of the sea, nor by the society of heavenly damsels (for ages without number). Each of them departs when our desires are satisfied.

8. It comes not from personal exertion, nor by the help of friends or relatives, nor by that of one's family; it proceeds from works; it is attached to good actions, and goes on one's back.

9. Hence, for one's own entire good and for good-will and friendly feeling for each other, let virtuous actions be

performed; let good conduct be persevered in, for those who do so suffer no pain.

10. Let Buddha be reflected upon; let the society of the virtuous be adopted; let delusion be avoided; constant, traditional good behaviour, and charity, and the aroma of mercy (are its requirements).

11. Let him who constantly takes to this religion look upon pain as impermanent and unspiritual. Effect proceeds from cause without a master, and is inert.

12. Whatever wealth exists of mine, whatever splendour, whatever knowledge and merit, they all are due to good actions, good conduct, traditional knowledge, and disillusion.

13. Follow me through good conduct, through tradition, through disillusion, through charity, through the controul of passions, and through humanity for the sake of welfare and friendship for all created beings.

14. It is not possible to accomplish salutary actions by the sound of speech; exert for success; act according to what you say.

15. Look not for another's leisure; always exert yourself with all possible assiduity. None can give without action, nor is anything accomplished without it.

16. Reflect well upon the pain which you have suffered in this world. Cessation and dispassion are difficult of attainment, and the world is eternally false.

17. Therefore, whenever opportunity offers, overcome all passions and sufferings by friendliness to all goodness, and by listening to the voice of Dharma.

18. Freedom from vanity, pride and ostentation, constant rectitude of purpose, becoming speech and honesty, are the qualities which you, who long for Nirváṇa, should cultivate to clear the road to it.

19. Dispel with the lamp of understanding (*prajṇá*) all delusion, sin and darkness, and rend asunder the knot of longing wickedness with the thunderbolt of true knowledge (*jṇána*).

20. How shall I unfold to you at length the extensive religion, pregnant with meaning? Remain not where any harm can result to religion.

21. In order that the Bodhi religion may be attained by him who is in quest of that nectar, and the same may be showered (on earth), adore him with purified mind, so that you may listen to the exposition of the great religion.

NOTES.

1. *Tushitakáyika*, p. 55. In order fully to explain the purport of this term it is necessary to advert briefly to the cosmogony of the Buddhists. The authorities are not unanimous on the subject, and it would take too much space to note all the differences observable in Buddhist works in Nepal, Ceylon, China and Mongolia. Enough may be, however, gleaned to show what the general idea is. In Nepal, according to the authorities cited by Mr. Hodgson (*Essays*, pp. 42 f.), the universe is made up of fourteen different classes of regions (*Bhuvanas*) placed in tiers one above the other. Some of these are solitary, others include several subdivisions. The order of their arrangement from the highest to the lowest stands thus :—

I. Agnishṭha Bhuvana. It is the abode of Ádi Buddha, and has no subdivision.

II. Bodhisattva Bhuvana. According to some there are ten subdivisions of this region; according to others, thirteen, namely 1, *Pramoditá;* 2, *Vimalá;* 3, *Prabhákarí;* 4, *Archismatí;* 5, *Sudurjayá;* 6, *Abhimukti;* 7, *Dúrañgamá;* 8, *Achalá;* 9, *Sádhumatí;* 10, *Dharmameghá;* 11, *Samanta-prabhá;* 12, *Nirupamá;* 13, *Jnánavatí.* These were made by Ádi Buddha himself, and are intended for Bodhisattvas of different grades.

III. Rúpa'vachara Bhuvana. It includes the following eighteen subdivisions, *viz.;* 1, *Brahmakáyiká;* 2, *Brahmapurohitá;* 3, *Brahma-prásádyá;* 4, *Mahá-brahmaná;* 5, *Paritábhá;* 6, *Apramánábhá;* 7, *Ábhásvará;* 8, *Paritasubhá;* 9, *Subhakitshná;* 10,

Anabhraká; 11, *Punyaprasavá*; 12, *Vṛihatphalá*; 13, *Arañgisattvá*; 14, *Avṛihá*; 15, *Apáyá*; 16, *Sudṛiśá*; 17, *Sudarsaná*; 18, *Sumukhá*. These are sometimes called *Brahma Bhuvanas*, because they are subject to Brahmá, and designed for the accommodation of his worshippers. They are the regions of semblance.

IV. Ká'má'vachara Bhuvana. It includes six subdivisions, namely; 1, *Chatur-mahárájiká*; 2, *Trayastriñśá*; 3, *Tushitá*; 4, *Yámá*; 5, *Nirmáṇaratí*; 6, *Paranirmáṇa-vasavartí*. These are regions of enjoyment subject to Vishṇu, who receives his worshippers there.

V. Arúpyavachara Bhuvana. Subject to Mahádeva, and subdivided into three; 1, *Nitya-yatnopáyá*; 2, *Vijnána-yatnopáyá*; 3, *Akinchinya-yatnopáyá*.

VI. Indra Bhuvana. Region of Indra.

VII. Yama Bhuvana. Region of Yama.

VIII. Su'rya Bhuvana. Region of the Sun.

IX. Chandra Bhuvana. Region of the Moon, including, as subdivisions, the regions of the planets and the stars.

X. Agni Bhuvana. The region of fire, also called *Agnikuṇḍa*.

XI. Váyu Bhuvana. The region of Air.

XII. Pṛithiví Bhuvana. The region of the earth.

XIII. Jala Bhuvana. The region of water.

XIV. Pátála Bhuvana. This includes seven subdivisions, of which six are the abodes of Daityas, and the last is the place of punishment for sinners. It has, according to some, eight subdivisions, according to others, 16, or 84. Burnouf, quoting the *Avadána-śataka*, gives the names of 16. (*Histoire*, p. 201) Most of them are noticed in the Hindu Puráṇas. Classes III to XIV are the handiworks of Manjuśrí.

The Tibetans, according to Georgi as summarised by Burnouf, (*Histoire*, pp. 599 f.) range the super-terrestrial regions in stages round the fabulous Meru mountain. The first stage represents the region of the Yakshas and other demons; the 2nd by the Garuḍas who, of half-human half-bird form, carry about a garland, whence their name S'ragdhará. The 3rd is that of the Nágas. The 4th is the abode of the Asúras. Next comes the home of the Chaturmahárájikas, and then successively the Trayastriñśas, the Yámas, the Tushitas, the Nirmáṇaratis, and so on. According to the authors of the first scheme, the dwellers in the classes II to IX have the common name of Devas; but a distinction is frequently made between the seniors and the juniors of each class, the former being called Devas, and the latter, Devaputras or sons of Devas. The class designation of each class is provided by the name of the region they occupy; thus the Devas of the Rúpávachara mansion are *Rúpávachara Devas*, the Devas of the Kámávachara mansion, *Kámávachara Devas*, &c. Their particular generic names are formed with the names of the subdivisions they occupy, such as *Brahmakáyika*, *Tushitakáyika*, &c., *i. e.*, having bodies of the regions of Brahmá, Tushita, &c.

Theoretically every division or subdivision has its special genus of Devas, and accordingly there should be nearly fifty genera; but in the literature of Nepal a much smaller number is noticed. The Avadána-śataka, in one place, gives the names of 23, and most of them occur in the Lalita-Vistara, along with some whose names do not fall within any of the classes noticed in the scheme. A remarkable one is that of S'uddhávása-káyika, which I have translated on pp. 3 and 4 as "Devaputras of auspicious homes and persons." It is possible, thought not probable, that the epithet is merely descriptive, and not intended to indicate any particular class. The Yakshas, Nágas, Garuḍas, &c. dwell in lower spheres, and have no claim to the epithet Deva.

Of the 23 genera noticed in the *Avadána-śataka*, detailed descriptions are nowhere given. The following brief notes are all I can offer in the necessarily limited space available to me here. I follow the order in which the names occur in Burnouf's work, and not that which they should occupy in the cosmographic scheme.

1. *Chatur-mahárájikas* also *Mahárájikas*. The four great kings or guardians of the four cardinal points. They occupy the same position which the *Lokapálas* do in the Hindu system. The short name occurs in the Puráṇas as that of one of the 220 kinds of Gaṇa Devatás, or demigods.

2. *Trayastriṅśas*, *lit.* thirty-three, meaning the Vedic gods, who are frequently so named in the Hindu S'ástras, and the development of which produces the thirty-three millions of gods. Of these

gods Indra is the chief; but in the Buddhist cosmos he is assigned a separate region.

3. *Yámas.* Protectors of the divisions of the day. According to the Vishṇu Puráṇa (I, vii.), Ákútí bore to Ruchi the twins Yajna and Dakshiṇá, who, marrying each other, had twelve sons, who became the Yámas. They flourished in the Manvantara of Svyambhuva. They reside in Maharloka. The Chinese and the Mongolian interpretation of the name supports the Indian theory. According to it, as rendered by Burnouf into French, "Les Yámas sont ainsi nommés parce qu'ils mesurent leurs jours et leurs nuits sur l'épanouissement et la clôture des fleurs de lotus," (p. 605).

4. *Tushitas.* The Vishṇu Puráṇa gives two accounts of these. According to one (B. I, c. VII) the Tushitas were borne of Kásyapa in the end of Sarochisha Manvantara. Wishing to be gods a second time they entered the womb of Aditi, and were born as the twelve Ádityas. In B. III. c. I, they are said to be the sons of Tushitá, wife of Vedaśiras. The Váyu Puráṇa gives a detailed account, but not corresponding with this. According to the Hindus they form one of the thirty-six orders of Devas.

5. *Nirmáṇaratis.* "Ceux qui trouvent leur volupté dans leurs transformations miraculeuses." Burnouf says, "The name and the role of these divinities appertain exclusively to the Buddhists, and I do not find any thing among the Bráhmans to correspond." The Vishṇu Puráṇa describes them as a class of gods numbering thirty. They flourished in the 11th Manvantara, (III. 26,). Adverting to these, he says they are not intended by the Buddhist term.

6. *Paranirmita-vasavartí.* "Ceux qui disposent à leur gré des formes qu'ont revêtues les autres." They are not noticed in Hindu works, but apparently they are connected with the Máras.

7. *Brahmakáyikas.* "Ceux qui forment la suit de Brahmá."

8. *Brahma-purohitas.* "Les ministres de Brahmá."

9. *Mahábrahmás.* "Les grands Brahmás." A fourth class of Brahmás is noted by Hodgson with the name of *Brahma-parisadyas*, which Burnouf renders into "ceux qui composent ensemble de Brahmá." These four inhabit the four regions of Brahmá. The Puráṇas relate the origin of various beings from the person of Brahmá while he was immersed in meditation; but as these did not multiply, he at last

created some sons who issued from his mind. They are all necessarily Brahmaputras or sons of Brahmá, but to mark the superiority of the latter they are called Mánasaputras, mind-born sons. The former may, therefore, be aptly described Brahmakáyikas, or born of the body of Brahmá. The second may be similar to, or the same with, the Brahmarshis or Brahma-sages, the Buddhist term meaning 'the priests of the class Brahmá.' The third may be likened to Prajápatis. Anyhow they are obviously imitations of Bráhmaṇic legends.

10. *Parittábhas*. Limited light.

11. *Apramáṇábhas*. Measureless light.

12. *Abhásvaras*. Full of light—*spiritus fulgens clarus*. (Voc. Pentaglot.) The three last are characterised by the possession of light. The first two are not noticed by the Hindus, the third forms a class of Gaṇa Devatás, or demigods. They number 64.

13. *Parittaśubhas*. Of limited purity—*exiguarum virtutum*. Georgi.

14. *Apramáṇaśubhas*—of measureless purity—*Virtutum infinitarum regio*. Georgi.

15. *Subhakritsnas*. Of absolute purity—*Pureté ètandu*. Voc. Pentaglot. These three are characterised by their varying degrees of purity. Their names do not occur in Hindu works, but the last is probably a variant of the Hindu Subhásvaras, a class of Pitṛis, mentioned in the Vishṇudharmottara and the Vahni Puráṇas.

16. *Anabhrakas*. Cloudless—*qui est sans nuage*, Burnouf. They are not noticed by the Hindus.

17. *Punyaprasabhas*. Burnouf translates this term in three different ways: 1st. Ceux dont l'origine est dans la purité: 2nd, ceux qui produisant la purité: 3rd, ceux dont les productions ou les descendants sont purs. He gives his adhesion to the first.

18. *Bṛihatphalas*. Of abundant fruition—"ceux qui ont les grandes récompenses."

19. *Avṛihas*. "Ceux qui ne s'étendent pas." Burnouf.

20. *Atapas*. Painless,—"ceux qui sont exempts de souffrance." Burnouf. Remusat gives—spiritus sine mœrore et le ciel sans fatigue.

21. *Sudṛiśas*. Beautiful,—"Spiritus bonus visus, or, le ciel de Dieux qui voient admirablement tous les mondes."

22. *Sudarsanas.* Of handsome appearance—*Bonus apparens.* Remusat.

23. *Akanishṭhas.* "Ceux qui ne sont pas enferieurs." Burnouf. *Altissimus.* Georgi. A name of Buddha according to the Hindus.

2. *Prásáda*, p. 56. The word which I have translated into "initiatory light of religion," and briefly "light," is in Sanskrit *dharmálokamukha*, which literally rendered should be "the mouth of the light of religion." M. Foucaux translates it into "porte evidente de la Loi." The word mouth has been used metaphorically to convey the idea of the light being the entrance which leads to the perfection of religion, *i. e.*, these virtues of faith, contentment, joy, affection, controul of the cravings of the flesh, &c., are the essentials without which the ultimate end of Buddhism cannot be attained. Thus they are initiatory lights or duties which must be primarily attended to.

3. *Káyasamvara*, p. 57. M. Foucaux renders this word into gaieté, but samvara means to controul and not to embellish, and the cleansing the body is best effected by controulling the cravings of the flesh, and not by indulging in gaiety.

4. *Triśaraṇa-gamana*, p. 57. The trinity of the Buddhists forming the three asylums, *śaraṇa*.

5. *Káya-gata-smṛiti*, p. 59. This word is repeated in the text with the statement that "it promotes a right understanding of the nature of the body," but as no other term has been repeated, and two or more effects are, when necessary, included under one head, I suspect the repetition is a copyist's blunder. It is not given in the Tibetan version.

6. *Ásaya*, p. 60. The *Daśabhúmiśvara* describes ten *ásayas* or "aspirations" to be the characteristics of the second or Vimalá stage of Buddhist perfection. These are 1st, desire for simplicity; 2nd, for tender-heartedness; 3rd, for activity; 4th, for consulting others; 5th, for equality; 6th, for doing good; 7th, for purity; 8th, for impartiality; 9th, for large-heartedness; 10th, for magnanimity. See my 'Analysis of the Sanskrit Buddhist Literature of Nepal,' p. 82.

7. *Adhyásayoga*, p. 61. The *Mahávastu Avadána* differs from the *Daśubhúmiśvara* both in the names and in the order of arrangement

of the ten stages. According to it the 2nd stage is named, not Vimalá but, Varddhamáná, a name which does not occur in the latter. This stage, it says, is distinguished by twenty *Adhyásayas* or 'higher aspirations,' (*Adhyásayoga*) and these are :—1st, *Kalyána Adhyásaya* or aspiration to do good ; 2nd, *Snigdha A.* the state of mind in which it is never moved by anger; 3rd, *Madhura A.* desire to please women by service ; 4th, *Tikshṇa A.* knowledge of this world and of the world to come ; 5th, *Vipenda A.* active exertion to do good to all creatures ; 6th, *Vichitra A.* charity without ostentation ; 7th, *Aparyádána A.* profuse charity. 8th, *Anupahata A.* power of resisting temptation. 9th, *Asádháraṇa A.* uncommon diligence for the good of all animated creation. 10th, *Unnata A.* contempt for the doctrines of the Tírthikas ; 11th, *Ahṛipana A.* pursuit of virtue for other than enjoyment. 12th, *Anivartya A.* firmness in faith in Buddha in spite of temptations ; 13th, *Akṛirtima A.* aversion to the state of merchants, Pratyeka Buddhas and others ; 14th, *Suddha A.* desire for supreme good and contempt for all worldly gains ; 15th, *Driḍha A.* determination in spite of opposition ; 16th, *Svabháva A.* contempt for gifts not given with a good will ; 17th, *Tṛipta A.* contentment ; 18th, *Puṅgala A.* aspiration for omniscience ; 19th, *Ananta A.* charity without any desire for return ; 20th, (Not given in the only MS. at my disposal.)

8. *Dána Páramitá*, p. 61. For the ten Páramitás, *vide* Note 16, p. 11.

9. *Four collected things*, p. 61. These are :—1, alms, *dána ;* 2, kind speech, *priya-vachana ;* 3, wealth-bearing occupation, *artha-kṛiyá ;* 4, community of wealth, *samánárthatá.*

10. *Ten supernatural powers*, p. 61. The powers are :—1st, the power of appreciating the merits of objects ; 2nd, that of appreciating the merits of men of different kinds : 3rd, that of knowing the different essences which lead to Mukti ; 4th, that of knowing the character of other people ; 5th, that of knowing the consequences of good and bad actions ; 6th, that of evading mundane pain ; 7th, the knowledge of the importance of meditation ; 8th, that of recalling to mind the events of former existences ; 9th, that of the purity of the celestial eye ; 10th, that of destroying all mundane pains. These are all included in the generic term of the " eye of religion," *Dharmachakshu.* This eye with four others are attained in the third stage

of perfection. See my 'Analysis of the Sanskrit Buddhist Literature of Nepal,' p. 117.

11. 109th, p. 62. The total number is 109 as in the Tibetan version, but the number wanted is 108. In my MSS. there are 110, of which one is apparently a repetition, as stated in note 5.

CHAPTER V.

PREPARATIONS FOR DESCENT.

Bodhisattva's parting address. Request of the Devaputras. Appointment of Maitreya to the Vice-gerency of Tushita. Discussion on the form in which the Bodhisattva should enter his mother's womb. Manifestation of eight pre-ordained signs in the palace of S'uddhodana. Máyádeví's resolve to perform a fast. Devas resolve to follow the Bodhisattva. Máyádeví visited by Apsarasas. Devas undertake to protect her. Bodhisattva performs miracles in Tushita. The condition of the several regions of the universe at the time. Devas carry forth the Bodhisattva on their shoulders. Corroborative Gáthás.

Thus, Bhikshus, the Bodhisattva, having, through this religious Gáthá, exhibited, and expounded, (the religion and thereby) exhilarated, gratified and befriended the great godly assembly, addressed the assembly of Mañgalya Devas.[1] "I shall proceed, venerable sirs, to the Jambudvípa. I have already performed the duties of a Bodhisattva, and, by charity, by kind speech, by good services, and by accepting these as equals, invited mankind to the four kinds of blessings. It would, therefore, be unbecoming and undutiful on my part, sirs, if I do not be thoroughly conscient of the absolutely perfect knowledge (*samyak-sambodhi*)."

Now the Devaputras of the class Tushitakáyika, crying, held the feet of the Bodhisattva, and thus addressed him: "This noble mansion of Tushita, the abode of the noblest of beings, will, without your presence, cease to be resplendent."

To the great and godly assembly said the Bodhisattva: "Henceforward Maitreya Bodhisattva will instruct you in religion."

Then the Bodhisattva appointed Maitreya Bodhisattva to the office of Vice-gerent, and, taking off from his own head his silken turban,[2] placed it on that of Maitreya. He then said: "when I

10

am gone thou shalt instruct these good people in the absolutely perfect knowledge."

Now the Bodhisattva, having established Maitreya Bodhisattva in the mansion of Tushita, asked the great godly assembly: "In what form, venerable sirs, shall I enter the womb of my mother?"

One of them said, "Lord, you should do so in the form of a human being."

Another said, "let it be in the form of S'akra."

Another suggested, "it should be in the form of Brahmá."

A fourth observed, "let it be in the form of a Mahárájika."

The fifth would have it, "in the form of Vaiśravaṇa" (*Kuvera*).

The sixth, "in the form of a Gandharva."

The next wished him to assume, "the form of a Kinnara."[3]

Another would have it that he should appear "in the form of a great serpent" (*mahoraga*).

Another, "in the form of Maheśvara" (S'iva).

The next wished him to assume "the form of Chandra" (the moon).

The next suggested, "let it be in the form of Súrya" (the sun).

Another said, "let it be in the form of a Garuḍa."[4]

Among them there was one of the name of Ugratejá, a Devaputra of the class Brahmakáyika, who had formerly been a rishi, and was firm in the absolutely perfect knowledge. He said: "since he will come to instruct Bráhmaṇs who read the Mantras and the Vedas and the S'ástras, the Bodhisattva should enter the womb of his mother in the form befitting that purpose."

"How should that be?"

"It should be in the form of a noble elephant of great size, having six tusks.[5] He should be covered with golden net-works, and pleasing in appearance; he should have well-blooded veins, manifest and well developed beauty, and be endowed with all auspicious marks."

Hearing this, the Bodhisattva manifested himself as one versed in the Vedas and the S'ástras of the Bráhmaṇs, and endowed with the thirty-two marks which he was afterwards to bear.

Thus, Bhikshus, the Bodhisattva, having, while in Tushita, ascertained the time of his birth, observed the eight pre-ordained signs in the palace of the king S'uddhodana.

What were the eight signs?

That palace was devoid of grass, dust, thorns, gravel, hardness and dirt; it was well watered, well adorned, (or well purified,) well aired, freed from darkness and dust, unaffected by gadflies, mosquitoes, flies, insects and reptiles, showered over with flowers, and well under controul. This was the first pre-ordained sign that was manifest.

Patraguptas,[6] parrots, mainas, (*Gracula religiosa*,) cuckoos, geese, herons, peacocks, brahminy ducks, *kunálas*,[7] sparrows, *jívas*, *jívakas*[8] and other birds of many-coloured plumage, and pleasing and agreeable voice, dwellers of the great mountain Himálaya, had all come to the palace of the king S'uddhodana, and, settling on the pavilions, doors, gates, windows, rooms, towers, and temples, sounded, in delight and good feeling, each its own peculiar note. This was the second pre-ordained sign.

The various fruit and flower trees in the delightful gardens and pleasure-grounds of the king S'uddhodana, all blossomed and flowered, though not in season. This was the third pre-ordained sign.

The tanks of the king S'uddhodana were full of water, and covered with millions over millions of lotus flowers and leaves of the size of cart wheels. This was the fourth pre-ordained sign.

Again, in the noble house of the king S'uddhodana, various articles of food, such as clarified butter, oil, honey, molasses and sugar, though extensively consumed, were never exhausted, and always appeared full. This was the fifth pre-ordained sign.

Again, in that excellent house of the king S'uddhodana, the extensive inner apartments resounded with the self-evolved delightful music of the trumpet, drum, *paṇava*,[9] *tuṇava*,[10] víṇá, flute, *vallaka*,[11] *sampaláḍa*,[12] &c. This was the sixth pre-ordained sign.

Moreover, in that excellent house of king S'uddhodana, whatever vessels of gold, silver, ruby, pearl, lapis-lazuli, conch-shell, marble, coral, &c. there were, they all looked cleaned, purified, lustrous and full. This was the seventh pre-ordained sign.

Furthermore, owing to its cleaned and purified state, its being enlightened by the slanting rays of the moon and the sun, and its exhilarating the body and the mind, that house was everywhere aglow. This was the eighth pre-ordained sign.

Máyádeví had bathed, anointed her person, made her arms heavy with various ornaments, and arrayed herself in a dress of thin texture and blue colour. She was full of affection, delight and gratification. She was attended and served by ten thousand maids. Proceeding to the music-hall where king S'uddhodana was seated at ease, she took her seat on his right side, on an excellent chair covered with a network of jewels. There seated, she, with a benign countenance, free from all affectation, and smiling face, addressed him in these verses :—

"Honorable sir, and protector of the religion of the earth, listen to my request. I solicit of thee, O king, a blessing. Deign to grant it. Listen with benign attention to the request which excites my mind and thought.(1)

"I shall adopt the noble fast of the gods, penance and good conduct, (*Devavrataśílavaropavása*,) for the endowment of the eight members of my body. With affection for the world, with freedom from all feeling of mischief, with pure thoughts and fullness of love—I shall do to others what I do for myself.(2)

"With mind divested of all frivolity, vanity, covetousness, and all carnal passions, I shall, O king, commit nothing that is false. Abiding in truth, avoiding everything cruel and harsh, I shall indulge in no unrighteous or frivolous talk.(3)

"Freedom from all evil designs, faults, receiving of presents, delusions and vanity, elevation above all foolishness, satisfaction with my own wealth, constant occupation, retirement from my chamber, and non-indulgence in viciousness,—these are the ten duties which I shall perform.(4)

"O king, entertain no wish for my society, as long as I shall be engaged, surrounded by fame, in the fast of good conduct (*śilavrata*). Nor shall you, O king, be without virtue: all night through, do encourage my fast of *śilavrata*.(5)

"It is my earnest wish, my lord, that I should quickly ascend the highest tower of the palace of Dhártaráshṭra, and, surrounded by my female companions, repose, lying on a soft well-scented bed sprinkled with flowers.(6).

"No warders, nor disturbers, nor vulgar people, nor uncongenial ones should approach me; nor shall my form ever cross (their sight); nor sounds, nor scents other than agreeable and sweet should I perceive.(7)

"Those who are now in prison, liberate them all; and make all men rich with the gift of good clothes, food, drinks, carts with yokes of bullocks, and horse-carriages; do thou bestow, these for seven nights together for the gratification of the earth.(8)

"Let there be no dispute or quarrel, nor angry words; let there be friendly feeling among each other, and peaceful salutary thoughts. In this abode let men, officials, warders, Devas be full of joy, and engaged in enjoyment for their good.(9)

"Let not there be any soldiers who inflict punishment, nor wicked punishers, nor oppressors, nor rebukes, nor punishment. Let all be in peaceful mind, thoughtful of friendship and good. Do you look upon all the crowd as thy only son."(10)

Hearing this earnest appeal, the king replied: "Let everything be as you wish. Ask whatever you desire; and whatever you ask, the same shall I instantly grant you."(11)

The king, ordered all his courtiers to embellish the tower on the top of the palace, and to sprinkle therein delightful flowers, to bestrow it with incense and essences, and to set up over it umbrellas and canopies on serried posts tall as palm trees.(12)

"Place (said he) twenty thousand mail-clad warriors armed with clubs, spikes, arrows, spears and swords, round the delightful Dhritaráshṭra palace for the protection and for dispelling all fears of the Deví.(13)

"Surrounded by her maidens she is like a heavenly damsel. She is bathed, anointed and well-dressed. Let the music of a thousand clarions rise around, for the gratification of the lady.(14)

"Let her, like a goddess in the grove of Indra, neglecting her jewels and tiara, rest on her precious and comfortable bed-stead with jewelled feet, covered with rich bedding, and strewn over with flowers."(15)

Now, Bhikshus, the four great kings (of the four quarters), S'akra the sovereign of the Devas, Suyáma the Devaputra, Santushita, Sunirmita, Paraṇirmitavasavartí, Sárthaváha son of Mára, the lord of strength Brahmá, the priest Brahmottara, the priest Subrahmá, Prabhávyúhábhásvara, Maheśvara, Nishṭhágatas of the class S'udhávásakáyika, Ekanishṭha—these and other Devas by hundreds of thousands assembled together, and thus addressed each other: "It would be unbecoming and ungraceful in us, venerable sirs, to allow the Bodhisattva to depart alone without a second. Which of us, sirs, can calmly bear the idea that the Bodhisattva should alone descend, dwell in the womb, be born, grow up, entertain himself with wooden play-things, partake of the entertainments of the inner apartments, depart therefrom, undergo awful penances, ascend the Bodhimaṇḍala, overpower Mára, attain the Bodhi, and set the wheel of religion in motion,—and all with the desire of attaining the final Nirváṇa for the peace of mind, for the welfare of the mind, for benevolence, and for calmness of the mind?" At that time the following Gáthás were resounded.

Who can forego following the handsome one who is always of contented mind? Who can prevent him from carrying out whatever he wishes in virtue, form and speech?(1)

If he lists he can always in loving spirit enjoy amorous pleasures in the company of the best of Apsarasas in the palace of the lord of three times ten.[13] Do ye follow that moon-like face ? (2)

We shall follow that being of stainless glory who can, if he likes, enjoy, in the city of the Devas in the delightful grove of Miśraka, covered with flowers like powdered gold. (3)

We shall follow the great person who, if he liked, could enjoy along with the wives of the Suras, in the car of Chitraratha, or in the garden of Nandana, amidst avenues formed of the petals of Mándárava flowers. (4)

If he wished he could assume mastery over the Yámas, or over the Tushitas, or supreme power: his worship takes place everywhere in the universe. We shall follow such a being of endless glory. (5)

If he wishes he can enjoy in the delightful Nirmitapura, or in the complaisant home of the Vasavartí gods; he can conceive everything in his mind. We shall follow such an owner of the noblest qualities. (6)

He is the great lord (*Mahes'vara*); he has nothing wrong in his mind; he is proficient in every science; he is the sovereign of lust; he has attained the fulness of Vaśitá.[14] Proceed forth in the company of such a beneficent being. (7)

He wishes to surpass the region of Kámadhátu in order to attain the domain of Brahmá; he sustains fourfold vigour. That great personage is worthy of our following this day. (8)

Again, his mind may be diverted to the greatest empire among the mortals. We shall follow that ocean of jewels, that giver of fearless felicity, that upholder of profuse virtue. (9)

He is the lord of the earth, the noblest of sons, the owner of countless wealth; he owns a large family, and has destroyed all his enemies. That beneficent being is going forth; let us follow him. (10)

He owns beauty, enjoyment, supremacy, noble deeds, fame, power, and merit, and his mandates are obeyed on earth. Let us follow that sovereign of Brahmá, knowing him to be the only resource.(11)

Those who long for the greatest object of desire among mortals, the highest felicity in the three worlds, the felicity of meditation and that of discrimination, let them follow the Lord of religion.(12)

Whoever wishes to destroy passions and faults, whoever desires to overcome all afflictions, let him quickly follow him who owns peace of mind, superior peace of mind, perfect peace of mind, and exercises complete controul over his thoughts.(13)

Let him follow the owner of merit, knowing him to have learnt the lessons of all the Jinas, to be full of absolute knowledge, to have roared like a lion with the ten transcendental powers.(14)

He has closed the road to destruction, and of his own accord thrown open the pleasant path of the six emancipations, for passage by the eight corporeal members. Follow him who has brought to a close the way to changes.(15)

Whoever wishes to worship the Sugata, to hear of religion from that kind one, whoever wishes to attain noble merits, let him follow that ocean of merit.(16)

If you wish to remove the cause of birth, disease, death and pain, and to rend asunder the bonds of worldliness, follow him whose conduct is as pure and as expansive as the sky.(17)

In order to redeem yourself and others, follow the dear one, knowing him to be endowed with all the noble signs and merits, conceivable on earth.(18)

He is full of humanity, meditation, and knowledge; he is grave and of awful aspect; whoever wishes for salvation let him quickly follow that king of physicians.(19)

For the attainment of these and other merits of different kinds, for friendliness and cessation of transmigration, follow the wise one who, for the sake of perfection, is full of accomplished penance and is replete with all merits.(20)

Hearing these words eighty-four thousand Devas of the class Chatur-mahárájika assembled together. So did a hundred thousand

Devas of the class Trayastriñśa, and a hundred thousand each of Yámas, Tushitas, Nirmáṇaratis, and Paranirmitavasavartis, sixty thousand Devas of the class Márakáyikas, who had acquired sufficient merit by good works in former existences, as also sixty-eight thousand Brahmakáyikas. Many hundreds of thousands of Akanishṭha Devas also came there. Other Devas from the east, the south, the west and the north, came by hundreds of thousands. Among them those who were most liberal-minded addressed these Gáthás to the godly assembly.

"Listen, O, ye lords of the immortals, to these words. In this twofold world whatever beings there are, renouncing them, and all wealth, desirable objects, and longings, he has given himself to the felicity of meditation: let us follow this noble and pure being.(1)

"His feet are tied; he is in the womb; he is a noble one, worthy of adoration, and full of greatness: we should adore him. He is protected by virtue; he is a saint *(rishi)*; and without protecting him in his incarnation the mind cannot be dissatisfied.(2)

"Let us recite with the music of clarions and other instruments the beauty and the merits of the ocean of merit; we shall thereby gladden the heart of all mortals and Devas; and hearing it there will be no dissatisfaction in the mind of the noble Bodhi.(3)

"We shall shower flowers on the king's house, redolent as it is with the aroma issuing from the burning of the finest black agallochum, smelling which gods and men, will be happy, elated, and free from decay and disease.(4)

"With Mándárava flowers and with Páríjáta flowers, with camphor and superior camphor, as also with well-blown red lotus[15] we shall pour showers on Kapila, for the worship of him who has accomplished all former duties.(5)

"As long as the untainted of three filths[16] dwells in the womb, as long as the destroyer of decay and death is not born, so long shall we follow him with cheerful mind; it is our wish that so long we shall perform the worship of the intelligent one.(6)

"They attain high reward, who, among men and gods, behold the seven steps[17] of the pure being, besprinkled with aromatic waters by numerous S'akras and Brahmás.(7)

"As long as he lives among men, as long as the destroyer of the pains of lust dwells in the gynacæum, as long as he does not proceed forth renouncing his kingdom, so long shall we with cheerfulness follow him.(8)

"As long as he does not spread the grass on the earth of the (Bodhi) Maṇḍa,[18] as long as he does not come in contact with the Bodhi after overpowering Mára, as long as he instructs not tens of thousands of Bráhmaṇs after setting the wheel of religion in motion, so long shall we perform profuse worship of the Sugata.(9)

"As long as he does not overcome the three thousand regions by his Buddha career, as long as he does not translate millions over millions of men to immortality, and the contented does not himself ascend the road to Nirváṇa, so long none of us shall forsake the high-minded noble saint."(10)

Now, beholding the exquisite person and beauty of the Bodhisattva the idea struck the heavenly nymphs of the class called Kámadhátvis'vari, "How should that lady be who will sustain in her this pure and noble being?" Impelled by curiosity, they took most exquisite flowers, pastiles, lamps, essences, garlands, unguents, powdered sandal-wood, and clothes, and, in the fulness of their heart, and in the position they had acquired by former good deeds, at that moment disappeared from the city of the immortals. They proceeded to the great city of Kapila abounding in gardens by hundreds of thousands, to the great palace of Dhṛitaráshṭra, in the abode of king S'udhodana, where every room was pure and resplendent. There, these ladies with dishevelled dress, enveloped in auspicious and untainted glory, with arms loaded with beautiful ornaments, pointed out with a finger the sleeping Máyádeví, and then, rising high in the sky, recited the following Gáthás.

Beholding the bewitching beauty of the Bodhisattva the Apsarases of the city of the immortals wondered, what sort of a lady must she be who is to be the mother of the Bodhisattva ?(1)

They then, taking flower-garlands in their hands, in great curiosity repaired to the house of the king. Taking flowers and unguents they joined their ten fingers in salutation.(2)

With dishevelled dresses and of playful form they pointed at her the palm and finger of their right hand, and said "behold Máyádeví in repose, and well observe the beauty of a human female.(3)

"We pride ourselves on the exquisite beauty and form of the Apsarases, but, beholding the wife of the king, we should renounce all such ideas.(4)

"This meritorious lady, who is to be the mother of the noblest soul, is like another Rati. Even as jewels are best set on a proper article, even such is this lady in the house of the Deva.(5)

"From the sole of her foot and the palm of her hand to the top of her body every part is delightful to excess; looking at her the eye can never be satiated, the more you behold her the more the mind and thought are delighted.(6)

"Her noble face is resplendent as the moon on the sky, and her body is resplendent with light. She is stainless as the sun, lustrous as the moon, and her spirituality casts its radiance over her.(7)

"Her complexion is lustrous even as the precious metal gold, or as burnished gold. The soft sweet-scented tresses on her head rival the black bee in colour.(8)

"In her eyes rests the glory of the lotus petal, while her pure teeth own the lustre of the sky. Slender is her waist like the bow, and swelling are her sides without a depression.(9)

"Her thighs and legs represent the trunk of the elephant; her knees are well-formed, and the limbs are becomingly tapering; even and rosy are her palms and soles: verily she is a goddess manifest and no other."(10)

Seeing the lady, the mother of Jina, dwelling thus, the heavenly nymphs sprinkled flowers on her, respectfully walked round her person, and then in a moment returned back to their celestial abodes.(11)

Now, the four guardians from the four quarters, S'akra, Suyáma as also Nirṛiti, the Devas, Kumbháṇḍas, Rákshasas, Asuras, Mahoragas, and Kinnaras exclaimed.(12)

"Proceeding before the noblest of beings, the greatest of men, protect his car. While on earth commit no fault even in your mind, nor injure any human being.(13)

"Armed with swords, bows, arrows, spears and falchions, and abiding under the sky, do ye all with all your attendants, watch the noble mansion in which dwells Máyádeví.(14)

"Knowing that the time of descent has arrived, do ye, sons of Devas, with cheerful hearts, proceed to the mansion of Máyá, and, holding in your hands flowers and unguents, salute her with the ten fingers of your folded hands.(15)

"Descend, descend, thou pure being, lord of mankind. This day is the proper time. O lion of disputants, feeling mercy and compassion for all created beings, now descend to bestow the gift of religion."(16)

Now, Bhikshus, at the time of Bodhisattva's descent, many hundreds of thousands of Bodhisattvas, all linked together by unity of caste, and dwellers of Tushita, proceeded from the east towards the Bodhisattva for his adoration. Along with them came Devas of the four Chaturmahárájika class, eighty-four thousand Apsarases, and hundreds of thousands of Thirty-three, of Yámas, of Tushitas, of Nirmáṇaratis, of Paranirmitavas'avartis, with eighty-four thousand Apsarases resounding their clarions.

Now the Bodhisattva, seating himself, in the presence of all the gods, on the most virtuous throne of S'rígarbha, in the great tower, surrounded and followed by Bodhisattvas, Devas, Nágas and Yaksas without number, issued forth from the abode of Tushita. When proceeding on, he caused a light to issue forth from his person. By that most extensively spread, far-expanding, unperplexed, glorious light, transcending all other light, these three thousand great thousands of regions[20] became resplendent. Even in the frontier regions which, from beginning, were enveloped in visible darkness and gloom, where these powerful and majestic sun and moon, which are called the great lords Mahes'a, do not by their light give light, nor by their colour bring out colour, nor by their heat give heat, and they are neither heated nor made manifest—where such beings as are produced cannot see their own extended hands,—even there at that time a great and bright light became manifest, and through its brightness, the people there beheld and recognised each other. They exclaimed, "how has this come to pass? how has this arisen?"

These three thousand great thousands of regions became the scene of eighteen supernatural occurrences of six kinds. There were shaking, great shaking, and complete shaking. There were cracking, great cracking, and complete cracking. There were motion, great motion, and complete motion. There were confusion, great confusion, and complete confusion. There were running, great running, and complete running. There were roaring, great roaring, and complete roaring. At the end it was depressed, at the middle it was raised; at the middle it was depressed, at the end it was raised. At the eastern side it was depressed; at the western side it was depressed. At the eastern side it was raised; at the western side it was raised. At the southern side it was depressed; at the northern side it was raised. At the northern side it was depressed; at the southern side it was raised. At that time pleasing, gratifying, endearing, exciting, delightful, exhilarating, indescribable, charming, inoffensive, unalarming sounds were audible everywhere. No person at that time felt any hatred, or fear, or awe, or stolidity. Again, at that time neither the light of the sun, nor that of the moon, nor that of Brahmá, S'akra and the guardians of the regions, was perceptible. All who were in hell and all creatures in the region of Yama were, at that time, free from all suffering, and full of pleasure. No being was at that time afflicted by disease, or hatred, or delusion, or envy, or vanity, or conceit, or hypocrisy, or haughtiness, or anger, or malice, or anxiety. All beings at that time were full of the feeling of friendship and benevolence, feeling as if they were all in the company of a father and a mother. Unexpectedly supernatural clarions by tens of thousands of millions resounded delightful sounds. Devas innumerable carried forth the pavilion on their heads and shoulders and hands; while hundreds of thousands of Apsarases, placing themselves in front and behind, on the left side, and on the right, each employing her own song, in melodious musical voice bepraised the Bodhisattva.

This day begins the profound worship of thee who hast acquired merit by former good works, who hast been purified by the ordinance of true knowledge, of thee whose long night has passed and the dawn of goodness has appeared.(1)

Thou didst, of yore for tens of millions of Kalpas, give away in largesses dear sons, wives and land. The fruition of thy benefactions now shower on thee in the form of flowers.(2)

Thou, great master, didst weigh out thy own flesh for thy beloved hungry and thirsty birds. Through the fruit of thy benefactions even those who dwell in the region of the dead shall obtain food and drink.(3)

Thou didst, of yore for tens of millions of Kalpas, cherish the obligation of uninterrupted good conduct *(s'íla)*, and the fruit of thy goodness is that thy senses have been purified and saved from destruction.(4)

Thou didst, of yore for tens of millions of Kalpas, reflect on forbearance *(kshánti)* and learn the truth, and the fruit of that forbearance has now resulted in friendliness to gods, men and creation.(5)

Thou didst, of yore for tens of millions of Kalpas, cherish untainted and excellent vigour *(víryá)*, and the fruit of that vigour now shines firm as the mount Meru.(6)

Thou didst, of yore for tens of millions of Kalpas, hold meditation *(dhyána)* with great pain, and the fruit of that meditation now removes all pain from all created beings.(7)

Thou didst, of yore for tens of millions of Kalpas, reflect on pain-assuaging knowledge *(prajná)*, and the fruit of that knowledge is now resplendent in great light.(8)

In kindness to all beings thou hast acquired the pain-assuaging virtue of friendliness *(maitri)* to all creatures and exalted delight even in those who hate you. Salutation be to thee, the Brahma-like Sugata.(9)

Salutations be to the sage who has risen above the meteor light of Prajná, who is the remover of all faults, darkness, and delusion, who has become the eye to show the right way to the three thousand chiefs.[21](10)

Salutations be to the Sugata, who is proficient in the knowledge of the supernatural powers, *(riddhis,)* the director to the right path, the learned in the greatest good, who fully emancipates all enslaved creatures.(11)

Thou art thoroughly proficient in all means. Thou showest the way to unfailing departure. Thou followest the duties of the world, but never mixest with the world.(12)

Having examined all great longings and faults, thou desirest that which is good and becoming; what more can be said than that even the hearing of thee produces profuse faith, devotion and virtue.(13)

Everything is become dull in the abode of Tushita since he has gone to Jambudvípa, to awaken hundreds of millions of beings, sleeping in pain.(14)

The rich, and flourishing town is this day bustling with uncountable crowds of Devas. The home of the king is resounding with sweet music from the clarions of heavenly nymphs.(15)

That lady of exquisite beauty whose son he will be, is resplendent in the fulness of virtue and good deeds. The light of her beauty irradiates the three thousand regions.(16)

Nor is there in that city any covetousness, or fault, or quarrel, or dispute; through the glory of the excellent being every one is abiding in friendliness and feeling of regard for each other.(17)

The royal family of the king, born in a Chakravarti dynasty, is thriving. The city of Kapila, rich in treasuries of jewels, and full of wealth, is all aglow.(18)

Yakshas, Rakshas, Kumbhâṇḍas, Guhyakas, Devas and Dánavas with Indra at their head, who are now the guardians of the noble being, will ere long attain salvation (*moksha*).(19)

For us, who for the enhancement of virtue bepraise thee, O leader, do thou enhance our devotion and respect, so that we may quickly attain the perfect Bodhi, even as thou, noblest of beings, hast done.(20)

NOTES.

1. *Mangalya Devas*, p. 73. It is doubtful if the word *Mangalya* can be accepted as a generic noun implying a particular class of Devas. It does not occur under any of the heads given in note 1, p. 65. As a common noun it would mean simply auspicious. But, seeing that there are other classes mentioned in the Lalita-Vistara besides those included in the note, I am disposed to think it means a class.

2. *Silken turban*, p. 73. The Sanskrit text *paṭṭa-maula* is a compound of *paṭṭa*, meaning "silk" or "turban," and *maula*, "the head," "a lock of hair on the crown," "braided hair tied round the head like a turban," "a tiara," "a diadem." M. Foucaux renders the Tibetan version of the whole passage into "et le Bôdhisattva ayant ôté de dessus sa tête la tiare et le diadème, les mit sur la tête du Bôdhisattva Mâitrêya." (p. 51). Translating from the Sanskrit Dr. Lefmann has "Indem nam der Bôdhisattva von seinem eigenen haupte tiara und diadem und legte sie auf das haupt des Bôdhisattva Mâitrêya" (p. 33). The rendering in either case is due to the importance attached in Europe to the crown as an emblem of royalty. In India this idea does not exist; nowhere is any importance attached to the crown as a necessary token of rank or office. Whereas the giving of turbans is a mark of esteem and trust, and the giving of one's own

turban is always looked upon as a special mark of esteem and confidence. Among friends the exchanging of turbans is the most highly prized memento of attachment. The turban may be set off with jewels, but it is the turban that is valued as a token of mutual confidence; and not the jewels set on it. I feel pretty certain, therefore, that the word under notice means a turban of silk cloth, and not a turban and a diadem. *Paṭṭa*, moreover, primarily means silk, not turban, the latter meaning being a secondary one resulting from the fact of turbans being often made of silk, even as in English cloth stands for dress, and it is preferable to accept the primary meaning of words, when admissible, to secondary ones. It may be noticed too that the Bodhisattva is described as wearing a turban (*ante*, p. 3), but nowhere has a crown been assigned him.

3. *Kinnara*, p. 74. A class of demigods, having the human form with the head of a horse. These beings were noted for their musical attainments. They figure prominently both in Hindu and Buddhist legends. *Vide* my "Buddha-Gayá," p. 155.

4. *Garuḍa*, p. 74. A class of demigods having the form of a bird, with a human head. These beings have a second name *Śrag-dhara*, or carriers of flower garlands. In Buddhist sculptures they are met with very extensively, flying in the air and carrying garlands for the adoration of the Bodhi tree and other sacred objects. Mr. Burgess, in the "Cave Temples of India," confounds them with the Kinnaras. In Hindu legends they are often mentioned, and the chief of them is said to be the vehicle of Vishṇu. This chief was born of Káśyapa by Vinatá; his form on the occasion was that of a large bird, but without a human head. *Vide* Wilson's Vishṇu Puráṇa, II, 73.

5. *Six tusks*, p 74. The belief in the existence of a species of elephant with six tusks is common both to the Hindus and the Buddhists. Such a species, however, not being known to Indian fauna, I have been induced to believe that it is a reminiscence of the palæozoic Indian hippopotamus, an animal of elephantine proportions with six large projecting teeth. Dr. Falconer has shown at great length that such reminiscences of animals of former ages exist in connexion with the gigantic tortoise (*Colossochelys atlas*), the one-tusked elephant, and other animals, and there is nothing to preclude the possibility of some vague idea of the hippopotamus being preserved.

12

The figures of this animal as shown in sculpture appears to Mr. Theobald as a rude and somewhat ideal representation of the real animal. (*Vide* my Buddha-Gayá.) It should be added, however, that in sculptures delineating Buddha's birth the animal shown is an ordinary elephant. In the Chinese version of Máyá's dream it is said that "she thought she saw a six-tusked white elephant, his head coloured like a ruby (or red pearl) descend through space and enter her right side." (Beal's Romantic Legend, p. 37.) The Burmese version omits the six tusks. According to it "Opposite this mount, and facing the cave where Maia sat surrounded by her attendants, rose another mount, where Phraalong, under the shape of a young elephant, was roaming over its sides in various directions. He was soon seen coming down that hill, and, ascending the one where the princess lay on her bed, directing his course towards the cave. On the extremity of his trunk, lifted like a beautiful string of flowers, he carried a white lily. His voice, occasionally resounding through the air, could be heard distinctly by the inmates of the grotto, and indicated his approach. He soon entered the cave, turned three times round the couch whereon sat the princess, then standing for a while, he came nearer, opened her right side, and appeared to conceal himself in her womb." (Bigandet, I, p. 29.) In Burmese inscriptions and other records the six tusks are, however, frequently mentioned.

6. *Patraguptas*, p. 75. The word means "protected by their wings," but to what particular species of bird the term is applied I cannot make out.

7. *Kuṇálas*, p. 75. I have failed to identify this bird also. It may be the *Munál* pheasant.

8. *Jívas, Jívakas*, p. 75. This is obviously a mislection of Jívaṇjíva which means the Chakora or Greek partridge.

9. *Paṇava*, p. 75. A percussion instrument closely resembling, if not identical with, the *Váñyá* of our times. It is thus described in the *Saṅgíta-náráyaṇa*. It is made of earth or metal, about a cubit in length and of the shape of a Dhatura flower, the mouth being about half a cubit wide. The mouth is covered with goat skin held in position with thongs or hempen cords. On the middle of the skin is applied a paste to give the proper tone, and it is played upon with the middle finger of the left hand. This description applies in

every detail to the Váñyá, except the shape, which, instead of being like a Dhatura flower, is elongated and globular.

धत्तूरकुसुमाकारः पक्वो धातुजोऽथवा ।
स्थूलयोऽपि भवेत्तस्य प्रमाणो वा तदन्यथा ॥
सार्द्धहस्तं भवत्यास्य वेष्टनं परिकीर्त्तितम् ।
तन्मुखं वस्त्रचर्म्मेण कुर्य्याद्दाच्छादितं पुनः ॥
तच्चर्म्म पट्टसूत्रेण बद्धं वा चर्म्मरज्जुना ।
वारि स्निं मध्यभागेऽस्य प्रदेयञ्च स्वद्रवत् ॥
नाति सूक्ष्मं न च स्थूलं ध्वनिगाम्भीर्य्यहेतवे ।
वाद्यते वामहस्तस्य मध्यमाङ्गुलिना स्वयम् ॥

10. *Tuṇava*, p. 75. I know of no musical instrument of this name, but I take it to be a variant of *Tuntaví*, which was a one-stringed lute of which the modern Ekatárá is the representative. It had for sounding board a gourd-shell mounted with skin, a staff of bamboo, a wooden bridge, and a key at the end of the staff for tuning the chord. The following is its description as given in the *Sañgíta-náráyaṇa*.

तुन्तवीलक्षणं प्रोक्तं पूर्व्वसङ्गीतकोविदैः ।
सार्द्धहस्तमितो दण्डः सूक्ष्मवंशेन निर्म्मितः ॥
चर्म्मणाच्छादितालावु दण्डमूले नियन्त्रिता ।
दण्डाग्रे कीलकश्चैकः संयता तत्र तन्त्रिका ॥
दारवजां पट्टिकां कृत्वा ककुभोपरि विन्यसेत् ।
धृत्वा तां दक्षहस्तेन वादयेत्तेन पाणिना ॥

11. *Vallaka*, p. 76. This is a fully developed lute, and is the same with the modern *sitár*. The *Sañgíta-náráyaṇa* calls it *vallakí*, and gives a full description of it. According to it the staff should be made of wood or bamboo well polished. Its length should be 10 fists or about 30 inches, and its breadth 5½ fingers. Eighteen fingers at the top should constitute the head, and here the keys, made of horn, should be attached. Between the head and the body of the staff there should be a bridge of an arched form. The sounding board or the body of the instrument should be 18 fingers wide and sufficiently deep. There should be a bridge, made of horn, on the body, and the chords should be of pure brass and steel. The instrument should be held by the left hand and the chords pressed with the fingers of that hand on the stops, and played with the right hand.

दशाङ्गुलि मितो दण्डो द्वावत्नी वंशकोऽथवा ।
गुडको मध्यभाकारः खादिराद्यैश्च निर्मितः ॥
षडादशाङ्गुलं दीर्घं निरन्ध्राः प्रकीर्त्तितम् ।
सार्द्धपञ्चाङ्गुलं दण्ड प्रान्तस्थच निकल्पितम् ॥
मध्यं पञ्चाङ्गुलं प्रोक्तं अग्रमूलं सुसन्धितम् ।
मध्यान्ते कर्णिका च स्यात् पञ्चाङ्गुलिमिता मता ॥
अर्द्धचन्द्राकृतिः सा तु पतिता प्रष्ठदेशतः ।
एवञ्च ककुभं तत्र नीचाद्ध्वे नियोजयेत् ॥
षडादशाङ्गुलमुखं चतुस्युक् चादरर्भकम् ।
दण्डान्ते कीलका स्थाप्यास्तन्त्रीणां तत्र बन्धनम् ॥
पित्तलेनातिमृदुना निर्मितानां तथायसा ।
एतास्तु तारवाद्दिव्यस्तिष्ठन्ति पट्टिकोपरि ॥
पञ्चाङ्गुलिमिता सा तु तस्या चतुष्कोणोर्द्धता ।
मदनस्य च सिक्थस्य योगेन सुदृढीकृता ॥
स्थापिता चक्रमध्ये तु प्रभाद्दिवर्णनिर्मिता ।
एतैरवयवैर्युक्ता मत्तकी परिकीर्त्तिता ॥
तान्तु वामकरे धृत्वा वेन सम्पीड्य तन्त्रिकाम् ।
वर स्थानं निरूप्याथ दक्षिणेन च पाणिना ॥
वादनीया सावधानै रागाणां मर्म्मकोविदैः ।
पुस्तीवेषु बह्वीर्वरामेस्था विचिषता ॥

I am indebted to my friend Rájá Saurendramohan Tagore for the quotations above given.

12. *Sampatáḍa*, p. 76. I have not been able to identify this instrument. Its name does not occur in any of the musical works to which I have access.

13. *The Lord of three times ten*, p. 76. This is the Vedic style of indicating the Devas, who originally numbered thirty.

14. *Vasitá*, p. 79. Entire control over the longings of the flesh. It includes both the cravings of the organs as well as the failings of the intellectual faculties, and thus comprehends the objects of the two terms *yama* and *niyama* of the Hindu writers.

15. *Red lotus*, p. 81. The word in the Sanskrit text is *sphára-virochamána*, a compound of *sphára* "well blown," and *virochamána* "gorgeous." If I could accept the word *tatha* preceding it as an expletive, the epithet could be taken as an adjective "gorgeously full-blown," qualifying *mandárava*. But this cannot be done. The little

word is obviously a copulative conjunction, and *virochamána* must mean a flower, but not knowing of any flowers of that name, I have taken it to mean the red lotus, the most gorgeous flower in India. *Virochana* is the name of the *Calotropis gigantea*, the *Andersonia rohitaka*, and one or two other plants, but they do not bear a sufficiently rich flower to be worthy of name here.

16. *Three filthes*, p. 81. The three qualities of goodness, foulness and darkness which, according to all Indian philosophers, are the sources of evil. To rise above them is the great aim and object of philosophy.

17. *Seven steps*, p. 82. S'ákya, immediately after his birth, advanced seven steps forward towards each of the four quarters of the globe by way of symbolically subduing the universe. See Chapter VII. Both the Chinese and the Burmese versions give the miracle, but in the latter, the new-born child instead of walking seven steps, jumps "over a distance of seven lengths of a foot." (Bigandet, I, p. 37.)

18. *Maṇḍa*, p. 82. This is an abbreviation of Bodhi Maṇḍa, the terrace under the banian tree at Buddha-Gayá on which the saint spread some kúśa grass and, sitting thereon, performed the last great meditation which disclosed to him the true knowledge. See Chapter XIX.

19. *Thirty-three*, p. 84. Another well-known epithet for the Hindu gods.

20. *Three thousand great thousands of regions*, p. 84. All the regions extant in the universe are reckoned at three thousand, and the qualification "great thousands" appears to be merely a rhetorical flourish. The qualification is not unfrequently omitted. See verse 16, p. 87.

21. *Three thousand chiefs*, p. 87. The sovereigns of the three thousand regions which constitute the Universe.

CHAPTER VI.

THE DESCENT.

Bodhisattva enters his mother's womb. Máyá's dream. The dream expounded. The abode of Máyá. Gods of different kinds present houses. The jewelled house Ratnavyúha. Celestials come to see the house. Description of the house. The lotus-essence. Morning visitors. Midday visitors. Vesper visitors. Condition of Máyá. Miracles performed by her. Visit of Bodhisattvas. Corroborative Gáthás.

Thus, Bhikshus, the winter having passed away, in the fulness of the Spring season, in the month of Vaiśákha, when the sun was in the constellation Viśákhá, the trees were covered with leaves, and loaded with exquisite flowers and blossoms. The earth was covered with a carpet of green. The evils of great heat or cold were then absent, and everywhere there was calm and quietness. At such a time the Bodhisattva, the eldest in the three regions, and adored of creation, seeing that the proper season had arrived, that the moon was on the 15th day of its age and in perfect fulness, renounced the mansion of Tushita, and, calling to mind the tradition, entered, in the form of an elephant, of a yellowish white colour,[1] having six tusks, crimson veins, golden teeth, and perfect members, the womb of his mother who had been purified by the rite of Poshadha.[2] Entering the womb of the mother, he occupied the right side, and lay on that side, never turning to the left.

Máyá Deví, sleeping peacefully on an excellent bed, dreamt a dream [which she described thus] :

"A noble elephant, white as silver or snow, having six tusks, well proportioned trunk and feet, blood-red veins, adamantine firmness of joints, and easy pace, has entered my belly.

"Such a delightful form I had never before seen, nor heard, nor conceived; it produced in me the same corporeal and mental feeling of joy which one enjoys on being immersed in meditation."

Now, Máyá Deví rose from her auspicious bed, with her ornaments and dress in disorder, but in the fulness of delight, pleasure and joy of body and mind, and, descending from the tower, attended and preceded by her maids, repaired to the Aśoka grove. Seated at ease in that grove she despatched a courier to King S'uddhodana with the message, "May it please my lord to come; the Deví desires your presence."

The king was agitated with delight by the message, and, rising from his noble seat, proceeded, attended by his ministers astrologers, courtiers and priests, to the As'oka grove; but he could not enter it. Near the entrance he felt himself very heavy, and, when standing for a moment at the door, became thoughtful, and then recited the following Gáthá:

"I cannot call to mind if I have ever felt in my heroic head such a heaviness of my body as I do to-day. I am not able to enter my own family house. Ah! could I ask of some one what will happen to me to-day!"

Now, the Devas of the class S'uddhávásakáyika, (pure in body and dwelling) assuming semi-developed forms, came under the sky, and addressed the king S'uddhodana in a Gáthá.

"O king, the noble Bodhisattva, full of the merits of religious observances and penances, the adored of the three thousand regions, the possessor of friendliness and benevolence, the sanctified in pure knowledge, renouncing the mansion of Tushita, has acknowledged sonship to you by entering the womb of Máyá. Join your ten nails, bend down your head, and enter the grove, O king, with a humbled, devout mind."

[The king did so] and beholding Máyá in her greatness, said, "Dear one, what may I do for your gratification?"

The Deví said, "I desire to know why a noble and beautiful elephant, bright as snow or silver, more glorious than the sun or the moon, with well-formed feet and well-proportioned body, having six tusks, and joints of adamantine firmness, has entered my belly? I behold the three thousand regions all resplendent and free from darkness, and ten millions of Devas singing my praise. I have no fault, nor anger, nor delusion. In peaceful mind I feel the bliss of meditation.

"Noble king, quickly invite to this home, Bráhmaṇs well-versed in the Vedas and the Upanishads[3] that they may truthfully expound my dream—whether it forbodes good or evil to our family."

Hearing this, the king forthwith sent for Bráhmaṇs versed in the learning of the Vedas and the S'ástras. Máyá, standing before the Bráhmaṇs, addressed them (saying), "Listen to the nature of the dream I have seen."

The Bráhmaṇs said, "Relate to us, Devi, the kind of dream you have seen; after we have heard it we shall expound it."

The Deví said, "a noble and beautiful elephant, bright as snow or silver, more glorious than the sun or the moon, with well-formed feet and well-proportioned body, having six tusks and joints of adamantine firmness, has entered my belly.—Relate unto me the purport of this."

Hearing this speech, the Bráhmaṇs said, "Know ye with high satisfaction that no evil will befall thy family. Unto thee will be born a son endued with all auspicious signs, the noblest of the royal race, a Chakravartí, a noble one,—one who will, again, renouncing his home, the abode of pleasure, with disinterested affection for the whole creation, become a Buddha, the observed of the three regions, who will gratify the three regions with the best of nectar."

Having thus explained the purport of the dream, and enjoyed the refreshments offered by the king, and accepted the dresses[4] presented to them, the Bráhmaṇs retired.

Thus, Bhikshus, king S'uddhodana, having heard the five Bráhmans, expounders of dreams, and interpreters of signs,[5] was greatly pleased, delighted, gratified and steeped in good-will; he treated the Bráhmaṇs with a profusion of dressed food of vari-

LIST OF BOOKS FOR SALE

AT THE LIBRARY OF THE

ASIATIC SOCIETY OF BENGAL,

No. 57, PARK STREET, CALCUTTA,

AND OBTAINABLE FROM

THE SOCIETY'S LONDON AGENTS, MESSRS. TRÜBNER & CO.

57 AND 59, LUDGATE HILL, LONDON, E. C.

BIBLIOTHECA INDICA.

Sanskrit Series.

Chaitanya-chandrodaya, Náṭaka, 3 fasci.	Rs.	1	14
Srauta Sútra, A's'valáyana. 11 fasci.		6	14
——— Láṭyáyana, 9 fasci.		5	10
S'ankara Vijaya. 3 fasci.		1	14
Daśa-rúpa, 3 fasci.		1	14
Kaushitaki Bráhmanopanishad, 2 fasci.		1	4
Sánkhya-sára, 1 fasci.		0	10
Lalita-vistara. 6 fasci.		3	12
Taittiríya Bráhmaṇa. 24 fasci.		15	0
Taittiríya Sañhitá. 31 fasci.		19	6
Taittiríya Áraṇyaka, 11 fasci.		6	14
Maitri Upanishad, 3 fasci.		1	14
A's'valáyana Grihya Sútra, 4 fasci.		2	8
Mimáñsá Darsana, 14 fasci.		8	12
Táṇḍya Bráhmaṇa, 19 fasci.		11	14
Gopatha Bráhmaṇa, 2 fasci.		1	10
Átharvana Upanishads, 5 fasci.		3	2
Agni Puráṇa, 14 fasci.		8	12
Sáma Veda Sañhitá, 37 fasci.		23	12
Gopála Tápaní, 1 fasci.		0	10
Nrisiñha Tápaní. 3 fasci.		1	14
Chaturvarga Chintámani, 36 fasci.		22	8
Gobhilíya Grihya Sútra, 10 fasci.		6	4
Piñgala Chhandah Sútra, 3 fasci.		1	14
Taittiríya Prátis'ákhiya, 3 fasci.		1	14
Prithiráj Rásu, by Chand Bardai, 4 fasci.		2	8
Rájatarangini,		4	0
Mahábhárata, vols. III. and IV.,		40	0
Puráṇa Sangraha.		1	0
Páli Grammar, 2 fasci.		1	4
Aitareya Áraṇyaka of the Rig Veda, 5 fasci.		3	2
Chhándogya Upanishad, English, 2 fasci.		1	4
Sáñkhya Aphorisms, English, 2 fasci.		1	4
Sáhitya Darpaṇa, English, 4 fasci.		2	8
Brahma Sútra. English,		1	0
Kátantra. 6 fasci.		6	0
Kámandakíya Nítisára, 4 fasci. (Fasci. 1, out of stock.)		2	8
Bhámatí, 8 fasci.		5	0
Aphorisms of Sandalya, English, Fasci. 1.,		0	10
Vayu Purána, 6 fasci.		3	12
Kathá Sarit Ságara. English Translation, 6 Fasci.		6	0
Prakrit Lakshanam, fasci. 1.,		1	8

Arabic & Persian Series.

Dictionary of Arabic Technical Terms. 20 fasci., complete, Rs.	25	0
Risálah-i-Shamsiyah, (Appendix to Do. Do.),	1	4
Fihrist Ṭúsí. 4 fasci.	3	0
Nukhbat-ul-Fikr,	0	10
Futúh-ul-Shám, Wáqidí, 9 fasci.	5	10
Futúh-ul-Shám. Azadí. 4 fasci.	2	8
Maghází of Wáqidí, 5 fasci.	3	2
Isábah, 28 fasci., with supplement,	20	14
Táríkh-i-Fírúz Sháhí, 7 fasci.	4	6
Táríkh-i-Baihaqí, complete in 9 fasci.	5	10
Muntakhab-ut-Tawáríkh, vols. I. II. and III., complete in 15 fasci.	9	6
Wís o Rámín, 5 fasci.	2	3
Iqbálnámah-i-Jahángírí, complete in 3 fasci.	1	14
'Álamgírnámah, 13 fasci., with index,	8	2
Pádsháhnámah, 19 fasci., with index,	11	14
Muntakhab-ul-Lubáb, by Kháfí Khán, 19 fasci., with index,	12	12
Áín-i-Akbarí, Persian text, 4to., 22 fasci.	27	8
Áín-i-Akbarí, English translation by H. Blochmann, M. A., vol. I,	12	4
Farhang-i-Rashídí, 14 fasci., complete,	17	8
Nizámí's Khiradnámah-i-Iskandarí, 2 fasci. complete,	2	0
Akbarnámah. 17 fasci. with Index,	20	0
Maáṣir-i-'Álamgírí, by Muhammad Sáqí, complete, 6 fasci., with index,	3	12
Haft Ásmán. history of the Persian Maṣnawí,	1	4
Ṭabaqát-i-Náçirí, English translation. by Raverty, 10 fasci.	10	0
Ṭabaqát-i-Náçirí, Persian text. 5 fasci.	3	2
History of the Caliphs, (English Translation,) 5 fasci.	5	0

MISCELLANEOUS.

Journal of the Asiatic Society of Bengal from vols. XII to XVII, 1843-48, vols. XIX to XX, 1850-51, to Subscribers at Re. 1 per number and to non-subscribers at Re. 1-8 per number; vols. XXVI, XXVII, 1857-58, and vols. XXXIII to XLVIII, 1864-79, to Subscribers at 1-8 per number and to non-subscribers at Rs. 2 per number.

Asiatic Researches, vols. VII. to XI. and vols. XVII. to XX. each, Rs.	10	0
Do. Do. Index,	5	0
Catalogue of Fossil Vertebrata,	2	0
——— of Arabic and Persian Manuscripts,	1	0
Tibetan Dictionary,	10	0
——— Grammar,	8	0
Notices of Sanskrit Manuscripts, 14 fasci.	14	0
Istiláhát-i-Súfiyah. Edited by Dr. A. Sprenger, 8vo.	1	0
Jawámi' ul-'ilm ir-riyází, 168 pages with 17 plates, 4to.	2	0
Aborigines of India, by B. H. Hodgson,	3	0
Examination and Analysis of the Mackenzie Manuscripts, by the Rev. W. Taylor,	2	0
Han Koong Tsew, or the Sorrows of Han. by J. Francis Davis,	1	8
'Ináyah, a Commentary on the Hidáyah, Vols. II. IV.,	16	0
Analysis of the Sher Chín, by Alexander Csoma de Körös,	1	0
Khazánat-ul-'ilm,	4	0
Sharáyat-ul-Islám,	4	0
Anís-ul-Musharrihín,	3	0
Catalogue Raisonné of the Society's Sanskrit MSS. Part I, Grammar,	2	0
Moore and Hewitson's Descriptions of New Indian Lepidoptera, Part I, with 3 Coloured Plates,	6	0

BIBLIOTHECA INDICA;

A

COLLECTION OF ORIENTAL WORKS

PUBLISHED BY THE
ASIATIC SOCIETY OF BENGAL.
NEW SERIES, No. 473.

THE

LALITA-VISTARA,

OR

MEMOIRS OF THE EARLY LIFE OF S'ÁKYA SIṄHA.

TRANSLATED FROM THE ORIGINAL SANSKRIT.

BY

RÁJENDRALÁLA MITRA, LL. D., C. I. E.,

FASCICULUS II.

CALCUTTA:
PRINTED BY J. W. THOMAS, AT THE BAPTIST MISSION PRESS.
AND PUBLISHED BY THE
ASIATIC SOCIETY, 57, PARK STREET.
1882.

LIST OF BOOKS FOR SALE

AT THE LIBRARY OF THE

Asiatic Society of Bengal,

No. 57, PARK STREET, CALCUTTA,

OBTAINABLE FROM

THE SOCIETY'S LOND...
57 AND 59, LUDGATE HILL, LONDON,

BIBLIOTHECA INDICA.

Sanskrit Series.

No.	Title	Rs.	As.
1.	Atharvaṇa Upanishads, Fasc. I—V @ /10/ each	3	2
2.	Áśvaláyana Gṛihya Sútra, Fasc. I—IV @ /10/ each	2	8
3.	Agni Puráṇa, Fasc. I—XIV @ /10/ each	8	12
4.	Aitareya Araṇyaka of the Rig Veda, Fasc. I—V @ /10/ each	3	2
5.	Aphorisms of Ṣáṇḍilya, Fasc. I	0	10
6.	Aphorisms of the Vedánta, Fasc. III—XIII @ /10/ each	6	14
7.	Brahma Sútras, Fasc. I	1	0
8.	Bhámatí, Fasc. I—VIII @ /10/ each	5	0
9.	Bṛihat Araṇyaka Upanishad, Fasc. I—XI @ /10/ each	6	14
10.	Ditto English Translation, Fasc. I—III @ /10/ each	1	14
11.	Bṛihat Saṃhitá, Fasc. I—III, V—VII @ /10/ each	3	12
12.	Chaitanya-Chandrodaya Náṭaka, Fasc. I—III @ /10/ each	1	14
13.	Chaturvarga Chintámaṇi, Fasc. I—XXXVII @ /10/ each	23	2
14.	Chhandogya Upanishad, Sanskrit Fasc. I—VI @ /10/ each	3	12
15.	Ditto English, Fasc. I and II @ /10/ each	1	4
16.	Categories of the Nyáya Philosophy, Fasc. I and II @ /10/ each	1	4
17.	Daṣa Rúpa, Fasc. I—III @ /10/ each	1	14
18.	Gopatha Bráhmaṇa, Fasc. I and II @ /10/ each	1	4
19.	Gopála Tápaní, Fasc. I	0	10

(Continued on third page of cover.)

ous kinds, and, having honored them with rich dresses, bade them adieu. He also presented at that time, at the four gates of the great city of Kapilavastu and at all the city alms-houses and highway crossings, largesses in profusion. Food for the hungry, drink for the thirsty, clothing to the ill-clad, vehicles to those who wanted them, as also essences, garlands, unguents, powdered sandal-wood, beds, shelters, and service, whatever were needed, were given in honor of the Bodhisattva.

Now, Bhikshus, it thus occurred to the king S'uddhodana: "in what sort of a room would Máyádeví be comfortably lodged?" At that moment the four great kings of the quarters approached him, and said: "There is little cause for your anxiety, king; rest at ease, and leave everything to us; we will provide for the accommodation of the Bodhisattva."

Now, S'akra, king of the Devas, approached him, and said:

"Even the best house of the thirty-three protectors of the tower is vile; I shall provide the Bodhisattva with a house as good as Vaijayanta, (the palace of Indra)."

Next, Suyáma, a Devaputra, approached the king, and said:

"At the sight of my mansion ten millions of S'akras are overpowered with wonder; I shall place that Suyáma palace at the service of the venerable Bodhisattva."

Then, Tushita, a Devaputra, approached the king, and said:

"Even the very charming house in which the renowned one dwelt among the Tushitas, shall I place at the service of the Bodhisattva."

Next Sunirmita, a Devaputra, approached the king, and said:

"Most charming is my excellent house, decorated with a profusion of jewels; I shall bring it down, O king, for the worship of the Bodhisattva."

Then Paranirmita-vas'avartí, another Devaputra, approached the king, and said:

"Whatever gorgeous palaces there may be resplendent in the region of desire (*Kámadhátu*), they all lose their glory in the presence of mine; I shall bring that beautiful, auspicious, jewelled palace, and present it, O king, for the worship of the Bodhisattva. It is endowed with a profusion of exquisite flowers, and scented with all sorts of aromatic substances; I shall bring it down to wherever the Deví chooses to dwell."

Thus, Bhikshus, all the chiefs of the Devas, who can put on any form they wish (or of the class Kámávachara), erected their respective palaces in the noble city of Kapila. By the king S'uddhodana a superhuman palace, unattainable even by Devas, was duly furnished. By the power of his Mahávyúha Samádhi, the Bodhisattva beheld the presence of Máyádeví in every one of these houses, and, entering it, took his seat, as on a bedstead, on the right side of Máyádeví's womb. Each of those chiefs of Devas felt gratified with the thought—"It is in my house that the mother of the Bodhisattva has taken her dwelling, and not elsewhere." Thereof the proof:—

"Through the influence of the Mahávyúha Samádhi, each thinking that it was his own creation, all the Devas had their object fulfilled, and the king's desire was fully gratified."

Now, among that godly assembly this idea struck some of the Devaputras. Even the Devaputras of the class Mahárájakáyikas have fearlessly descended to the rank odour of human habitation, but the question is—how the Bodhisattva, who excels all the liberal-minded Devas of the class Thirty-three, the Yámas, and the Tushitas, and all others—who is the aroma of purity, the jewel of beings,—should abandon his celestial form and the abode of Tushita, and take his place for ten months in the womb of a mother in a stinking human abode?

Now the venerable Ánanda,[6] inspired by the divine power of Buddha, thus addressed the lord: "It is wonderful, my lord, that Tathágata should have said that censurable is the abode in the womb of a mother, so is the indulgence in desires; and it is more wonderful, my lord, how, having excelled everything, and become a Bodhisattva, the lord should abandon Tushita, the home of gods, and take his place in the womb of a mother in a stinking human abode? I cannot venture, my lord, to relate what your lordship had before deigned to expound."

The lord said: "Wish you, Ánanda, to behold the felicity of Ratnavyúha[7] which the Bodhisattva enjoyed on the womb of his mother?"

He replied; "this is, my lord, the time, this, O Sugata, is the moment--O Tathágata, do thou display that enjoyment of the Bodhisattva, beholding which we may be gratified?"

The lord, accordingly, made a sign. Thereupon Brahmá, the lord of the earth, along with sixty-eight hundred thousand Brahmás, disappearing from the Brahmaloka, stood before the lord. He then saluted with his head the feet of the lord, thrice circumambulated his person from the right side, and with joined hands stood, saluting the lord. The lord, perceiving his presence, thus addressed him: "Do you know, Brahmá, the decimensial Bodhisattva enjoyment which I have enjoyed for ten months in the womb of my mother?"

He replied, "it is even so, lord, so it is, Sugata."

The lord said, "where is it now? Can you show it, Brahmá?"

He replied, "lord, it is now in the Brahmaloka."

The lord said, "then, Brahmá, do you exhibit, to these people, the decemensial Bodhisattva enjoyment, so that they may thereby know how it is decorated."

Thereupon Brahmá, the lord of the earth, thus addressed his companion Bráhmaṇas: "Do you abide here while I bring down the Bodhisattva enjoyment." He then saluted with his head the feet of the lord, disappeared from the presence, and instantly returned to Brahmaloka.

Then Brahmá, the lord of the earth, thus addressed the Devaputra Subrahman: "Do you, sir, retire from this place, and proclaim in the Brahmaloka, everywhere in the homes of the Thirty-three, and sound forth that we shall bring down to the Tathágata, the jewelled mansion of Bodhisattva enjoyment,[8] (*Ratnavyúha*) and those among them, who wish to behold it, should quickly come to the place." Then he, along with eighty-four hundreds of thousands of millions of tens of millions of Devas, taking up the jewelled mansion of Bhodisattva enjoyment, placed it on an enormous Brahmá car, three hundred yojanas in expanse, and carried it, surrounded by many millions of Devas, to Jambudvípa.

At that time a great concourse took place of Kámávachara Devas, anxious to proceed to the presence of the lord. Then was the jewelled mansion of the lord's enjoyment embellished and decorated with celestial clothing, garlands, incenses, flowers, music, and other objects of enjoyment. It was surrounded by Devas of the class Maheśa. S'akra, king of the Devas, placing himself in the ocean of Mahásumeru,[9] held forth from a distance a palm-leaf umbrella, and, turning his head towards it, watched the house attentively, but could not catch even a glimpse of it. Much less could the Devas of the classes Mahes'a and Bráhmaṇa, and other gods of the class Thirty-three, as also Yámas, Tushitas, Abhinirmáṇa-ratis and Paranirmáṇa-vasavartis, not to talk of S'akra, the king of the gods—they were all stupified.

Now, the lord suppressed the sound of the celestial music. Why did he do so? Because it was calculated to madden the inhabitants of Jambudvípa.

Now, the four great kings of the quarters approached S'akra, the king of the Devas, and said; "O king of the Devas, what should we do? We cannot have a sight of the jewelled house of Bodhisattva enjoyment."

To them replied he; "what can I do, venerable sirs, for even I cannot obtain a sight of it. But we can proceed to the presence of the lord, and there obtain a sight."

They said, "then, king of the Devas, do what you think best, so that we may quickly have a sight of it."

S'akra said; "Come along with me."

In an instant the super-excellent sons of Devas appeared before the lord, and, placing themselves on a side, raised their heads and beheld the lord.

Then Brahmá, the lord of the earth, along with eighty-four hundreds of thousands of millions of tens of millions of Devas carried the jewelled mansion of Bodhisattva enjoyment to the

Tathágata. The mansion was in every way worthy of the Bodhisattva. It was a handsome palace, four-sided, four-cornered, with a pavilion on its top, of the height worthy of an infant six months old, (*Sanmásajáta-dárakah.*)[10] In the middle of the pavilion there was a bedstead fit for an infant six months old. (*Sanmásajáta-dáraka bhitti-phalakah*).[11] The house was so painted that the equal of it could not be found in the regions of the Devas, of the Máras, or of the Brahmás. The Devas were struck with wonder at the sight of its shape and colour. Their eyes were quite dazzled. Brought to the side of the Tathágata, it looked exceedingly lustrous, radiant and effulgent. Glowing like a thing made by a skilful goldsmith, and devoid of every defect, the pavilion verily appeared at that time most splendid. Therein appeared the bedstead of Bodhisattva enjoyment, the like of which in make and colour nowhere in the regions of the Devas was to be seen, except in the three dimpled lines on the neck of the Bodhisattva. The cloth in which the Mahábrahmá (the great Brahmá), was arrayed appeared dim in the presence of the Bodhisattva's bedstead—it seemed very like a weather-beaten black blanket, (*Váta-vṛishṭyávihatah kṛishṇa-kambalah*).

Within the first pavilion there was another jewelled pavilion made of Uragasára sandal-wood,[12] which was worth as much gold as would equal in bulk a thousand earths ;—it was with such wood that the whole of the pavilion was veneered—such was the second pavilion. It stood firm but detached. Within it there was a third pavilion of the same kind. In that third pavilion, redolent with exquisite aroma, was the bedstead placed and arranged. Of that Uragasára sandal-wood the colour was like that of lapis-lazuli. The redolent pavilion again was covered on the outside with exquisite flowers, which seemed as if the merit of the Bodhisattva's former good acts had been smeared on it.

Again that jewelled palace of Bodhisattva enjoyment, though hard and unbreakable as adamant, was nevertheless as soft to the touch as the down on the pod of the *Abrus precatorius*.[13]

And in that house was to be seen the houses of all the Devas who were able to assume all shapes at their fancy.

On the night when the Bodhisattva entered the womb of his mother, a stalk arose from the water below the earth, and, penetrating through sixty-eight hundreds of thousands of yojanas of the great earth, bore a lotus high up in the region of Brahmá.[14] None, however, saw that lotus, except ten hundred thousand Bráhmaṇa choristers (of that region). In that lotus had been deposited the essence of the three thousand of regions, their radiance and their sap. Mahábrahmá placed the essence in a vase made of lapis lazuli, and brought it before the presence of the Bodhisattva. Bodhisattva accepted it, and drank it out of favour to Mahábrahmá. There was not a being living who could drink that vigorous essence and remain at ease, except the next coming Bodhisattva who had acquired the fullness of all the stages of Bodhisattva perfection.

What were the works through the influence of which the essence remained in the Bodhisattva?

For having for long nights practised the duties of a Bodhisattva; for having given medicine to the sick; for having fulfilled desires of longing people; for protecting those who sought his shelter; for daily offering to Tathágatas, to Chaityas, to S'rávakas, to Saṅghas, and to his parents, the first share of flowers, fruits and tasteful substances, before partaking of any of them himself. These were the works in recognition of which Mahábrahmá brought to him the nectariferous essence.

Moreover, at that time all and every place of superhuman excellence as regards enchantment and pleasure, were visible in that pavilion. Through the influence of the Bodhisattva a couple of vestments, each like the aggregate of a hundred thousand pieces[15] appeared in that jewelled house of Bodhisattva enjoyment, the like of which could not appear in any human habitation, except in that of the next coming Bodhisattva. Nor was there any superestimable form, or sound, or odour, or taste or touch in existence, which was not perceptible in that pavilion. That pavilion was so enjoyable, so highly enjoyable, so well-executed within and without, so well-established, so soft to the touch like the down on the pod of the *Abrus precatorius* that its comparison could no where be had.

This is the nature of Bodhisattva, this is the idea in the contemplation of the affluent one, that he would be born in the human region, and, having acquired perfect Sambodhi, turn the wheel of the law. It is on the right side of the womb of the lady whom he accepts as his mother that the pavilion and the jewelled house exist. Renouncing Tushita, the Bodhisattva takes his seat on the bedstead in that pavilion. Nor is the Bodhisattva born as a fœtus made of consolidated bubbles and fleshy fibres. No, he appears with all his body and its members fully developed and marked with all auspicious signs, and in a seated position.

The sleeping Máyádeví in a dream perceived that the noble elephant had entered into her body. And when S'akra, the king of the Devas, the four regents of the quarters, twenty-eight commanders of Yaksha soldiers, and the chief of the Guhyakas, of the Yaksha race in which descended Vajrapáṇi, came to know that he was seated in his mother's womb, they became united and watchful.

There were in attendance on him four goddesses, namely, Utkhílí, Utkhalí, Dhvajavatí, and Prabhávatí. When they knew that the Bodhisattva had entered his mother's womb, they became constantly watchful and protective.

S'akra, the king of the Devas, when he knew that the Bodhisattva has entered his mother's womb, became, along with five hundred Devaputras, united to guard him.

Again, when the Bodhisattva had entered his mother's womb, his body assumed a form which appeared like a grand fire on the top of a mountain—a mountain fire which is visible even in a densely dark night at a distance of a yojana,—and visible from a distance of five yojanas. Thus did his effulgence spread from the womb of his mother. His complexion was luminous, pleasing, agreeable; and seated on the bedstead in the pavilion, he looked exceedingly beautiful, like the lapis-lazuli set on native silver;[16] and remaining in her fixed position, his mother could always see him in her womb. As the lightning flashing from the clouds enlightens everything, even so did she see the Bodhisattva in his mother's womb, by his beauty, by his radiance, and by his colour cast a blaze of light first on the jewelled pavilion; then on the second or the scented pavilion; next on the third or scented pavilion; then on the whole of his mother's nature; then on the sofa on which he was seated; then on the whole house; then, issuing forth from the top of the house, the light made the eastern side luminous; and so on the southern, the western and the northern, the upper the lower sides, and the ten quarters to the extent of two miles on each side.

At dawn of day the four great kings of the quarters along with twenty-eight Yaksha captains and five hundred Yakshas came there to have an audience of the Bodhisattva, and to pray, to serve, and to listen to religious instruction. The Bodhisattva, perceiving their approach, lifted his right hand, and with a finger pointed out seats for them. They took the seats pointed out to them, and, seeing the Bodhisattva in his mother's womb, and of a form like an image of native silver, moving his hand, cogitating, and then putting down his hand, derived great pleasure, satisfaction, and gratification. The Bodhisattva, perceiving their feeling, lifted his right hand, moved it, reflected, and saluted his mother. Knowing then that they were seated, he by his virtuous speech interested them, encouraged them, welcomed them, and gratified them. When they felt a desire to retire, he prevented them. When the four kings thought "the Bodhisattva has now given us leave," they thrice circumambulated his person and that of his mother, and then departed. This is the cause, this the reason, why the Bodhisattva when the night had passed away, had lifted his right hand, cogitated and, after the cogitation, put down his hand. Afterwards when others, whether women, or men, or boys, or girls, came to visit him, he entertained them in the same way, and then his mother welcomed them.

Thus, Bhikshus, when the Bodhisattva was in his mother's womb, he became well practised in welcoming people; and there was not a Deva, nor a Nága, nor a Yaksha, nor a man, nor any superhuman being who could first welcome the Bodhisattva. To all, the Bodhisattva offered welcome first, and then did his mother.

When the morning had passed away and midday had commenced, the supereminent S'akra, king of the Devas, as also the most eminent Devaputras of the class Thirty-three, came there to have an audience of the Bodhisattva, to pray to and serve him, and to listen to religious instruction. The Bodhisattva from a distance perceived them coming, welcomed them by lifting his gold-coloured right hand, and with a finger pointed them to their respective seats. S'akra could not disobey the order of the Bodhisattva. He and his companions took the seats assigned them. The Bodhisattva, perceiving that they were seated, by his virtuous speech interested them, encouraged them, welcomed them, and gratified them. When the Bodhisattva moved his hand, his mother turned towards it. To the others the idea struck,—"it is to us the Bodhisattva has offered welcome." Each thought—"it is with me that the Bodhisattva is talking,—me he is welcoming."

Then the shadow of S'akra,[17] king of the Devas, and of the gods of the class Thirty-three became apparent in the pavilion. Nowhere can such pure Bodhisattva enjoyment be had as by the Bodhisattva in his mother's womb.

When S'akra and the other gods felt a desire to depart, the Bodhisattva perceived their feeling, gave them leave by lifting his right hand, then cogitated, and then, knowing that it had been understood, put down his hand. Nor did he thereby hurt his mother. S'akra and his companions perceived that the Bodhisattva had given them leave, so they thrice circumambulated his person and that of his mother, and then departed.

When the midday had passed away and the vesper had arrived, Brahmá, the lord of the earth, attended and beserved by hundreds of thousands of Devaputras of the class Brahmakáyika, taking the essence of vigour from the lotus (p. 102) proceeded towards the Bodhisattva, to have his audience, to pray to him, to worship him, and to listen to religious instruction. The Bodhisattva, perceiving that Brahmá was coming along with his attendants, welcomed them by lifting his gold-coloured right hand. With a finger he also pointed out to them their respective seats. Brahmá was not able to disobey the order of the Bodhisattva. He and his companions sat on the seats assigned them. The Bodhisattva, knowing that they were seated, entertained them with virtuous speech, welcomed them, encouraged them, and gratified them. When he moved his hand Máyádeví turned towards it. Each of the gods thought, "it is to me that the Bodhisattva is addressing,—with me he is speaking." When Brahmá and his companions felt a desire to retire, Bodhisattva perceived it, and, by way of giving his sanction, raised his gold-coloured right hand, and then waved it, and, after waving it, cogitated, and, after waving and cogitating, by way of conclusion waved again his hand. Thereby he did not hurt his mother. Then this thought struck Brahmá and his attendant Devaputras of Bráhmic form, "the Bodhisattva has given us leave." Thereupon they thrice circumambulated his person and that of his mother, and retired. Bodhisattva, knowing that they had understood the hint, put down his hand.

Then came many thousands of Bodhisattvas from the east and from the south, from the west and from the north, from above and from below, from all the ten quarters of the globe, in order to have an audience of the Bodhisattva, and to pray to him, to worship him, to listen to religious instruction, and to sing the hymn of religion. On their approach the Bodhisattva evolved from his body a light, and with it produced a large array of thrones. Having done so, he made the guests take their seats thereon. When he perceived they were seated, he asked them, and questioned them, about all the details of this, his great translation. None, however, at this time saw him, except Devaputras of his rank.

This, Bhikshus, is the reason, this the cause why the Bodhisattva had, on the expiry of the night, evolved the light from his body.

Nor did, Bhikshus, the body of Máyádeví become heavy on the Bodhisattva's entering her womb; on the contrary it attained lightness, softness, subtility. Nor did she feel any of the pains incident to the condition of pregnancy. Nor was she oppressed by the heat of desires, envy and delusion. Nor did she think of the affairs of lust, malice, or cruelty. Nor did she perceive or feel any cold, or heat, or hunger, or darkness, or dust, or pain. Nor did any shadow of an offensive form, sound, smell, taste, or touch approach her. No unpleasant dream ever disturbed her. No feminine frivolity, no wickedness, no envy, no pain incident to females oppressed her. At that time the mother of the Bodhisattva was, like Panchaśikhodaya, immersed in the discharge of the ten domestic duties and civility.[18] No longing arose in her mind with regard to any man. Nor did that feeling arise in any man with reference to the mother of the Bodhisattva. All men, women, boys and girls in the city of Kapilavastu and elsewhere in the countries of the Devas, the Nágas, the Yakshas, the Gandharvas, the Asuras, and the Garuḍas, having seen the mother of the Bodhisattva, were at ease and full of memory. The wicked all quickly retired from the place. Those who were affected by many diseases,—by diseases of the ears, or of the nose, or of the tongue, or of the lips, or of the teeth, by the itch, or the goitre, or sores in the chest (*uragaṇḍa*), or leprosy, or mania, or epilepsy, or fever, or rheums, or distempers resulting from disordered bile and the rest,—sought her, and the mother of the Bodhisattva placed her right hand on their heads. Thereupon they were immediately freed from their complaints, and they retired to their respective homes. Moreover, Máyadeví took up clumps of grass from the earth, and gave them to diseased persons, and the moment they obtained the gift, they became free from all diseases. Whenever she looked towards her right side she beheld the Bodhisattva in her womb, even as a person beholds his own face in an untarnished mirror. Seeing him, she became satisfied, excited, affected, delighted and soothed in mind with affection.

When the Bodhisattva was in his mother's womb exquisite clarions poured forth delightful music all day and night. Excellent flowers fell in showers. The Devas sent down rain in due season. The winds blew according to their appointed time. The seasons changed in due order, and the stars ran their appointed course. The kingdom was in peace and prosperity, and in no way distressed. The S'ákyas, in the great city of Kapila, as also other people, eat and drank, enjoyed and played, conversed and gave alms, and performed religious ceremonies. During the season of the resplendent moonlit sky, for four months,[19] they remained in-doors, and passed their time in play and enjoyment. The king, S'uddhodana, forsaking all worldly affairs, and the society of even pure women, and adopting the life of a Brahmachárí, engaged himself in religious work, even as if he had retired to a grove of penance[20] (*Tapovana*).

Thus, Bhikshus, did the coming Bodhisattva remain in glory in the womb of his mother. Then he invited the Venerable Ánanda :[21] "Do you wish, Ánanda, to see the jewelled house of Bodhisattva enjoyment wherein the Bodhisattva flourished in the womb of his mother?"

Ánanda replied, "Yes, I wish to see it, Lord, I wish to see it, Tathágata."

He showed it to the Venerable Ánanda, to S'akra, the king of the Devas, to the four guardian kings of the quarters, and to other gods and men. Beholding it, they were satisfied, excited, affected, delighted and steeped in a feeling of affection.

Brahmá, the lord of the earth, then carried the jewelled house back to Brahmaloka, and established it there as a monument (*chaitya*).

Then the Lord again addressed the Bhikshus, saying: "Thus, Bhikshus, during the ten months' sojourn of the Bodhisattva in his mother's womb thirty-six tens of thousands of Devas and mortals were engaged in the practice of the the duties of the three Yánas.

In support of this are the following Gáthás:

"When Bodhisattva, the noblest of men, was in his mother's womb, the earth with all the forests on it, the product of the transformation of the six,[22] quaked. (1).

"Hosts of Devas, refulgent as gold, and decorated in every way, beheld with delight the king of religion—(2)

"seated in his great pavilion, decorated with innumerable jewels. The hero and leader had ascended it and placed himself therein. (3).

"It was redolent with the aroma of the most fragrant sandalwood, and its floor was loaded with all the most precious jewels of the three thousand regions. (4).

"Penetrating through many thousands of regions the lotus essence of vigour became manifest for the meritorious. (5).

"That substance, refulgent in virtue, had been for seven nights prepared in the region of Brahmá, and had been brought to the Bodhisattva by the mighty Brahmá himself. (6).

"There was not a being in existence who could drink and digest that essence prepared by Brahmá, except the well-behaved Bodhisattva. (7).

"The vigour of virtue of many kalpas was reposited in that essence, and by drinking it the thought and understanding of man becomes purified. (8).

"To adore the leader, S'akra, Brahmá and the guardians of regions came three times to the presence of the Bodhisattva. (9).

"They prayed to him, worshipped him, heard of the noble religion, circumambulated his person, and retired as they had come. (10).

"Bodhisattvas, anxious for religion, came to him seated on the resplendent throne formed of the essence of creation, and bright as gold. (11).

"Women and maidens, who happened to be afflicted by being possessed by demons,[23] or by insanity, running about naked and covered with dust, (12)—

regained their senses by the sight of Máyá, and, being endowed with memory, understanding and correct notions, returned to their homes. (13).

"Those who were afflicted by disorders resulting from wind, or bile, or phlegm, those who suffered from diseases of the eye, or the ear, or the body or the mind, (14),

or were overpowered by diseases of various kinds—they all became free from their diseases on Máyá placing her hand on their head. (15).

"Or taking up a tuft of grass from the earth she gave it to diseased persons, and they immediately became cured. (16).

"And having acquired ease and freedom from disorders, the people repaired to their respective homes, (and this happened because) there dwelt the king of physicians and lord of medicines in her womb. (17).

"Whenever Máyádeví looked at her person, she beheld the Bodhisattva seated in her womb. (18).

"Even as the moon is surrounded by stars, so was the lord Bodhisattva adorned by his auspicious signs. (19).

"Neither passion, nor envy, nor delusion affected him. Neither lust nor desire for cruelly ever assailed him. (20).

"He lived with a contented mind, with a delighted mind, in love and calmness. Neither hunger nor thirst, neither cold nor heat, affected him. (21).

"Always did excellent clarions resound without a cause, and flowers of exquisite odour always fell in showers. (22).

"Neither did gods, nor birds, nor men, nor superhuman beings at the time hurt or injure each other. (23).

"All of them were enjoying, and playing, and giving away food and drink in charity. With minds full of contentment and joy, they were all resounding the vow of festivity. (24).

"Everything was under the government of mercy. The clouds rained in due season, and grass and flowers and annuals all sprouted forth in vigour. (25).

"For seven nights jewels rained in profusion in the palace of the king, and all poor persons took them, enjoyed them, and gave them away. (26).

"There lived not such a being as was poor, or in pain, for all were immersed in festive joy as in the garden of the celestia king on the top of the Meru. (27).

"The king of the S'ákyas, pure in every respect, forsook all regal duties, and devoted himself to religion. (28).

"Entering the grove of penance (*Tapovana*) he asks of Máyádeví, "how do you feel in health, holding the noblest of being in you?" (29).

NOTES.

1. *Yellowish white colour*, p. 94. This is not in keeping with the comparison subsequently given. "Yellowish white" cannot be compared with silver or snow. Naturally the so-called white elephant is of a yellowish white or tawny colour, and the phrase closely confirms it. "White as silver or snow" must, therefore, be looked upon as the result of poetical license in the Gáthás.

In the Burmese version no elephant is mentioned.

2. *Poshadha*, p. 94. This is the rite or fast to which reference is made on p. 76. It was also called Uposhadha and Ashṭamí. See my Analysis of 'the Sanskrit Buddhist Literature of Nepal,' p. 262.

3. *Bráhmaṇs well versed in the Vedas and the Upanishads*, p. 96. In the Chinese version the king is made to order some maid-servants to proceed to the chief minister, Mahánámaputra, and desire him to send for eight Brahmaṇs, to wit, Yajna-bhadanta, Visaka-bhadanta, I'śvara-bhadanta, Piṇḍu-bhadanta, Brahma-bhadanta, and the three sons of Káśyapa. The maids conveyed the order to the warder at the gate, one Rojana, who went to the prime minister, and brought the minister and the Bráhmaṇs to the king. The Bráhmaṇs being named no mention is made about their knowledge of the Vedas and the Upanishads. The number of Bráhmaṇs in my text is limited to five. In the Tibetan version as rendered into French the words are "Bráhmanes tres-habiles á expliquer le sens du Rig-Veda et des Çástras," (p. 63). In the Chinese version the reference to the Hindu śástras was probably not deemed proper to be

introduced. It is worthy of note, however, that the Sanskrit text should have named works which do not relate to astrology.

In the Chinese text the reply given by the astrologers is in substance the same as in Sanskrit, but it includes some additional matter which is said to be contained in certain Gáthás. These have been thus rendered into English by Mr. Beal.

"If a mother in her dream, behold
The Sun Deva enter her right side;
That mother shall bear a son
Who shall become a Chakravarti Rája.
If she sees in her dream
The Moon Deva enter her right side,
That son, born of that mother,
Shall be, of all kings, the chief.
If the mother, in her dream, behold
A white elephant enter her right side,
That mother, when she bears a son,
Shall bear one chief of all the world (Buddha);
Able to profit all flesh;
Equally poised between preference and dislike;
Able to save and deliver the world and men
From the deep sea of misery and grief."

(*Beal's Romantic History of Buddha*, p. 38.) These Gáthás do not occur in the Sanskrit text.

4. *Accepted the dresses presented them*, p. 96. Here we have a clear reference to Khilats, which most people in the present day believe to be an institution of Muslim origin.

5. *Expounders of dreams and interpreters of signs*, p. 96. It is not the duty of high caste Bráhmaṇs, according to the Hindu custom and *Smṛiti* rules, to expound dreams and interpret signs. The task is relegated to half-caste Bráhmaṇs called Daivajṇas, who cultivate astronomy and astrology. The text does not mark the difference.

6. *Now the Venerable A'nanda*, p. 98. This para. does not occur in all my MSS., but there is no reason to doubt its authenticity. The work is being related by S'ákya to his congregation, and the thread of the narrative, though frequently broken, turns up every now and then to preserve consistency. The object here is to show

that the exhibition of the Ratnavyúha took place long after the birth of the sage. It was to gratify the congregation that the exhibition was made; but it did not form a part of the narrative of the occurrences at the time of gestation. The exhibition is in some respects the counterpart of the microcosm exhibited by Kṛishṇa to Arjuna in the Bhagavadgítá. Its displays how the sage could command Brahmá to carry out his behests.

7. *Felicity of Ratnavyúha*, p. 99. The Sanskrit words are *Ratnavyúham bodhisattva-paribhogam.* Word for word the meaning is "jewel, collection, Bodhisattva, and enjoyment." The Tibetan counterpart of the phrase has been rendered by M. Foucaux into *l'exercise précieux qui fut l'occupation du Bodhisattva*, (p. 66). It is evident, however, that the word *Ratnavyúha*, has been used, not in its ordinary lexicographical meaning, but in a technical sense to imply a house, palace, tower or some other substantial structure. It is subsequently described to be "quadrangular and quadrilateral" to be surmounted by pavilions, to be decorated with cloth, garlands, and unguents, to have one of its pavilions veneered with a precious kind of sandal-wood, and to be carried about in a huge car,—descriptions which cannot be consistent with exercise, or felicity, or enjoyment. I take it, therefore, to be a house, a palace, or a tower, in the sense of some structure fit for habitation. The Burmese version has nothing to say about the phantasmagorial palaces built by the Devas nor of the Ratnavyúha. It is content with saying that on the Bodhisattva's entering his mother's womb, "four chiefs of Náts, from the seat of Tradoomarit, armed with swords, kept an uninterrupted watch round the palace, to avert any accident that might prove hurtful to the mother or her blessed fruit. From 10,000 worlds, four Náts, from the same seat, were actively engaged in driving away all Bilous (hobgoblins) and other monsters, and forcing them to flee and hide themselves at the extremity of the earth." Bigandet, p. 32. Describing the mother, it says, "Maia, free from every disordered propensity, spent her time with her handmaids in the interior of her apartments. Her soul enjoyed, in a perfect calm, the sweetest happiness; fatigue and weariness never affected her unimpaired health." Her womb is described to have "resembled an elegant Dzedi." Bishop Bigandet explains the Dzedi to be "a religious edifice of a conical form, supported on a

square basis, and having its top covered with what the Burmese call an umbrella, resembling in its shape the musical instrument vulgarly called *chapeau chinois* by the French. On each side of the quadrangular basis are opened four niches (? one on each side) in the direction of the four cardinal points, destined to receive statues of Buddha." This description shows clearly that the Dzedi is no other than the well-known *chaitya*, which, though latterly used to indicate a funeral or memorial tumulus, originally meant a temple or sacred place. The sacred personage being in it, the womb is very aptly compared to a temple. Our text, not satisfied with this simple comparison, makes a Ratnavyúha of it, distinct from the womb, and then lodges it in the region of Brahmá as a sacred monument to be put into requisition whenever desired. The whole of the description of this Ratnavyúha is a fanciful protraiture of the womb as a bassinet.

8. *The jewelled mansion of Bodhisattva enjoyment*, p. 99 For convenience of treatment the original Sanskrit has been rendered here and elsewhere in slightly varying forms.

9. *The ocean of Mahásumeru*, p. 100. Meru or Sumeru, means the great mountain which is fabled to stand on the centre of the earth, and round which the seven oceans and continents are located. The epithet *mahá* added to it would imply the great Sumeru mountain. In the text the word Mahásumeru is qualified by the epithet *samudra*, "ocean." I have nowhere noticed any mention made of an ocean named Mahásumeru. In composition *samudra* is sometimes used to imply the verge or end, the ocean being the verge or limit of land, and the two words therefore may, in the text, mean the outermost limit of the great Sumeru mountain. It may also be made to mean the ocean which surrounds the great Sumeru. In the French version of the Tibetan text the word Sumeru is omitted.

10. *Of the height worthy of an infant six months old*, p. 101. Though the tower is brought on a car 60 yojanas in expanse, its pavilion is limited to only the size of an infant six months old. Consistency in figures and measurements is an obligation to which the authors of the Maháyána sútras are nowhere amenable.

11. *A bedstead for an infant six months old*, p. 101. The Sanskrit words are *Sanmásajátasya dárakasya bhitti-phalakah*. The

first word means "of one born six months," and the second "of a boy." The third word is a compound of *bhitti* and *phalaka*. *Bhitti* means the walls of a room, and thence the boundary line, and *phalaka* "a plank," or "a bar of wood." Put these together I come to "a bedstead, the bars of whose boundary, (*i. e.*, the framework) are fit for an infant six months old;" in other words a bassinet large enough for an infant of the age of six months. The three words being separated by case-affixes, the meaning has become dubious. Had they been compounded into one word, they would have been more consonant with the genius of the Sanskrit language.

12. *Uragasára sandal-wood*, p. 101. *Uraga* means a serpent, and *sára* an essence, *i. e.*, the wood that has the essence of serpents in it. It is popularly believed that forests of sandal-wood are more or less infested by cobras, and the sandal-tree which is most infested by cobras produces the finest wood. Another very highly prized variety of the sandal-wood is called *gos'írsha*, or "of the head of the cow." It is so named from its being produced on a mountain called Gośírsha. (*Burnouf's Histoire du Buddhisme indien*, p. 619.)

13. *As soft to the touch as the down on the pod of the* Abrus precatorius, p. 101. The Sanskrit original of this is *Kuchilindika-sukha-sañsparsha*. M. Foucaux renders it into "Elle est douce au toucher comme un vêtement de Kâtchalindi" (p. 32.) Commenting on it he says, "les deux manuscrits sanscrits écrivent Kâtchilindi. Cet mot, dont je ne trouve nulle part l'explication, est le nom d'une étoffe, et peut-être celui de l'endroit où on la fabriquait." (p. 19.) Elsewhere he adds, "Le Pouráṇas donnent ce nom au pays situé sur la côte de Coromandel, depuis Cuttack, jusqu'aux environs de Madras. Les editions tibetaines ont écrit *Kalinga;* le manuscrits sanscrits ont Kálindika et Kâtchilindika." (p. 72.) The words "*sukha* 'pleasant,' and *sañparsha*, 'touch'" are of obvious import; the only doubtful word is the first, and it does not occur in any Sanskrit dictionary. To assume then that it is the name of a country, and deduce therefrom that some soft stuff of that country is meant are rather venturesome. The word Káchinchika in Sanskrit means the *Abrus precatorius*, and as the down on its pods is of a velvety character, as soft to the touch as possible, I have accepted it to be the right meaning. The Indians are peculiarly fond of drawing their comparisons from natural objects,

and the *Abrus*, commonly called *kuncha*, *guncha*, or *rati*, is so abundant everywhere that the comparison to an Indian is very homely. I must add, however, that the Chinese version as rendered into English by Mr. Beal is "soft as Kalinda cloth." (*Romantic Hist. of Buddha*, p. 43).

14. *Bore a lotus high up in the region of Brahmá*, p. 102. The story of this miraculous lotus does not occur in the Burmese version.

15. *A couple of vestments, each like the aggregate of a hundred thousand pieces*, p. 102. The Sanskrit words are *s'atasahasravyúham náma vásoyugam*. The translation is correct word for word, and I fancy the purport is a pair of patchwork coverlets made of many bits of cloth. In the Tibetan version M. Foucaux reads, "Un assortiment de vêtements nommé Centmille-vêtements," (p. 71.) The word *náma* in the text obviously does not mean "named" but "like," and is intended to imply a comparison. If we take it to mean name, *sáta-sahasravyúha* would be the technical name of patch work—by no means an inappropriate name. Patchwork coverlets are extensively used by hermits in India, but they are also largely made as fancy articles for the use of householders and men of rank: rugs of patchwork are very common all over northern India, and they are highly prized.

16. *Like the lapis-lazuli set on native silver*, p. 104. I am doubtful as to the accuracy of "native silver" as a correct rendering of *játa-rúpa*, but I can suggest nothing better.

17. *Then the shadow of Sakra*, p. 105. I have failed to grasp the purport of this description.

18. *Like Panchaśikhodaya, immersed in the discharge of the ten domestic duties and civility*, p. 107. I know not who this Panchaśikhodaya is, and my text requires that the word should mean a person. Mr. Foucaux renders it into "Les cinq bases de l'étude." The ten domestic duties are: Avoiding (1) evil designs, (2) faults, (3) receiving of presents, (4) delusions, (5) and vanity, (6) elevation above all foolishness, (7) contentment, (8) constant occupation or avoidance of idleness, (9) retirement from one's chamber, (10) non-indulgence in viciousness. I do not clearly understand the 9th. *Ante*, p. 76.

19. *During the season of the resplendent moonlit sky, for four months*, p. 108. The rainy season, when the moon-light is the most

pleasant. Owing to the rains the S'ákyas could not betake to outdoor sports, and so they entertained themselves within their houses.

20. *Grove of penance*, p. 108. Men, when tired of life, retire to a grove to pass the remainder of their lives in austerity and divine contemplation, and S'uddhodana, like them, retired for the time from worldliness, to remain pure. Brahmacharya is continence, such as Vedic students are required to adopt. S'uddhodana observed the rules of continence.

21. *Then he addressed the Venerable Ánanda*, p. 108. The clue of the dialogue between the Lord and Ánanda, which was broken by the narrative of the miraculous bassinet, is now taken up to keep up the continuity of the life as narrated by the Lord to his congregation.

22. *Transformation of the six*, p. 109. I suppose the five elements and Prakriti are meant by the six; but I am not sure.

CHAPTER VII.

THE BIRTH.

Thirty-two omens. Máyá's request to go to the Lumbiní garden. Preparations for departure. The procession. Ramble in the garden. The Plaksha tree. The birth. Reception of the babe by Brahmá. Miracles. The babe's first acts. Miraculous occurrences. Bhagaván and A'nanda on faith in the Bodhisattva. Adoration of Máyá by Apsarases. News of the birth carried to the king. The king's rejoicings and benefactions. Naming of the Prince. Adoration of Máyá by goddesses. Auspicious hymn. Death of Máyá. Procession to Kapila. Welcome by the S'ákyas. Gautamí appointed foster-mother. Asita's reflections—departure to Kapila,—reception there, and prognostications. Thirty-two primary and eighty subsidiary marks on the Prince's body. Gáthás about Asita. Adoration by Devaputras. Corroborative Gáthás.

Thus, Bikshus, ten months having elapsed, and the time for the birth of the Bodhisattva having arrived, thirty-two omens became manifest in the garden attached to the palace of king S'uddhodana. What were the thirty-two omens? (1) All the flower plants there budded, but did not blossom. (2) In the tanks blue lotuses, (*Nymphæa cerulea*) pink lotuses, (*Nelumbium speciorum*) lilies, (*Nymphæa esculenta*), and white lotuses put forth buds, but did not flower. (3) Flower and fruit trees sprouted from the earth and bloomed, but bore no fruit. (4) Eight trees grew forth and twenty hundreds of thousands of stores of innumerable jewels came up to view. (5) In the gynacæum mines of jewels became exposed. (6) Fountains poured forth scented water, both cold and hot, and redolent of aromatic oils. (7) Young lions came down from the sides of the Himavat mountain, joyfully walked round the city of Kapila, and sat by its gates bearing no enmity against any being. (8) Five hundred young elephants of a yellowish white colour came, and, in the presence of king S'uddhodana, scratched the earth with their trunks and feet. (9) Heavenly nymphs with golden zones appeared standing with their hips touching each other in the gynacæum of the king. (10) Semiophide Nága damsels, with various articles of worship, appeared pendant under the sky. (11) Ten thousand Nága damsels holding peacock's feathers became visible under the sky. (12) Ten thousand well-filled jars appeared going round the great city of Kapilavastu. (13) Ten thousand celestial damsels, carrying vases filled with scented water[1] on their heads, became apparent. (14) Ten thousand daughters of Devas appeared standing with parasols, flags and pennons in their hands. (15) Many hundreds of thousands of Apsarases appeared awaiting with conch-shells, clarions, drums, banners, and bells in their hands. (16) The air seemed still, and did not blow. (17) Rivers and currents stood still, and did not flow. (18) The chariots of the sun, and the moon, and the stars and the celestial constellations stopped their courses. (19) The constellation Pushya became manifest. (20) Mines of jewels became exposed in the house of king S'uddhodana. (21) Fire ceased to burn. (22) Jewels appeared pendant under net-works over towers, palaces and gateways.[2] (23) Reprehensible odours were nowhere present. (24) Various agreeable smells seemed to circulate everywhere. (25) The voices of crows, owls, vultures, wolves and jackals were no longer audible.[3] (26) Agreeable sounds resounded everywhere. (27) The whole of man-kind appeared to have retired from labour. (28) Banks and low grounds on earth all became even and level. (29) All roads, crosses, courtyards, highways and market places were covered with flowers so as to be flat like the palm of the hand. (30) All pregnant women gave birth with comfort and ease. (31) The presiding gods and goddesses of Sála forests having made half bodies with leaves appeared saluting them. These were the thirty-two prevalent omens[4] that became apparent.

Now, Máyádeví, perceiving that the time for the Bodhi-sattva's birth had arrived, and impelled by the vigour of the Bodhisattva, repaired, at the first watch of night, to the king, and addressed him in these Gáthás:

"'Lord, listen to my wish[5] as I relate it unto you. It is my earnest desire that I should immediately proceed to the garden. Should it not be to your annoyance, or harm, or trouble, I would quickly repair to the pleasure-garden. (1).

"'You have become wearied by penance and constant devotion to virtue, and I am confined for a long time, carrying within me the pure being. The noble Sál trees in serried lines are in blossom; it is fit, therefore, O lord, that I should go to the garden ground. (2).

"'It is the noble season of spring, the delighter of women; the black bees are in murmur; the koels are in full song; many-coloured and pure (pollen) powders from the flowers are flying in the air; dear one, accord your permission that I may proceed without delay.' (3).

"Hearing these words of the lady, the king, in delight and joy of mind, thus addressed his courtiers: 'Place in array my vehicles harnessed to elephants and horses, and my chariots, and decorate the precious Lumbiní garden.[6] (4).

"'Let twenty thousand elephants of the colour of the cloud, like the blue mountain, housed in golden networks, decorated with gold and jewels, with bells hanging on their side—noble six-tusked elephants—be placed in array. (5).

"'Let twenty thousand horses of the colour of snow or silver, with noble manes of the colour of munja fibre,[7] covered with golden networks set with little bells,—swift as the wind, and worthy the vehicle of royalty,—be placed in order. (6).

"'Quickly set in array twenty thousand men, veterans in warfare, longing for fight with heroes, armed with swords, bows, arrows, iron spears, lassoes, and falchions; so that they may without delusion, guard the noble Máyá and her suite. (7).

"'Decorate the Lumbiní garden which, in its wealth of flowers, is like the Nandana garden of the Súras, with jewels and gold in profusion;—with precious stuffs of various kinds set off all the trees; and having done so report to me.' (8).

"These commands having been heard, the Lumbiní garden was immediately decorated.

"The courtiers then exclaimed: 'Success, success attend thee, O king! May thy life be long! Lord, without waiting we have already done everything according to thy command and are awaiting thy pleasure.' (9).

"The noble king was satisfied. Entering his excellent apartment, he thus commanded his warders:

'Issue orders so that those who are well-affected towards me and those who wish to please me may all decorate themselves for my gratification. (10).

"'Let all be cheerful. Let every one put on soft and pleasant dresses of diverse colours in choice fashions, and redolent with delightful essences and aromatics. Let them have pearl necklaces pendant on their chests, and let all appear fully ornamented. (11).

"'Let lutes, monochords, and mriḍangas,[7]—let vínás, flutes, and mukuṇḍas,[8]—let clarions by hundreds of thousands—raise their charming music, and so entertain all that even gods by hearing the sweet sounds may long for their goddesses. (12).

"'In this noble chariot let Máyádeví ascend, and none other, whether man or woman. Let women of various ranks drag that car, causing no diversion, nor the slightest distraction.' (13).

"When Máyá issued forth from her apartment to the gate, she heard loud cheers proceeding from the diversified army of elephants, horses, chariots and foot soldiers stationed at the king's gate; the sound was such as to cause commotion even in the ocean. (14).

"That beautiful chariot was set off, by the king's orders, with a hundred thousand tinkling bells and a thousand chauris; it had a jewelled throne, and around it jewelled trees, rich in foliage and flowers. (15).

"In that chariot geese, herons and peacocks raised a pleasant carol; parasols, standards, flags and pennons were uplifted; little bells suspended from networks tinkled around; it was set off by stuffs of different kinds. Heavenly damsels came to the sky to behold it. (16).

"They broke forth in pleasant sweet cheers, and bepraised her, when Máyá took her seat on the throne, and the three thousand earths formed of sixfold modifications quaked. The damsels showered, too, choice flowers after whirling them in the air. (17).

"This day will the noblest of beings be born in the garden of Lumbiní. The four guardians of the quarters are carrying that chariot. Indra, lord of the gods, is purifying the road, and Brahmá is marching in front to restrain the wicked. (18)

"Immortals by hundreds of thousands are, with joined hands, saluting her. The king, in delight, is beholding the procession. For such a god among gods, such should be the rejoicings—for him, whom the four guardians of the quarters, Brahmá, Indra and the other gods (19).

"offer such profuse homage. This pure being is manifest; there is none other in the three regions who is worthy of such homage. Should any Deva or Nága, S'akra or Brahmá, or the guardians of the quarters, venture to accept it, the crown of his head would immediately burst open. But to this greater god all homage is becoming." (20).

Now, Bhikshus, Máyádeví proceeded forth attended by her suite. She was guarded by eighty-four thousand well-appointed horse-cars, eighty-four thousand well-appointed elephant-cars, eighty-four thousand brigades of heroic, veteran, sturdy soldiers clad in impenetrable mail and armour. She was preceded by sixty thousand S'ákya maidens. She was guarded by forty thousand S'ákyas, old, young and middle-aged, all born agnates to the king S'uddhodana. She was surrounded by sixty thousand musicians of king S'uddhodana's inner apartments, all engaged in singing and music, playing on clarions and other instruments. She was surrounded by eighty-four thousand Deva damsels, by the same number each of Nága damsels, of Gandharva damsels, of Kinnara damsels, and of Asura damsels, proceeding in different arrays, decorated with a profusion of ornaments, and engaged in singing, music, or pleasant conversation. The whole of the Lumbiní garden was redolent with scented waters,[9] and besprinkled with choice flowers. All the trees in that noble park were clad with leaves, flowers and fruits out of season. That park was decorated by Devas, even as the Miśraka Park[10] is adorned by them.

Now, Máyádeví, having entered the park and descended from her chariot, sauntered about in the company of human and heavenly damsels. Rambling from tree to tree, strolling from one parterre to another, now looking at this tree, then at another, she came near the waved-leaved fig tree (*Ficus infectoria*, Plaksha.[11]) It was the noblest of many noble trees, with well-disposed branches, bearing fine leaves and blossoms, covered with exquisite flowers, redolent of aroma, having clothes of various colours suspended from it[12], resplendent in the lustre of numerous jewels, having its root, trunk, branches and leaves set with all kinds of jewels, having well-disposed and far extending branches, standing on ground even as the palm of the hand, covered with verdant green rivalling in colour the throat of the peacock, and soft to the touch like the down on the pod of the *Abrus precatorius*. About it dwelt the mothers of former Jinas, and around it resounded the music of Devas. It was auspicious, stainless, and pure. By the calm spirit of hundreds of thousands of S'uddhávásakáyika Devaputras, it was bent. It was bepraised by the bent heads of those who bore matted hair as their crown, (*i. e.*, hermits). This Plaksha tree did the lady approach.

Now, that Plaksha tree, feeling the glory of the Bodhisattva, lowered its head and saluted her. Now, Máyádeví, extending her right hand, resplendent as the lightning on the sky, held a branch of the Plaksha tree, and, looking playfully towards the sky, stood there yawning. At that time sixty hundreds of thousands of Apsarases, along with Kámávachara Devas, engaged themselves in her service.

Thus did the Bodhisattva remain thriving in the womb of his mother. And when ten full months had passed, forth from the right side of his mother,[13] he issued, with full memory, knowing everything, and undefiled by any uterine dirt, such as usually attaches to others.

At this time, Bhikshus, there were present before him S'akra, the lord of the Devas, and Brahmá, lord of the earth,[14] and they respectfully and intelligently and in full memory received the Bodhisattva under cover of a beautiful piece of silk cloth.[15]

Brahmá, lord of the earth, and his suite of Brahmakáyika Devaputras plucked out the tower in which the mother of Bodhisattva had dwelt during her pregnancy, and carried it away to Brahmaloka for the purpose of erecting a chaitya on it, and worshipping it.

No Bodhisattva should be received by any human being, therefore was the Bodhisattva first received by the Devas.

Immediately after his birth the Bodhisattva alighted on the earth; and at that time, piercing through the earth, a noble lotus appeared for the newly-born Mohásattva Bodhisattva. The two Nága kings, Nanda and Upananda, remaining in semi-developed form under the sky, bathed the Bodhisattva by pouring two streams of water, one hot and the other cold.[16] S'akra, Brahmá, the guardians of regions, and the Devaputras by hundreds of thousands, who had come there, bathed the new-born Bodhisattva with scented water and well-blown flowers, and sprinkled the same about him. Two chámaras, and a jewelled umbrella became manifest in the sky. The Bodhisattva, seated on the noble lotus, beheld the four quarters; he beheld it with the sight of a lion—with the sight of a Mahápurusha.

At that time further birth being precluded by the maturation of the fruit of his former good works, the Bodhisattva obtained a transcendental sight,[17] through which he beheld to the utmost the three thousand great thousand regions, along with all their towns, market towns, villages, provinces, kingdoms, and capitals, together with all the gods and human beings dwelling there. He perceived, too, the mind and habits of all created beings. Perceiving them, he looked to ascertain whether there was any person equal to him in good conduct, in meditation, in thorough knowledge, and in the exercise of all virtuous actions; but nowhere in the three thousand great thousand regions did he see any.

Now then, the Bodhisattva, dauntless and fearless as a lion, and unagitated, calling to mind and contemplating on the eight objects of reflection,[18] and knowing the mind and habits of all beings, advanced seven steps towards the east,[19] saying, "I shall be the easternmost (foremost) in all virtuous actions, the source of all goodness." While he advanced, the beautiful, white, wide-extended umbrella and the auspicious chámaras, advanced along with him in the sky, and where he set his foot there sprouted forth lotuses. In this way he next advanced seven steps towards the south, saying, "I shall be worthy of reward (*dakshiṇiya*) from gods and men." Towards the west he advanced seven steps, and, stopping like a lion at the seventh step, with a cheering voice declared, "I am the eldest on the earth; I am the noblest on the earth; this is my ~~western~~ (or last) birth; I shall bring to an end all birth decay, death and pain." He advanced seven steps towards the north, and said, "I shall be subsequenceless (without a north) among all creation." He advanced seven steps downwards, and said, "I shall destroy Mára and his army; I shall shower on hell the rain of the cloud of the great religion, and blow out the fire of the nether regions, so that they may be restored to happiness." He advanced seven steps upwards, and, casting his look above, said, "I shall be the observed of all who live above." These were the words that were said by the Bodhisattva.

At that time the three thousand great thousand regions learnt well from this voice that this was the knowledge of things produced by the maturation of the works of the Bodhisattva.

When the Bodhisattva is born for the last time and when he acquires the sequenceless absolute Bodhi, then with reference to him these and the like miracles become manifest.[20] Then, O Bhikshus, all beings were horripilated with delight.[21] Then frightful, horripilating, extensive earthquakes took place. Then superhuman celestial clarions sounded without being blown by any one. Then trees of every season bore flowers and fruits in the three thousand great thousand regions. Clear rolling sounds of the clouds were heard under the sky. The Devas slowly showered down from the cloudless sky small particles of rain. Delightful, mild, fragrant breeze loaded with many kinds of flowers, apparels, ornaments, and aromatic powders circulated everywhere. Free from darkness, dust, smoke and fog all the sides sparkled delightfully.

From above the sky loud, deep and grave sounds were heard. The refulgence of the moon, of the sun, of S'akra, of Brahmá, and of the Lokapálas was subdued. The whole of the three thousand regions became aglow with the touch of the highest pleasure, with the growth of the mental and corporeal pleasures of all beings, and with the resplendence of many thousands of variegated colours. All beings were devoted to the gratification of the newly-born Bodhisattva. They were all devoid of anger, malice, delusion, pride, dejection, disappointment, fear, covetousness, envy, and vanity. All were averted from all hurtful actions. The diseased got rid of their ailments. The hungry and the thirsty had their hunger and thirst subdued. Drunkards had their drunkenness removed. The insane got their reason back. The blind got back their power of vision, and the deaf their hearing. Those who had deformities in their mouth or other parts of their bodies had those defects removed. The poor obtained wealth, and the bound their freedom from bonds. The sufferings of those who dwelt in Avíchí and other hells were suppressed at the time. The brute creation were free from the pain of devouring each other, and the dwellers in the region of Yama suffered not from hunger, thirst, and the like. When the Bodhisattva, immediately after his birth, advanced seven steps, innumerable millions then stood firm on that adamantine spot, incalculable millions of hundreds of thousands of Buddhas from the ten quarters, of well regulated feet, of mighty vigour, thoroughly exercised in the great religion. The great Pṛithiví made herself manifest there, when the newly-born Bodhisattva of great power and vigour advanced seven steps. At that time the farthest bound of all regions become aglow in a resplendent light. Great were the sounds of singing and dancing at the time. Innumerable were the flowers, powders, essences, garlands, jewels, ornaments and apparels which were showered from the clouds. All creation was immersed in the highest delight. In short, inconceivable were the occurrences when, rising from all other regions, the Bodhisattva made himself manifest on this earth.

Now, the venerable A'nanda, rising from his seat, uncovering one shoulder, and resting on his right knee placed on the ground, saluted the Lord with joined hands, and thus addressed him: "Verily, Lord, the Tathágata was most wonderful to all creation. So was verily Bodhisattva fully endowed with the religion. The question then is, Why should he again acquire the sequenceless perfect knowledge ?[22] On this subject, Lord, I seek the asylum of the Lord Buddha four times, five times, fifty times, nay, many hundreds of thousands of times."

Thus beseeched, the Lord addressed the venerable A'nanda, saying—"there will be born in future times, A'nanda, many Bhikshus, of wreckless body, of thoughtless mind, devoid of good conduct, devoid of understanding, childish, ignorant, arrogant, haughty, puffed up, of evil propensity, of bewildered mind, full of gross desires, full of errors, impure, led by the ears, and dependant on their hearing, who will have no faith in this kind of purity of the Bodhisattva's descent from the womb. These, sitting aside, will thus speak to each other: 'Look ye, how inconsistent it is, that such should have been the glory of the Bodhisattva dwelling in the womb of a mother, amidst a mass of excrement and urine, that issuing from the right side of his mother's womb he was not besmeared with the filth of the womb! How can this be consistent!' These deluded persons will not be able to understand that the body of men of noble deeds is not produced in a mass of excrement and urine; that of such beings the descent from the womb is perfectly pure. It is from his mercy to created beings that the Bodhisattva, abiding in the womb, takes his birth on the region of the mortals. Remaining as a Deva he cannot set the wheel of religion in motion."

"Why so?"

"Not to let men, A'nanda, be in evil condition. The lord is Tathágata, Arhat, and the perfect knower; we are mere mortals; we cannot supply his place, and hence comes the evil condition. But to these deluded childish persons, devoid of religion, this will not be intelligible. That person is inconceivable by men; we should not, therefore, disbelieve him. Moreover, Ánanda, there will be some deluded persons who will boast of many virtuous actions, rejecting the religion of Buddha, immersed in gain, defiled with excrement, welcoming gain, and of vile caste, who at that time will not conceive the miraculous power of Buddha, much less of the greatness of the Tathágata in the form of the Bodhisattva.

Ánanda said: "Shall Bhikshus of such kind be born in future times, who will reject these auspicious Sútrántas, and be antagonistic to them?"

The Lord said: "Men of this kind, Ánanda, will reject the Sútrántas, be antagonistic to them, and in many and diverse ways adopt other means of purification. These worthless people will never be great."

Ánanda said: "Lord, what will be the lot of such evil-minded men? and what will be their means of salvation?"

The Lord said: "They shall have the same reward which has been, and will be, described by the lords Buddha of the past, the present and the future, for such beings."

Wonder-struck and horripilated, the venerable Ánanda exclaimed "salutation to Buddha." He then addressed the Lord: "Lord, my body is paralysed by hearing of the evil conduct of these wicked people."

The Lord said; "These men will be, Ánanda, not of good conduct, but of the most vicious conduct; and for their most vicious conduct they must fall into the great hell of Ávíchí."

"What is the reason of this?"

"Whoever, Ánanda, whether Bhikshus or Bhikshukís, or Upásakas or Upásikás, after hearing all these Sútrántas, do not liberate themselves from error, attain no faith in them, and respond not to them, shall fall into the great hell of Ávíchí after death. Mistrust not the Tathágatas, Ánanda."

"Wherefore?"

"Measureless is the Tathágata, profound, full, and unfathomable. Whoever, Ánanda, after hearing such like Sútrántas, rejoices thereat, and desire satisfaction, gratification and delight, they really will attain them. Really fruitful will be their human existence. They will have accomplished all good works: they will have given the greatest gifts: they will be free from the threefold destruction:[23] they will be the sons of Tathágata: they will succeed in every undertaking: they will derive the fruit of their faith: they will be well established in the kingdom; they will be contented, and the best of men; they will have mangled the sinful Mára; they will have crossed the wilderness of the world; they will have plucked the dart of grief; they will have attained all pleasant objects; they will have obtained the way to the asylum; they will be worthy of reward; they will be held worthy of respect and of rare ascendancy in this world."

"And what is the reason for this?"

"There are in this world men who have faith in this religion of the Tathágata—a religion which is like an army[24] against all worldly evil. They do not accept any low form of religion, (*lit.* root of good), and yet they may not be of one caste with me, or friends of mine."

"How so?"

"Some, A'nanda, become well affected and pleased by hearing; some become so by sight, and not by hearing; while others become so both by hearing and sight. Among them I am affected and pleased either by hearing or sight, being convinced of its truth. Hence the others are not bound to me by unity of caste or friendship. They should be delivered by the Tathágata because they betake to the Tathágata, because they are the followers of the merit of the Tathágata, because they are the dutiful worshippers of the Tathágata. To such frightened mortals as have sought shelter from me and practised all the Bodhisattva duties by me, I have given protection. What, moreover, the Tathágata enjoins is that, after knowing the sequenceless perfect Sambodhi, the Yoga should be performed.

Again A'nanda, that Tathágata who has done all this for you, has also, on mere hearing, removed all obstructions to the (attainment of the) Yána for his friends. Even those who travel a distance of a hundred yojanas towards him, are gratified even without seeing that friend of theirs ; what wonder then that they should be so by seeing him, and beholding these thoroughly established roots of welfare, and becoming Tathágatas, Arhats and perfect Sambuddhas, for they well know their former friends. Such men are friends of the Tathágatas as well as of me.

"How so?"

"Because, A'nanda, such a person becomes a dear friend and affectionate to the friend. A friend of such a friend becomes a dear one, and affectionate. Therefore, A'nanda, I enlighten you and inform you. Enlivening our faith we should take delight in unborn Tathágatas, Arhats and thorough Buddhas (*samyak sambuddhas*) so that, knowing us to be friends, they may fulfil our desires. Suppose, A'nanda, for example, that a man of good speech, of good conduct, and possessed of many friends, has an only son. When that person passes away, the son does not suffer, for his father's friends accept him as a friend. Even so, those who evince faith in me, are accepted as friends by me, for they are under my protection. And I say unto you, that the Tathágata has many friends, and those friends of the Tathágata are speakers of truth and not of falsehood. The truth-speaking friends of the Tathágata are Arhats and thorough Buddhas. Therefore, A'nanda, I say unto you that the Yoga should be performed with reverence."

Then, when the Bodhisattva was born, hundreds of thousands of millions of tens of millions of Apsarases, coming under the sky, rained on Máyádeví excellent flowers and pastiles, and aromatics and garlands and unguents, and clothes and ornaments. On this subject these (Gáthás may be quoted).

"At that time sixtyfold ten thousands of celestial Apsarases of auspicious, spotless, pure, golden effulgence, resplendent as the sun and the moon, and of delightful voice, arrived at the Lumbiní garden, and addressed Máyádeví, saying, 'be not dejected, we shall make you comfortable. (1).

"'Say, what you wish to be done, what we should do, what you desire? We are here abiding in affection for the advancement of your good. Be of ardent good cheer; grieve not in any way. This day, thou shalt quickly give birth to the noble physician who will be the destroyer of decay and death. (2).

"'These S'ála trees are resplendent with blossoms; these men on thy sides are waving a hundred thousand chámaras held in their hands; and this earth, the result of sixfold modifications, along with the ocean, is shaking, resounding in the sky; and now thou wilt give birth to a son that will be the noblest of mankind. (3).

"'Since an auspicious, pure, gold-coloured light pervades everywhere; since a hundred clarions are delightfully braying in unison in the sky; since a hundred thousand gods of pure homes and free from passions are bowing down in cheerfulness, thou wilt surely give birth to the merciful to creation. (4).

"'Even S'akra and Brahmá, even the guardians and other gods, pleased and gratified, and standing by thy sides, are saluting him with their hands. That lion among men, that leader pure of action, piercing thy side, will issue from thy womb like a mountain of gold.' (5).

"The two, S'akra and Brahmá, with joined hands, received the sage. Hundreds of thousands of fields quaked like beautiful pearls.[25] Perishing beings in all the three regions became happy; there was no affliction anywhere. Hundreds of thousands of immortals, scattered flowers from the sky. (6).

"The adamantine earth, possessed of vigour and might, stood still, when the great preceptor, the destroyer of decay and death, the noblest of physicians, the giver of the best medicine, standing on his two feet marked with a beautifully coloured lotus and a wheel, advanced seven steps, making most endearing exclamations in a profound voice. (7).

"Placing themselves under the sky the noble Brahmá and S'akra, the noble Deva, sprinkled pure, pleasant, fragrant water on the preceptor. The king of serpents sent forth two streams, one of warm and the other of cold water. Hundreds of thousands of immortals from the void above showered aromatic water on the preceptor. (8).

"Revered guardians of regions stood with their beautiful hands joined. The three thousand regions of the world with all their movables and immovables shook. (9).

"When the preceptor was born on the earth, a delightful light spread everywhere; destruction was stopped, all afflictions and pain were pacified. (10).

"The Maruts[26] showered flowers on the birth here of the leader of men. The hero of might and vigour walked seven paces. (11).

"Wherever on the earth he placed his foot there shot up auspicious and noble lotuses, and the ground was decorated with all kinds of jewels. (12).

"Then, having walked seven paces, the destroyer of decay and death, born like a great physician, put forth his profound voice. (13).

"The wise one, looking at the quarter, put forth these words full of meaning; 'I am the eldest of all creation; I am the noblest in all regions; I am the preceptor. (14).

"'This is my last birth.' This was said by the leader of men with a smiling face. He, the benefactor of regions, was honoured by the guardians of regions, by Maruts, by Indra, along with all chiefs of serpents, with a cheerful heart. He was bathed with streams of fragrant water by millions of Devas standing in the sky. (15-16).

"Having bathed with fragrant water the first born, the self-born, the Devas assembled in the sky, and paid homage to the noblest of men by holding forth large white umbrellas, chowries and valuable apparel. (17).

(The Apsarases said), "O Devi,[27] immense prosperity has been attained by you. Your son, endowed with all the signs of the jewel of a great race, is thriving: he is manifest as the lord of emperors (*chakravarti*). He, without enemies, the standard of the Jambudvípa, will be the lord of the only umbrella, master of the greatest stronghold, and king. Say, lady, what should we do (for you)?" (18).

After saying this the Apsarases became silent. People from[28] the great city of Kapilavastu having come, presented themselves before king S'uddhadana.

"Men having approached S'uddhadana thus addressed him with joy: 'Lord, great blessing has accrued to the royal family of the S'ákyas; twenty-five thousand sons have been born in the home of the S'ákyas:—all endowed with great power, naked,[29] and invincible.'

"Other men reported: 'Listen, Lord, to the joyful sound,—headed by Chhandaka eight hundred sons of maid-servants and ten thousand sons of free men have been born; and headed by Kanṭaka twenty thousand noble chargers of golden hue and tawny mane,[30] have been foaled. Many lords of castles have (1)

also been acquired by you, O noble king. Success attend your majesty! May it please your majesty to impart your behests, whether we should retire, or what should we do? You have acquired this greatness; we are your majesty's slaves: success attend you. Twenty thousand noble elephants caparisoned with golden networks (2)

"'and trumpeting, are ready to proceed to the royal mansion. Headed by Gopá sixty hundred powerful black calves have been born. Such have been the prosperous accessions in the noblest of noble mansions of the king. O Lord and king, do you yourself proceed and see everything with your own eyes.' (3).

"On the ocean of merit, the griefless Jina becoming visible in the resplendence of the brightness of his virtue, men and gods by thousands retired in delight."[31] (4).

Further, Bhikshus, on the instant the Bodhisattva was born there were alms given in profusion. Five hundred daughters of good family were brought forth. Ten thousand daughters headed by Yaśovati, eight hundred slaves headed by Chhandaka, ten thousand fillies, ten thousand colts, headed by Kanṭaka, five thousand elephant calves, and five thousand bovine calves,[32] were given under the royal orders for the young prince to play with. On the land of four times many millions of hundreds of thousands of islands asvaltha saplings were produced.[33] On the middle island (*antardvípa*) a forest of sandal trees came into being. For the enjoyment of the Bodhisattva five hundred gardens came into existence in the outskirts of the town. Five thousand mines, rising from the bowels of the earth, opened their mouths on the surface. Thus everything that was desirable to the king S'uddhadana, became subservient to him.

Then this idea struck king S'uddhodana, "what name should I give to the Prince?" Then this occurred to him: "since his birth everything has become profuse (*savártha-samriddháh*), let me name him SARVA'RTHASIDDHA, (one through whom every object has been attained)." Then with great ceremony and every propitious rite he declared "let the name of the Prince be Sarvárthasiddha," and named him accordingly.

Then, Bhikshus, after the birth of the Bodhisattva, his mother's flank became unbroken and scarless; as it was before so it became after.[34] Three water-wells became manifest, as also tanks of scented oil. Five thousand Apsarases, with well-scented oil,[35] approached the mother of the Bodhisattva, and enquired how easy had been the delivery, and how had she recovered from the exhaustion caused by it. Five thousand Apsarases, bringing excellent unguents, approached the mother of the Bodhisattva, and enquired, how easy had been the delivery, and how had she recovered from the exhaustion caused by it? Five thousand Apsarases, bringing pitchers filled with excellent scented water, approached, &c., &c. Five thousand Apsarases, bringing excellent baby linen, &c., &c. Five thousand Apsarases, bringing baby ornaments, &c., &c. Five thousand Apsarases, making excellent music with clarions, &c., &c. Foreign rishis versed in the five sciences,[36] came from beyond the bounds of Jambudvípa under the sky, and, placing themselves in front of S'uddhodana, resounded the language of blessing.

Thus, Bhikshus, for seven nights from the day of the birth

of the Bodhisattva in the Lumbini garden, he was with the music of the clarion and the táḍáva[37] beserved, respected, honoured and adored. Victuals and edibles and toothsome food were given away. All the S'ákyas, collecting together, shouted the acclaim of joy, and, distributing benefactions and performing virtuous actions, daily gratified thirty-two hundred thousand Bráhmaṇs, and gave away whatever people wanted. S'akra, the lord of the Devas, and Brahmá, assuming the form of pupils and sitting in front in that Bráhmanical assemblage, recited the following Gáthás:

"So that the world may become happy and all catastrophes may be removed this prosperity, the restorer of peace on earth, was born. (1).

"Even as the light of the sun and the moon and the gods beshrouded by darkness cannot shine, so for certain (it fails on) the rising of the light of virtue. (2).

"He, by whose birth in this region the eyeless have come to see, the deaf to hear, and the insane have regained their memory, (3).

"by the birth of which friendly person pains have ceased to afflict,—verily he will be worthy of the adorations of tens of millions of Bráhmaṇs. (4).

"Even as the S'ála trees are in good bloom and the earth is in peace, even so for certain will he be omniscient and worthy of the adoration of the world. (5).

"So that mankind may rise above helplessness and the great lotus may sprout,[38] verily will he, the greatly vigorous, be the lord of regions. (6)

"Even as the gentle breeze loaded with aroma is curative of human illness, so will he be the king of physicians. (7)

"These hundreds of passionless gods of Rúpadhátu devoutly and with joined hands shall salute him who will be all-merciful. (8)

"So that mortals may look on the Devas and the Devas may

look on men without hating each other, he shall be the accomplisher of his object. (9)

" So that all fires may be quenched, and the rivers may all become calm, and the earth may reel gently, he shall be the knower of the truth." (10)

Then, Bhikshus, on the seventh night after the birth of the Bodhisattva, Máyádeví departed this life. After her demise she was born among the Thirty-three Devas. Now, Bhikshus, it might occur to you that it was through the fault of the Bodhisattva she died. But you should not think so.

" And why?"

Because the span of her life was so ordained. The mothers of all former Bodhisattvas also died on the seventh night after their confinement.

" And what was the cause of that?"

Because on the delivery of the well-grown Bodhisattva with all his organs complete his mother's heart splits.

Now, Bhikshus, the Bodhisattva entered the great city of Kapilavastu with a retinue millionfold greater than that with which Máyádeví had seven days previously issued forth therefrom to retire to the garden. On his entry five thousand pitchers filled with scented stream water were carried before him. Five thousand maidens, holding peacock's tail chouries, marched before him. Five thousand maidens, holding palm-leaf fans, marched before him. Five thousand maidens, holding spouted urns full of aromatic water, marched before him, sprinkling the water on the road. Five thousand maidens, holding pieces of chintz,[39] marched before him. Five thousand maidens, holding fresh, variegated, long garlands, marched before him. Five thousand maidens, holding appropriate jewelled ornaments, marched before him, purifying the road. Five thousand maidens, carrying appropriate chairs, marched before him. Then five hundred thousand Bráhmaṇs, holding bells walked in procession before him, ringing auspicious music. Twenty thousand elephants, arrayed in beautiful ornaments, marched before him. Twenty thousand horses, richly caparisoned and decked with golden ornaments, paraded before him. Eighty thousand chariots mounted with white umbrellas, flags, pennons and networks of bells followed the train of the Bodhisattva. Forty thousand veteran heroes of majestic form, arrayed in invulnerable mail coats and breast-plates, followed the Bodhisattva. Under the sky illimitable and uncountable millions of millions of Devaputras of the class Kámávacharas followed the train, offering worship to the Bodhisattva with various collections of offerings. The magnificent chariot in which the Bodhisattva repaired had been decorated by Kámávacharas Devas with numerous collections of precious articles. Twenty thousand celestial maidens set off with numerous ornaments and holding jewelled threads (*ratna-sútra-parigṛihítáni*) dragged that chariot. Between every two Apsarases there was one human female, and between every two human females there was one Apsaras, but neither did the Apsarases feel the rank smell of the human females, nor did the human females feel bewildered by the beauty of the Apsarases: this was due to the glory of the Bodhisattva.

Now, Bhikshus, in the noble city called Kapila, five hundred houses had been built by five hundred S'ákyas for the use of the Sarvárthasiddha Bodhisattva. When the Bodhisattva entered the town, these S'ákyas placed themselves each by the gate of his own house, and with bent body and joined hands thus respectfully exclaimed: "Enter this house, O Sarvárthasiddha! Enter this, O Deva of Devas! Enter this, O pure being! Enter this, O giver of affection and joy! Enter this, O thou of spotless fame! Enter this, O thou universal eye (*samanta-chakshuh*)! Enter this, O thou unrivalled one! O thou of incomparable merit and vigour, of person marked with auspicious signs, of well ornamented body, enter this house." Having made this offering to the Prince they all shouted in joyous chorus, "Sarvárthasiddha! Sarvárthasiddha!"

With a view to gratify the desires of these persons, king S'uddhodana placed the Bodhisattva successively in their houses for a total period of four months, and then brought him to his own house. In that house, which was like an agglomeration of many jewels, the Bodhisattva took his abode. There all elderly S'ákya men and women assembled, and discussed the question as to who was there who could nurse and amuse and protect the Bodhisattva with due feelings of interest, friendliness, affection and calmness. Among them were five hundred S'ákya wives, and each of them said, "I shall nurse the Prince."

Then the S'ákyas, including the elders, men and women,[40] thus remarked: "All these wives are inexperienced[41] and thin and youthful; they are elated with the vanity of their youth and beauty; they are not fit to nurse the Bodhisattva at proper times. But here is the good matron Gautamí,[42] the sister of the Prince's mother; she is well able to bring up the Prince in a proper way; and at the same time approach king S'uddhodana." Then they in a body made the request to the great matron Gautamí; and the great matron Gautamí undertook to nurse the Prince. Now, thirty-two maid-servants were appointed for the Bodhisattva, eight as body-nurses to carry him about; eight as milk-nurses to give him nourishment; eight as cleansing-nurses to wash and dress him; and eight as play-nurses to amuse and play with him.

Then king S'uddhodana invited the S'ákyas to a meeting,[43] and held counsel with them as to whether the Prince would become an imperial sovereign, or whether he would retire as a houseless hermit?[43]

At that time there lived on the side of the noble Himavat mountain a great sage (*maharshi*) named Asita.[44] He was versed in all the five sciences, and lived with his nephew Naradatta. At the moment of Bodhisattva's birth he beheld many extraordinary, wonderful, magical occurrences. He saw Devaputras moving about in great joy under the sky, and, high in the void above, resounding the name of Buddha. The wish arose in his mind, "I must inquire into this mystery." With his intellectual eyes he surveyed the whole of the Jambudvípa. He beheld in the great city called Kapila, in the house of king S'uddhodana, a prince was born, who was refulgent with the light of a hundred virtues, who was the adored of all regions, who bore on his person the thirty-two signs of greatness. Having beheld this he addressed his pupil Naradatta:[45] "Know ye, my pupil, that a precious jewel has been produced in the Jambudvípa. In the great city of Kapilavastu, in the house of king S'uddhodana has been born a prince who is refulgent with the light of a hundred virtues, who is the adored of all regions, who bears on his body the thirty-two signs of greatness. Should he remain at home he will become a great sovereign, owner of a fourfold army, an emperor, victorious, virtuous, master of religion, ruler of countries, possessed of great might, and endowed with the seven jewels, and these will be the seven jewels, *viz.*, the jewel wheel, the jewel elephant, the jewel horse, the jewel ruby, the jewel wife, the jewel lord chamberlain, the jewel commander-in-chief. Unto him will be born a thousand sons, valorous, heroic, handsome, and oppressors of enemical armies. He will conquer the whole circle of the earth to the brink of the ocean through his impartial discipline, his arms, his religion, and his might, and reign over all with supremacy and power. Should he, however, retire from urban life to a hermitage, he will become a Tathágata, an Arhat, a knower of the perfect knowledge (*samyak-sambuddha*), a leader of unfailing policy, a lawgiver, and a perfect Buddha in this region. I should, therefore, proceed to see him."

Now, the great sage Asita, along with his nephew Naradatta, rose up like a goose in mid-air, and passed on to where the great city of Kapilavastu stood. Arrived there, he suppressed his miraculous power, entered on foot the city, and, arriving at the house of king S'uddhodana, stood at the gate. There the divine sage (*Devarshi*) Asita[46] saw hundreds of thousands of persons collected near the gate. Then, approaching the warder, he addressed him, saying, "Do you go and inform king S'uddhodana, that a sage awaits at his door."

"Be it so," replied the warder and, then proceeding to where king S'uddhodana was, joined his hands and said, "Be it known to your majesty that an old, emaciated octogenarian sage awaits at the gate, and says, 'I am anxious to visit the king."'

The king, having ordered an appropriate seat to be got ready for the sage, said to the warder, "Let the sage enter."

The warder, having retired from the royal court, said to the great sage, "please, enter."

Now the great sage Asita repaired to where king S'uddhodana was, and, standing before him, said, "Victory, Victory to the great king! May you rule all life through! May you conduct your royal duties according to law!"

Then king S'uddhodana, having welcomed him with the offering of Argha* and water for washing his feet, and enquired of his welfare, invited him to take a seat. Knowing then that the sage was comfortably placed, the king respectfully and with due regard addressed him thus: "I cannot say, O sage, that I have desired your visit. What may, please, be your object in coming here, and what do you require?"

Thus addressed, the sage replied, "Mahárája, a son has been born unto thee, and I am come with a desire to see him."

The king said: "The Prince is sleeping now, great sage; wait for awhile till he is awake."

The sage said: "Mahárája, great personages like him do not sleep long; such great personages are usually very wakeful."

Then, Bhikshus, through the blessing of Asita the Bodhisattva became awake. King S'uddhodana, with his two hands taking up the Prince Sarvárthasiddha,[47] carefully and gently brought him before the great sage Asita.

The great sage, beholding the Bodhisattva with his person adorned with the thirty-two signs of great personages and eighty subsidiary signs, with his body superior in excellence to that of S'akra, or of Brahmá, or of the guardians of regions, endowed with greater might than that of hundreds of thousands, with every member developed to perfect beauty, burst forth in this exclamation: "A wonderful soul has appeared in this

* Vide my *Indo-Aryans*, I, p. 380.

region!" Then rising from his seat, and joining his hands, he fell at the feet of the Bodhisattva, circumambulated his person, and, then taking him on his hands, sat in contemplation. He saw that the Bodhisattva had the thirty-two signs of greatness, which indicate for the bearer one of two careers, and no other. Should he remain at home he becomes a sovereign, possessing the fourfold army, and other attributes as described above. Should he, forsaking urban life and retire to a hermitage, he would become a Tathágata of great renown and a perfect Buddha. Beholding him thus, the sage cried much, shed profuse tears, and sighed deeply.

King S'uddhodana, seeing that the sage was greatly agitated, horripilated, crying, shedding tears, and heaving sighs, humbly asked him, "why do you cry? why do you shed tears? why do you heave deep sighs? May no evil befal the Prince!"

Asita replied, "I cry not, O Mahárája, for the sake of the Prince, nor is any evil to befal him. I cry on my own account."

"And what is the reason of it?"

"I am, Mahárája, an old, emaciated octogenarian. The prince Sarvárthasiddha is sure to acquire the sequenceless perfect knowledge, and, acquiring it, he will turn the wheel of the never-to-be-equalled religion, which cannot be turned by any S'ramaṇa, or Bráhmaṇa, or Deva, or Mára, or any other with the same religion. He will impart religion for the good and gratification of all beings, including gods. He will expound the religion which is auspicious at the beginning, auspicious at the middle, and auspicious at the end, of good purport, well arranged, unequalled, complete, perfectly pure, well-environed, includes Brahmacharya, and ends in virtue. Those, who follow religion by hearing it from us, will throw aside all trammels of caste, and be free from decay, disease, death, grief, lamentation, pain, melancholy, injury, and labour. By raining the water of true religion the Prince will gladden the hearts of those who are oppressed by the fire of passion, envy, and delusion. He will bring to the straight path of nirváṇa those wicked persons of vicious motives who are travelling in wicked ways. He will untie the bonds of those persons who lie fettered in the cage of worldliness and pain. He will create the eye of knowledge for those whose eyes are enveloped by the dense darkness of utter ignorance. He will pluck out the dart of affliction from the sides of those who have been pierced by it. For example, Mahárája, even as the fig blossoms[48] rarely and at some places, so on rare occasions, and at certain places, in course of millions of years, adorable Buddhas are produced on this earth. This Prince is one of them. He will for certain understand the sequenceless, perfect Bodhi knowledge. Having understood it, he will rescue hundreds of thousands of millions of persons from the ocean of worldliness, and establish them in immortality. But I cannot behold that Buddhist jewel, and hence it is, Mahárája, that I am crying, and am deeply grieved, and heaving deep sighs. I shall not be able to adore him. It is laid down in the Mantras, the Vedas, and the S'ástras, that it is not proper that the Prince Sarvárthasiddha should abide at home."

"Why so?"

"Because, Mahárája, the Prince Sarvárthasiddha is endowed with the thirty-two signs of a great personage."

"And what are the thirty-two signs?"

"They are: (1) the Prince Sarvárthasiddha has a coil of curly hair on his head;[49] this, great king, is the first sign of a great personage with which the Prince is endowed. (2) His hair is of a blackish deep blue colour like the neck of the peacock, and curling on the right side. (3) His forehead is large and even. (4) Between the eyebrows of Sarvárthasiddha there is a circle of hair of the colour of snow or silver. (5) His eyes are black like the eyelashes of the cow. (6) He has forty uniform, (7) closely set, (8) white teeth. (9) The voice of Prince Sarvárthasiddha is like that of a Bráhmaṇa. (10) His tongue is full of moisture; (11) it is large and slender. (12) His lower jaw is like that of a lion. (13) His neck is well raised. (14) The ends of his shoulders are raised like the saptachhada flower (*Alastonia scholaris*).[50] (15) His radiance is delicate,[51] and of the colour of gold; (16) and steady. (17) His arms are long and hanging. (18) The upper part of his body is like that of a lion; (19) the body of Prince Sarvárthasiddha is as long as his fathom.[52] (20) Every hair on his body is detached, ascending upwards, and turned on the right side. (21) His bottom is covered with hair. (22) His thighs are well developed. (23) His legs are like those of the gazelle. (24) His fingers are long. (25) Expansive are his hands and feet; (26) soft and fresh are his hands and feet; (27) with his fingers and toes joined with webs.[53] (28) His toes are long. (29) On the sole of each of his feet, Mahárája, there is a well executed white wheel, full of light and radiance, and having a thousand spokes, a felloe and a nave. (30) Even and well set are the feet of the Prince Sarvárthasiddha. By these thirty-two signs,[54] Mahárája, is the body of Prince Sarvárthasiddha endowed. Such signs, Mahárája, do not appear on Chakravartí kings; such signs appear only on Bodhisattvas. There are, besides, Mahárája, on the body of Prince Sarvárthasiddha eighty subsidiary signs; and endowed by them, the Prince cannot abide at home; he must retire to a hermitage."

"What are these eighty subsidiary signs?"

"They are: (1) The nails of the Prince Sarvárthasiddha are convex; (2) copper-coloured; (3) and smooth. (4) His fingers are rounded; (5) and well proportioned. (6) His veins are hidden; (7) so are his ankles. (8) His joints are close. (9) His feet are uniform, without irregularity. (10) His feet and heels are well spread. (11) The markings on the palms of his hands are smooth; (12) uniform (on both hands); (13) deep; (14) uncrooked; (15) and arranged in due order. (16) His lips are (red) like the Bimba fruit. (17) His speech is not loud. (18) His tongue is soft, fresh, and copper-coloured. (19) His voice is sweet and deep like the bellowing of the elephant, or the rolling of clouds; (20) in which the consonants are fully sounded. (21) His arms are long. (22) His skin is pure. (23) His body is soft; (24) large; (25) unemaciated; (26) unrivalled;

(27) well-adjusted; (28) and well-proportioned. (29) His knees are large, swelling and well developed. (30) Mahárája, the body of Prince Sarvárthasiddha is well rounded. (31) His body is well smoothed; (32) it is not crooked; (33) it is tapering. (34) His navel is deep; (35) not crooked; (36) and well fitted; (37) like a needle.[55] (38) He is frisky as a bull calf and as big. (29) Brilliant without any shadow. (40) Mahárája, the motion of Prince Sarvártha is stately like that of an elephant; (41) it is like that of a lion; (42) or like that of a bull; (43) or like that of a goose; (44) it is right-stepped.[56] (45) His waist is rounded; (46) it is not crooked. (47) His belly is like a bow. (48) His body is without perforations and faults, and of the colour of blue wood. (49) Mahárája, the canines of Prince Sarvárthasiddha are rounded; (50) sharp; (51) and regular. (52) His nose is well pointed. (53) His eyes are pure; (54) stainless; (55) laughing; (56) large; (57) and broad; (58) like the petals of the blue lotus. (59) Mahárája, the eyebrows of Prince Sarvárthasiddha are joined (with each other); (60) they are beautiful; (61) well-proportioned; (62) orderly; (63) and black. (64) His cheeks are big; (65) not unequal; (66) and faultless. (67) The bridge of his nose is not sunk. (68) Mahárája, the organs of Prince Sarvárthasiddha are well apparent; (69) and perfect. (70) His mouth and forehead are in keeping. (71) His head is full. (72) His hairs are black. (73) He is born with hair. (74) His hairs are appropriate; (75) sweet-smelling; (76) unrivalled; (77) untroublesome; (78) regular; (79) curly; (80) and whirled into the forms of S'rivatsa, Svastika, Nandyávarta, and Vardhamána diagrams. These are, Mahárája, the eighty subsidiary signs with which Prince Sarvárthasiddha is endowed. So endowed it will not be becoming the Prince to remain at home; for certain he will retire to a hermitage."

Pleased, exhilarated, gratified, glowing in affection and delight, by hearing this account of the Prince from the great sage Asita, King S'uddhodana, rising from his seat, fell at the feet of the Bodhisattva and recited this verse:

"Thou art bepraised by the Suras including Indra, and worshipped by Ṛishis; thou art the physician of the universe. I perform obeisance to thee, O Lord."

Then, Bhikshus, king S'uddhodana offered refreshment to the great sage Asita and his nephew Naradatta, and, having refreshed them, bade than adieu after offering them suitable presents of cloth &c.

Through his miraculous power the great sage Asita passed away through the sky, and reached his hermitage. There he thus addressed his youthful pupil Naradatta: "Naradatta, when you hear that the Buddha has become manifest on this earth, you should repair to him, and place yourself under his protection. Then the duration of your good, of your welfare, and of your gratification will be prolonged."[67]

The following (Gáthás) may be quoted on this subject:

"Beholding the Devas assembled under the sky to do honour to the Buddha, the celestial sage Asita, of Himáchala, felt highly gratified. 'How delightful (said he) to living beings is the name Buddha! It has brought joy on my body, and peace and gratification on my mind. (1)

"'Is the name Buddha that of a Deva, or an Asura, or that of a Garuḍa, or a Kinnara? How delightful and gratifying is this unheard of name!' With miraculous eyes he saw the ten quarters from the mountain and the earth to the ocean. He beheld wonderful and diversified forms, on the earth, on hills, on the ocean. (2)

"Their delightful splendour spreads wide, exhilarating the body. The cooling herbage on the crest of the mountain have sprouted; the trees are loaded with flowers, and crowned with various fruits. Shortly will the beautiful jewel be manifest in the three regions. (3)

"The earth appears like the palm of the hand, all smooth and untainted; the Devas, in great joy, are roaming about in the sky. Even as in the ocean home of the Nága king jewels sparkle wonderfully, so will the Jina jewel, derived from the mine of religion, be manifest in the continent of Jambu. (4)

"Since destruction is removed and pain departed, since beings are in happiness, since the Devas are roaming about in joy in the sky, since the sweet delightful sound of celestial music is audible, the jewel will surely appear in the three regions,—of him are these the premonitory signs. (5)

"Asita, with his miraculous eyes, saw the continent called Jambu. He saw in the house of S'uddhodana, in the noble city called Kapila, the mighty Náráyaṇa born,[58] endowed with all auspicious signs, merits and glory. Having seen this he was gratified and exhilarated, and his vigour increased. (6)

"Eagerly and quickly he came with wondering mind to the city of Kapila, and stood at the king's gate. Seeing many millions of persons collected there, the decrepit sage said:

'Charioteer,[59] quickly inform the king that a sage awaits at the gate.' (7)

"Hearing this, the charioteer instantly entered the royal palace, and thus reported to the king: 'Your majesty, an anchorite awaits at the gate—an exceedingly decrepit, tottering sage.'

"The king, to welcome the noble sage, gave orders to allow him to enter the palace. (8)

"Arranging for a proper seat for him, he ordered: 'Go instantly, and give him admission.' Hearing the charioteer's words, Asita was gratified, and professed satisfaction and pleasure. Like the thirsty longing for cold water or the oppressed after a hearty meal wishing for a bed, the sage was eager for the delight of beholding the noblest of beings. (9)

"(He said) 'Success be to thee, O king! May you reign for ever in happiness! May thy seat ever thrive, thou of controlled mind, of pacified passions, of excellent behaviour!'

"The king, welcoming the noble sage, said: 'Quickly relate, reverend sir, what is the object of your coming to this royal mansion?' (10)

"'A son of great beauty has been born unto thee; he is proficient in the Páramitás; he is of great vigour; he is halberded with the thirty-two signs, and endowed with the power of Náráyaṇa. To behold this son, the Sarvárthasiddha, lord of men, is my wish, and therefore have I come. I have no other object.' (11)

"'Sooth, you are welcome, and I am gratified by your visit; but you cannot see the lucky Prince now, as he is asleep. Well, you have to wait for a while if you wish to see the pure moon, spotless as the fullmoon, surrounded by the host of stars. (12)

"When the great charioteer, full of the light of the fullmoon, was awake, the king took the child of a body radiant as fire, more resplendent than the sun, glorious as the fullmoon, and said, 'O sage, behold the adored of men and gods, lustrous as the finest gold.'

"Asita beheld his two excellent and beautiful feet marked with the discus. (13)

"Rising then from his seat, and joining his two hands, he saluted the feet. Versed in the S'ástras, he, the noble sage, then took the child on his lap, and began to study him. He found the child shielded by excellent signs, and powerful as Náráyaṇa. Shaking his head, he, the versed in the Vedas and the S'ástras, perceived that there was one of two careers open to the child: (14)

"He would either be a mighty sovereign, emperor of the earth, or a Buddha, the noblest of men. Grieved in body and mind, he shed tears, and heaved deep sighs. The king became uneasy to know why should the Bráhmaṇ shed tears, and said to himself, 'I hope this Asita sees no evil pending on my Sarvárthasiddha.' (15)

"(He then asked) 'Explain, O sage, why you weep? Do you perceive any good or evil?'

'There is no evil or harm impending on your Sarvárthasiddha. I grieve much for myself, sire, since I am worn out and decrepit, and when this youth will attain Buddhahood, and preach the religion which will be respected by the world, (16)

"'I shall not have the felicity of beholding him. Hence it is that I am weeping. I know this for certain, O king, that whosoever has on his body the thirty-two noble and untainted signs, has one of two careers open to him, and not a third; he will either become a Chakravartí sovereign, or a Buddha, the noblest of men. (17)

"'This Prince is not desirous of sensuous objects, so he will be a Buddha.'

"Having heard this account from the sage, the king felt delighted and happy. Rising from his seat, and joining his two hands in respect, he saluted the Prince, saying, 'Thou art well-worshipped by Devas, thou art mighty, thou art bepraised by sages. (18)

"'Salutation to the accomplisher of the noble object, the adored of all in the three regions.'

"Asita then graciously said to his nephew, 'Listen to my words; when you hear that the Bodhi has become a Buddha, and is turning the wheel of the law on this earth, quickly come under the rule of the Muni; you will thereby acquire cessation (from all further transmigration.)' (19)

"Having saluted the feet of the Prince and performed circumambulation of his body, and accepted profuse and valuable gifts from the king, the noble sage said, 'This son of yours will gratify with religion all men and gods in this world.' Retiring then from Kapila, the sage repaired to his hermitage in the wilderness."[60] (20)

Then, Bhikshus, after the birth of the Prince, the Devaputra Maheśvara invited all the Devaputras of the class S'uddhávásakáyika, and thus addressed them: "Since, noble sirs, now that the great being, Bodhisattva, has taken birth in the region of the mortals, he who has for uncountable hundreds of thousands of millions of millions of years accomplished the duties of charity, good behaviour, mercy, vigour, meditation, knowledge as also fasts and penances; who is endowed with great friendliness, great mercy, and great contentment; who has acquired the neutral knowledge;[61] who is bent on promoting the happiness of all created beings; who has buckled on him the armour of firm vigour; who has acquired the good of the works performed by former Jinas; who is adorned with the signs of a hundred virtues; who is exercised in unfailing might; who is the overthrower of antagonistic intrigues; who is possessed of stainless, pure intentions; whose feet are well worshipped; who upholds the standard of the great knowledge; who is the destroyer of the might of Mára; who is the great merchant in the three thousand great regions; who is adored by both men and gods; who has performed the great sacrifice; whose object is the memory of the wealth of virtue; who is the destroyer of birth, decay and death; who is the well-born; who is born in the royal dynasty of Ikshâku;[63] who is the Bodhisattva awakening of the earth; he is sure ere long, appearing on the earth, to acquire the perfect Sambodhi knowledge. It is fit, therefore, that we should proceed to bepraise him, to show him respect, to worship him, and to pray to him, in order that thereby the pride and vanity of the vain Devaputras may be destroyed. Looking at us engaged in adoration, they, too, will adore the Bodhisattva, honour him, and worship him, and that will be for the lengthening the period of their desires, their welfare, and their happiness until they attain immortality. They will also hear of the success and prosperity of king S'uddhodana. Having thus adored the Bodhisattva, we shall return to our places."

Now the Devaputra Mahes'vara, surrounded by twelve thousand Devaputras, making everything in the great city of Kapilavastu resplendent by their light, came to the abode of king S'uddhodana, and, with the knowledge of the warder and the permission of the king, entered the house. He then, with his head, saluted the feet of the Bodhisattva, and, placing his scarf on one of his shoulders and circumambulating (the Bodhisattva) many hundred thousand times, sat aside, and, taking the child on his lap, encouraged king S'uddhodana (by saying), "Mahârâja, be gratified, be joyous."

"Why do you say so?"

" Since, Mahárája, the body of the Bodhisattva is adorned with the great marks and the subsidiary ones, and since the Prince has, by his colour, his vigour, and his prosperity, overpowered all celestial and human regions, therefore, king, he is sure to acquire the sequenceless perfect Sambodhi knowledge."

Thus, Bhikshus, the Devaputra Mahes'vara and his companion Devaputras of the class Suddhávásakáyika, having duly worshipped the Bodhisattva, and described him thus, repaired to their own homes.

On this subject these Gáthás:

" Informed of the birth of the ocean of merit, the god Sureśvara verily became anxious, saying, 'verily I must proceed and worship that precious saint whose worship is rarely to be heard even in many millions of kalpas.' (1)

" Attended by full twelve thousand Devas, all adorned with jewelled tiara, and full of motion, quickly repaired to the noble city called Kapila, and, halting at the gate of the king, (2)

told the warder, in pleasing accents, 'inform the king that we wish to enter the house.' On hearing these words the warder entered the house, joined his hands in supplication, and thus addressed the king: (3)

" 'Victory be to the Lord! May thou be prolonged in life! May thou long govern the people! There await at the gate beings resplendent with the light of profuse virtue, adorned with jewelled crowns, of quick motion, having faces like the fullmoon, and of steady radiance like that of the moon. (4)

" 'Sire, the shadow of these beings cannot any where possibly be seen,[63] nor have I heard the sound of their footsteps. Nor, walking on the earth, they raise any dust, and no one can be satiated by looking at them. (5)

" 'The light of their body spreads wide; their speech is so sweet that no human being has the like of it. They are grave, amiable, well-behaved, and of noble birth. I suspect they are gods, and not men. (6)

" 'They have in their hands excellent flowers, garlands, unguents, and silken vestments,[64] and appear full of respect. Doubtless, sire, the gods have come, anxious to see and worship the Prince, the god of gods.' (7)

"The king, having heard these thrilling words, said:

'Go and say, 'please enter the house.' Such grandeur and merit, such motion as you describe, cannot belong to men.' (8)

"The warder, with joined hands, thus addressed the gods, 'Ordered by the lord of men, you may enter.' Well satisfied and pleased, and carrying excellent garlands and essences, they entered the king's house which was like a celestial palace. (9)

"Seeing the noble gods entering the house, the king rose from his seat, joined his hands, and addressed them, "here are chairs with jewelled feet, favour me by taking your seats on them.' (10)

"Having taken their seats thereon, they, without pride or hauteur, said, 'Listen, king, the object with which we have come; there has been born unto you a son of profuse virtue, pure body, and well-worshipped feet, and we wish to see him. (11)

"'We know all rules, and are acquainted with all noble signs, and can foretell what is happening (anywhere) and what will happen. Lord of the earth, you are fortunate, drop all anxiety. We want to see the body adorned with the auspicious marks.' (12)

"The king with pleasure brought to the gods of high crowns, the Prince of resplendent complexion from the nursery, where he was surrounded by women. The three thousand regions quaked when the child was brought out of door. (13)

"The noble gods successively beheld the copper-coloured nails, pure as a spotless leaf and full of glory; then, rising from their seats, they of the nodding crowns saluted with their heads the Prince of immaculate light. (14)

"From his marks, from his appearance, from the resplendence of his virtue, from his head and crown, from his motion, from his eyes, from his spotless radiance, from the whirl of hair between his eye-brows, (they were perfectly satisfied that) he would perceive the Bodhi after overcoming Mára. (15)

"Reflecting on his merits they sang hymns in praise of the meritorious one, the knower of truth, the destroyer of darkness and pain. (They sang), 'soon will be manifest the true jewel, the remover of birth, decay, death, pain and woe. (16)

"'The whole of the three regions are in flames, heated by the threefold fire of wishes, desires and worldliness. Thou, learned one, by bringing forth the cloud of religion over the three thousand regions, wilt blow out the fire of pain with the water of immortality. (17)

"'Thou art of friendly speech, thou art full of mercy, thou art of amiable speech, thou art of unaffected sound and sweet words from thy celestial voice. Do thou send forth thy behest over the three thousand regions of the universe, and quickly proclaim the Boddhi? (18)

"'Despicable are the wicked Tírthikas; they are of vicious intent; they lie enthralled in the bonds of worldly attachment. Hearing of thy religion of nihility supported by every argument, they will run away like jackals before a lion. (19)

"'Piercing through the mass of ignorance, and the smoke of pain, for the manifestation of humanity, cast the rays of knowledge, and dispel the great darkness from the whole universe. (20)

"'On the birth of a being of such wonderful purity, men and gods have obtained the highest blessings. The road of vice is closed, and the wide road of the gods is made resplendent, glowing in light, by the purifier, the jewel among men.' (21).

"Then showering excellent flowers on the city named Kapila, circumambulating (the person of the Prince), respectfully singing hymns in his praise, and shouting 'Buddha, Buddha,' the Suras cheerfully returned to the sky." (22)

NOTES.

1. *Carrying vases filled with scented water*, p. 119. The reference to aromatic water is frequent both in Hindu and Buddhist writings, but I have failed to find any mention of the manner in which, and the articles with which, water was perfumed for use. As there is no mention anywhere of the rose flower, rose-water could not have been intended. The pandanus water is largely used now all over India, but the pandanus is not common in the North-Western Provinces. It is probable, therefore, that fennel and other seeds were used for perfuming water.

2. *Jewels appeared pendant under networks over towers, palaces and gateways*, p. 119. This is a poetical embellishment of a common practice. The practice of hanging nets over courtyards, and decorating them with artificial flowers, birds, and fishes made of tinsel and lightwood (*solá*) is to this day common all over India, and on the occasion of the Rása-pújá festival is held a *sine qua non*. It is often referred to in the Bhágavata Puráṇa. As large assemblages are generally held in courtyards covered over with awnings, this network under the awning serves as a pretty decoration. Sometimes the network is set up without the awning.

3. *The voices of crows, owls, vultures, wolves and jackals were no longer audible*, p. 119. The cries of these animals are believed to be portents of evil.

4. *These were the thirty-two prevalent omens*, p. 119. My MSS. supply only 31 omens, or rather merge two omens into one, and thereby reduce the total by one. The fourth in my text runs thus: "Eight trees grew forth, and twenty hundreds of thousands of stores of innumerable jewels came to view." In the Tibetan version the eight trees constitute one omen, and the stores another. The Burmese version refers to "thirty-two mighty wonders" (Bigandet I, p. 39), but does not name them in detail. The Rev. Mr. Beal has omitted the description of the omens in his translation from the Chinese version.

5. *Lord, listen to my wish*, p. 120. According to the Sanskrit and the Tibetan versions, Máyá herself desires to proceed to the garden of Lumbiní for a pleasure excursion. The season was the spring, the trees were covered with new leaves and flowers, and she longed for a change by way of recreation. The Burmese and the Siamese versions make the lady request permission to go to her father's country-house at Dewah to pass her time among her friends and relations, (Bigandet I, p. 34, and Alabaster's Wheel of the Law, p. 100). The Chinese version gives quite a different turn to the narrative. According to it Suprabuddha Grahapati, the father of Máyá, sent certain messengers to king S'uddhodana, at Kapilavastu, with this message, "as I am informed my daughter, Máyá, the queen of your majesty, is now with child, and already far advanced in pregnancy, and, as I fear that when the child is born, my daughter will be short-lived, I have thought it right to ask you to permit my daughter Máyá to come back to me and rest in my house; and, I have prepared for her reception the Lumbiní garden, and every proper amusement. Let not the king be displeased at the request, for, immediately the confinement is over, I will send my daughter to her home with you." S'uddhodana acceded to this request, had a proper retenue marshalled, and sent the queen to her father's house. (Beal, p. 42.)

6. *Lumbiní garden*, p. 120. The word here used is *udyána* or garden, but the word *vana* a 'wood' or 'forest' is also frequently used, and the inference is that it was a park, or a forest partially cleared to serve as a park. As the narrative stands in the Sanskrit and the Tibetan versions, this garden would seem to be a park belonging to S'uddhodana, but the quotation given above in the next preceding note shows that it belonged to the father of the lady, and was situated in the country of Dewah or Devadaha, also called Koli. It was once the kingdom of Devadatta, a cousin and inveterate enemy of Sarvárthasiddha. According to the Chinese text the garden was called after the name of the wife of the chief minister of Suprabuddha. See note 11 below.

7. *Mridañgas*, p. 121. A percussion instrument about two feet six inches long, thickest in the middle, and tapering towards both ends. The barrel is made of baked earth, and the ends, 6 inches in

diameter, are mounted with goatskin, partially covered with a thick paste to make it resonant. The instrument is very common in Bengal and northern India.

8. *Mukuṇḍa*, p. 121. I have failed to identify this instrument. Its name does not occur in any of the several works on musical instruments that I have consulted. I suspect my MSS. are corrupt here, and the word is wrongly spelt. In the French translation of the Tibetan text, the words are "Préparez des tambours d'airain, des luths, de flûtes, des harpes, des tambourins et cent mille clochettes au son agréable." (Foucaux, p. 84.)

9. "*Scented waters*," p. 122. See note 1, above.

10. *Mis'raka Park*, p. 122. One of Indra's gardens. It is described to be the most luxurious that human mind can conceive.

11. *Waved-leaved fig tree*, p. 123. The Sanskrit word is *Plaksha*, which is generally used to indicate the waved-leaved fig tree, *Ficus infectoria*, vernacular *Pákur*, and I have translated it accordingly. It is also applied to the *Hibiscus populneoides* and the *Ficus religiosa*. The Abhinishkramaṇa Sútra takes it for the *Jonesia Asoka*. The Chinese version gives *Palása* (*Butea frondosa*) for Plaksha, and the Burmese text makes it Engyin, or the *Shorea robusta*, while the Siamese version has *Simwaliwana*, which is obviously a corruption of *Sálmalivana* or a forest of S'álmali or silk-cotton trees—*Bombax heptaphyllum*. If Mr. Carlleyle's identifications of Kapilavastu with Bhuïlá Dih, 18 miles to the east of Fyzabad, and of Koli or Devadah with Bághnagar, be correct, (they have been accepted to be so by General Cunningham), we find a Sál forest between the two, about 8 or 9 miles away to the east of Kapilavastu, and the Sál therefore should be the correct version. (Arhæological Survey of India, XII.)

Nor is the name of the tree the only discordant point in the story. The manner of coming to the tree and the birth are differently related by the different texts. The Sanskrit and the Tibetan texts take the lady to the tree casually as she was rambling about in the garden. The Burmese text brings her to the park in her way to her father's house.

"Between the two countries an immense forest of lofty Engyin trees extends to a great distance. As soon as the *cortège* reached it, five waterlilies shot forth spontaneously from the stem and the main branches of each tree, and innumerable birds of all kinds, by their melodious tunes, filled the air with the most ravishing music. Trees, similar in beauty to those growing in the seats of Nats, apparently sensible of the presence of incarnated Buddha, seemed to share in the universal joy.

"On beholding this wonderful appearance of all the lofty trees of the forest, the queen felt a desire to approach nearer, and enjoy the marvellous sight offered to her astonished regards. Her noble attendants led her forthwith a short distance into the forest. Maia, seated on her couch, along with her sister Patzapati, desired her attendants to have it moved closer to an Engyin tree (*Shorea robusta*), which she pointed out. Her wishes were immediately complied with. She then rose gently on her couch; her left hand, clasped round the neck of her sister, supported her in a standing position. With the right hand she tried to reach and break a small branch, which she wanted to carry away. On that very instant, as the slender rattan, heated by fire, bends down its tender head, all the branches lowered their extremities, offering themselves, as it were, to the hand of the queen, who unhesitatingly seized and broke the extremity of one of the young boughs. By virtue of a certain power inherent in her dignity, on a sudden all the winds blew gently through the forest. The attendants, having desired all the people to withdraw to a distance, disposed curtains all round the place the queen was standing on. Whilst she was in that position, admiring the slender bough she held in her hands, the moment of her confinement happened, and she was delivered of a son.

"Four chief Brahmas received the newborn infant on a golden network, and placed him in the presence of the happy mother, saying, "Give yourself up, O Queen, to joy and rejoicing; here is the precious and wonderful fruit of your womb." (Bigandet I, pp. 35*ff.*)

The Siamese version is closely similar to this. According to it:

"Between the cities of Kapila and Dewadaha, there was in those days a forest of the most splendid trees, named Simwaliwana. It was a lovely spot. Interlacing branches, richly covered with foliage, sheltered the traveller as if he were covered with a canopy. The sun's scorching rays could not penetrate to the delicious shade. All over the trees, from their trunks to their very tops, bunches of flowers budded, bloomed, and shed their fragrant leaves, and unceasingly budded and bloomed again. Attracted by their sweet pollen, flights of shining beetles buzzed around them, filling the air with a melodious humming, like to the music of the heavens. There were pools full of lotuses of all colours, whose sweet scent was wafted around by gentle breezes, and whose fruit floated on the waters in all stages of ripeness.

"When the Queen Maia entered this forest, the trees, the inanimate trees, bowed down their heads before her, as if they would say, "Enjoy yourself, O queen; among us, ere you proceed on your journey." And the queen, looking on the great trees, and the forest lovely as the gardens of the angels, ordered her litter to be stayed, that she might descend and walk.

"Then, standing under one of the majestic trees, she desired to pluck a sprig from the branches, and the branches bent themselves down that she might reach the sprig that she desired; and at that moment, while she yet held the branch, her labour came upon her. Her attendants held curtains around her; the angels brought her garments of the most exquisite softness; and standing there, holding the branch, with her face turned to the east, she brought forth her son, without pain or any of the circumstances which attend that event with women in general.

"Thus was he born, on Friday, the fifteenth day of the sixth month of the year of the dog, under the astronomical sign Wisákhá." (Alabaster, p. 100).

The Chinese text makes the lady reach her father's home, and there spend some time (rather inconsistently with the terms of the message sent by Suprabuddha,) before the idea of going to the Lumbiní garden is mooted. It says—

"At length, in the second month of spring, on the eighth day, the constallation Kwei being now in conjunction, the king, accompanied by his daughter Mâyá, went forth towards the garden Lumbiní, anxious to see the beauties of the earth. Having arrived at the garden, the queen Mâyá stepped down from her chariot, adorned as we have before described, surrounded by dancing women, etc.; and so passed from spot to spot, and from tree to tree in the garden, admiring and looking at all! Now, in the garden, there was one particular tree called a Palasa, perfectly strait from top to bottom, and it branches spread out in perfect regularity, its leaves variegated as the plumage of a peacock's head, soft as kalinda cloth, the scent of its flowers of most exquisite odour. Delighted at the sight, Mâyá rested awhile to admire it, and gradually approached under the shade of the tree; then that tree, by the mysterious power of Bodhisattva, bent down its branches, and, forthwith, the queen with her right hand took hold of one; just as in the air, there appears a beautifully tinted rainbow stretching athwart heaven; so did she take hold of that curving branch of the Palasa tree and look up into heaven's expanse. Thus, standing on the ground, and holding the branch as we have described, with clasped hands and bended knee, the heavenly women who surrounded the queen, addressed her thus:—

> 'The queen now brings forth the child,
> Able to divide the wheel of life and death
> In heaven and earth, no teacher
> Can equal him;
> Able to deliver both Devas
> And men from every kind of sorrow,
> Let not the queen be distressed,
> We are here to support her!'

"At this time, Bodhisattva perceiving his mother, Mâyá, standing thus with the branch in her hand, then with conscious mind arose from his seat and was born." (Beal, p. 42-3.)

12. *Clothes of various colours suspended from it*, p. 123. This mode of decorating trees was at one time very common, and all Buddhist sculptures represent the Bodhi tree decorated with clothes hanging from its branches.

Nor was the practice confined to the Buddhists only. It seems to be extensively wide-spread and of great antiquity. The object is not always the same. In some cases it is, and was, intended to honour the tree itself as an old or beautiful or sacred one, as in the case of the plane tree which Xerxes saw in Lydia in his march to Greece and was so pleased with it that, according to Herodotus, he caused golden robes and ornaments to be hung over it. In others it is to honour the spirits of departed saints that clothes are put on trees, as we find on trees overhanging the graves of Muhammadan saints in India and Arabia. In others evil spirits, hobgoblins, and devils are allowed peace-offerings in that way, and numerous instances are met with all over the earth. Mungo Park noticed it in Africa, Sir John Lubbock cites instances among the Esthoneans in Livonea, Burton in Madagascar, Taylor in Mexico, and Sir John Franklin among the Cree Indians. In China and central Asia coloured or gilt paper is used more largely than cloth, but strips of silk are not wanting. They are offered to the manes, as well as to evil spirits. At Darjeling, among the Tibetan population, paper is used very largely, but cloth also is frequently seen. As far as I could ascertain from the people, the offerings were all intended to appease evil spirits; but, seeing that they hung little bits of cloth also on their chaityas, I had no reason to doubt that the dead were also honoured in the same way. In a paper, under the uncomely name of "Rag-bushes in the East," Mr. Walhouse has collected a large number of instances in all parts of the earth, (*Indian Antiquary*, IX, pp. 150*ff.*) and the curious reader will find the paper very interesting as showing the wide prevalence of the custom among very divergent and totally unconnected races. Doubtless as we see the offerings on the trees they are nothing but rags, but when offered they were not dirty rags, nor given as dirty rags, but as offerings the most convenient at hand. Cloth was wanted, and cloth was given without regard to its size. Similarly at Hindu S'ráddhas, when a man is too poor to afford an entire piece of cloth, small slips of cloth, or even a few bits of thread, are offered to the manes as emblems of entire pieces of cloth.

13. *Forth from the right side of his mother he issued*, p. 123. The Siamese version is silent on the subject, and leaves the idea that the birth was natural.

14. *There were present Brahmá and S'akra*, p. 123. The Siamese version is silent on the subject.

15. *Silk cloth*, p. 123. The word in Sanskrit is *divya-kaus'ika-vastra*, which in the Tibetan version, as rendered into French, is "vêtement divin de Káçi (Benares)" (Foucaux, p. 87). The Chinese make only S'akra receive the child on "a Kasika garment" (Beal, 44). The Burmese and the Siamese make Brahmá receive it on "a golden network." I take kauśika to be a variant of *Kausheya* "made of *kosha*" or cocoons, *i. e.*, silk. Kauśika cannot be a regular derivative of Káśí.

16. *Two streams of water, one hot and the other cold*, p. 124. The Burmese text does not notice these streams. The Siamese text brings down from heaven two streams of water, one falling "on the queen and one upon the Grand Being" (Alabaster, p. 102). According to the Chinese version the streams came from mid-air, and washed only the child. (Beal, p. 47).

17. *Transcendental light*, p. 124. This portentous light is distinct from the portents subsequently noticed. It is not referred to in the Burmese, the Siamese and the Chinese versions of the story. It has been, by some, alleged to be a variant of the star which guided the sages who went to visit Christ immediately after his birth.

18. *Eight objects of reflection*, p. 124. The objects of meditation mean the different forms of meditation. Hindu Yogís recognise these forms.

19. *Advanced seven steps towards the east*, p. 124. The different versions of the legend all recognise this miraculous occurrence, and the words put into the mouth of the child are substantially, but not literally, the same. The Bhágavata Puráṇa ascribes to the infant Kṛishṇa a miracle similar to this.

20. *These and the like miracles become manifest*, p. 125. The miracles are not given in the same terms nor in the same order in the different versions of the story as preserved among the Tibetan, the Chinese, the Burmese, and the Siamese nations. Evidently no great importance was attached to them.

21. *All beings were horripilated with delight*, p. 125. When adverting to the miracles the present tense is used, but in detailing them the text puts the verb in the past tense. This causes a hiatus in the narrative. I have closely followed the text.

22. *Why should he again acquire the sequenceless Bodhi knowledge?* p. 127. The question is a poser, and the Bodhisattva fails to meet it directly. In fact the idea of antiquity in regard to the religion of S'ákya was an after-thought, and had to be worked out by resort to subterfuges.

23. *Free from the threefold destruction*, p. 129. Physical, mental, and spiritual.

24. *A religion which is like an army*, p. 129. The word in Sanskrit is *aníka*, which implies a brigade consisting of horses, elephants, chariots and foot-soldiers.

25. *Quaked like beautiful pearls*, p. 131. I do not clearly understand the appropriateness of the comparison. Perhaps it means that the quaking of the earth was so gentle that it was as delightful as the sight of pendant pearls shaken by a gentle breeze.

26. *The Maruts*, p. 132. The word marut may mean the regent of the wind, or a god simply. It is not clear what is meant in the text.

27. *The Apsarases said, O Devi*, p. 132. The text has Deva in the masculine gender, and this would imply the king; but the address is obviously intended for the queen, and I, therefore, assume the text to be incorrect.

28. *People from the great city of Kapila having come*, p. 12. The narrative shows that Máyá went out of the city, whether it be for a ramble in a garden in the suburbs, or to her father's house, but S'uddhodana remained at home in the city. Why should these people then come to him *from* the city to announce the births and other auspicious occurrences in the city? The answer may be that the king was in the palace, and the people came from the city to the palace to report the occurrences; or that he had gone to the garden on hearing of the birth of his son and heir, and there, immediately after the birth, received the messengers. According to the Chinese version, Mahánáma of the family name of Basita, who was the chief or prime-minister of S'uddhodana, repaired along with his colleagues to visit the Lumbiní garden, and, standing outside the gate, noticed the miraculous occurrences, and engaged himself in conversation with his companions as to their cause, when a maid-servant came out of the garden and communicated to them the news of the birth. Thereupon, Mahánáma immediately returned to Kapilavastu, and reported the birth to the king, who, along with his officers, proceeded to the Lumbiní garden to behold his son and heir.

"Having arrived at the outer gate of the garden, they immediately despatched a messenger to the queen to congratulate her on the auspicious event of the birth and its attending circumstances, and to express the king's desire to see the child. To which the queen made reply, 'Go! tell the king he may enter the garden!' Then a woman in attendance, seeing the king in the garden, took the child in her arms, and, approaching the king, said, 'The royal babe salutes his father.' To whom the king answered, 'Not so! first of all send him to the Bráhmaṇ ministers in attendance, and afterwards let him see me!' Then the nurse forthwith took Bodhisattva to the place where the Bráhmaṇs were. At this time the chief minister (Kwo sse), and the Bráhmaṇs, having looked at the child, addressed S'uddhodana in the following terms of congratulation, 'All honoured be the king, and prosperous for evermore! Even as we see that this babe will prosper! even so may the king and all the S'ákya race increase and ever flourish. Mahárája! this child will certainly, and of necessity, become a holy Chakravartin monarch!'

"At this time, queen Máyá, the mother of Bodhisattva, beholding S'uddhodana and the ministers, her face glowing with joy, immediately inquired of the king in these words, 'Mahárája! recite to me, I pray you, the distinguishing signs of one who is to become a Chakravartin monarch! Tell me, I pray you, what these are that my heart may also rejoice!' Then S'uddhodana Rájá desired the Bráhmaṇ ministers to explain and point out the distinctive signs of a Chakravartin monarch." (Beal, p. 50). The Bráhmaṇs, thereupon, explain the signs on the babe which betokened great prosperity. In our text the signs are expounded by Asita.

29. *Naked*, p. 133. I fail to perceive the appropriateness and force of this epithet. I suspect the text is corrupt.

30. *Tawny mane*, p. 133. The object is to imply chestnut horses, which were always held in greater estimation than horses of other colours. See my 'Indo-Aryans,' I, p. 333.

31. *Retired in delight*, p. 133. The text here is incomplete, consisting of only half a distich, and the accuracy of the translation is therefore questionable. The purport, too, is not apparent.

32. *Bovine calves*, p. 133. *Kapilá* means a young she-elephant, but as the preceding word *kareṇu* implies both male and female elephants, I take the following word to mean bovine calves. In the vernacular of Bengal in the present day *kapilá*, corrupted into *kaïlá*, is used to indicate a cow-calf.

32. *As'vattha saplings were produced*, p. 134. The Sanskrit words are *chaturṇám cha dvípakoṭiśatasahasráṇám madhye pṛithiví-pradeśe aśvatthayashṭih prádurabhút*. They may be rendered into "On the land in the middle of the four times many hundreds of

thousands of tens of millions of islands an aśvattha staff was produced." A staff pure and simple is, however, no part of any Buddhist paraphernalia; it is held in no estimation, and in the vast volume of Buddhist literature extant, in which the mantle, the alms-bowl and other articles are so frequently mentioned, a staff is never adverted to. This rendering, therefore, cannot be accepted as correct. The Tibetan version of the text, as rendered into French, has *s'éleva de la terre la tige d'un Açvattha*, (Foucaux, p. 97) and this is obviously the right meaning. The object of the text is to show that along with the sage, were born Yaśodhará, his wife; Chhandaka, his charioteer; *Kanṭaka*, his favourite horse, and most of those who subsequently became his foremost disciples. And as the aśvattha tree also formed an integral part of his faith, it is but natural to suppose that his biographers should include it among the productions of the time of his birth. The merit of dedicating the aśvattha tree is highly extolled, and even Hindus try to avail themselves of it by such dedication, and in the Bhagavadgítá Kṛishṇa describes himself as the aśvattha among trees. In the Sui Behar inscription reference is made to a dedication of it by a Buddhist. Dr. Hoernle, however, thinks differently. Misled by the word yaṭhi, he says:—

"What the *yaṭhi* is, I do not know; perhaps others who are better acquainted with the practices of Buddhism may be able to explain it. The word, in the modern form *láṭh*, is applied to monumental pillars, like the well-known stone pillars of Allahábád, Dehli, Banáras and other places; but that can hardly be the meaning of the word here. The word is also applied to a monk's staff. This, at first sight, would seem to be a much more likely meaning. The *áropaṇa* 'setting up' or 'assuming' of a staff might be a ceremony indicating the assumption of a high clerical office (as in the case of a Bishop's staff or crook). Or 'putting up (putting aside) the staff' might be a euphemism for 'death;' the monk having died, his *yaṭhi* may have been enshrined by the two pious ladies. It is impossible to avoid connecting in one's thoughts the curious shaft which pierces the tower, and the mouth of which was closed with the copperplate that bears the inscription, with the *yaṭhi* mentioned in that inscription as having been enshrined. Can it be possible that the shaft was the receptacle of the *yaṭhi*? The dimensions of the shaft, no doubt, are large; but the *yaṭhi* need not have been a real mendicant's staff, or at least only such a one *pro forma;* in reality it might have been an object more like the famous *láṭh* or iron pillar of Dehli; perhaps ornamented with jewels and precious stones." ('Indian Antiquary,' Vol. X, Nov. 1881, p. 327.)

Doubtless the ordinary meaning of *yashṭi*, is a staff; but according to Wilson it also means "a creeper." (Dictionary, *sub voce*). Taking a staff to be the radical meaning it would by metonymy stand for the trunk of a tree, and the staff may then well stand for the whole tree. The word *áropaṇa*, rendered into "setting up" or "assuming," comes from the root *ruh* "to grow from seed," "to grow as a tree," "to sow seed." The only word used for planting all over northern India, is *rohná*, whence *roá*, &c. It is used in contradistinction to *vap* or *voná*, "to sow broadcast." The conjecture about "a ceremony indicating the assumption of a high clerical office (as in the case of a Bishop's staff or crook)" is due solely to the familiarity of the learned gentleman with the European idea of the staff of office, but it is not common in India. It is true that among one sect of the Hindus, the Daṇḍís, the assumption of the *daṇḍa* or staff is synonymous with retirement from worldly life to ascetic mendicancy, and the Daṇḍís do always carry about a thin bamboo switch as the emblem of their mode of life; but there is literally nothing to show, (and we have enough in the literary remains of the Buddhists to show all the details of their monastic lives,) that the ceremony of assuming a staff formed any part of it. The idea of the crook has come from the Biblical metaphor of the shepherd and his flock, the shepherd holding the crook over his lambs to lead them to the right path. There is no such metaphor current among the Buddhists, and to the best of our information never was, and it would be futile, therefore, to identify the yaṭhi with the crook. To Europeans the idea of the crook may not, at first sight, strike as inconsistent, but there is nothing but a fancied similitude to support it.

The word is in the singular number in the original, but I have changed it into the plural to make it consonant with the innumerable islands referred to. As in the case of Kaṇṭaka a single horse was wanted, and yet twenty thousand colts were produced, so for a single tree required for the sage to sit under during his meditation a great many were produced. Besides, we are dealing not with facts but fancies, and therefore there is nothing to stand in the way.

34. *As it was before so it became after*, p. 134. The incident is not noticed by the southern Buddhists. Is it possible to suppose that the case was one of difficult parturition, and an operation, something like the Cesarean operation, had to be performed and that led to the mother's death? The idea of the operation was not unknown in India. In the case of Eve the absence of a mother suggested the unnatural expedient.

35. *With scented oil*, p. 134. The use in India of oils richly perfumed was, it would seem, as common before as it is now. It is a pity we have nothing left to show the process followed in preparing such oils.

36. *Foreign ṛishis versed in the five means*, p. 134. Who the foreigners were, there is nothing to show. Their knowledge of the five means is indicated by the word, *panchábhijnáh*. According to the Pentaglot Vocabulary the five sciences are, 1st, "La science pareille a'un miroir; 2nd, la science de l'égalité (des substances); 3rd, la science de l'observation; 4th, la science de l'achévement de ce qu'il faut faire; 5th, la science des régions de la Loi (*Dharma*)." *Apud* Foucaux, p. 98.

37. *The music of the clarion and the táḍava*, p. 135. I can find no account of the *táḍava* in any Indian work on music. If the word could be taken to be *shaḍava* it would mean an instrument with six strings arranged in a hexatonic style, but it occurs as táḍava in several Buddhist works.

38. *The great lotus may sprout*, p. 135. It is not clear whether this refers to the great lotus which shot forth from the bottom of the earth and yielded the essence for the nourishment of the sage during his fœtal state, (p. 102), or merely a poetical imagery to imply his birth. Probably it means the former.

39. *Pieces of chintz*, p. 136. The Sanskrit term is *vichitra-paṭolaka*, lit. "many coloured cloth." This is not included in the Tibetan version.

40. *The S'ákyas including the elders, men and women*, p. 138. The Sanskrit words are *mahallaka-mahallakádyáh S'ákyáh*. Wilson, in his Dictionary, explains *mahallaka* to mean, "an eunuch employed

in a harem," and adds "*mahalla* said to mean the inner apartments probably the Arabic word محل and *kan* added." In his *S'abdakalpadruma*, Sir Rájá Rádhákánta assigns this meaning to mahallika, but for mahallaka gives 'warder of the inner apartments' (*antahpura-rakshaka*) without adding that the warder should be a eunuch. He quotes *Jaṭádhara* and the *S'abdaratnávalí* for its synonyms, of which the former gives *samidalla*, *kañchukí*, *sthápatya*, *Sauvidalla* and *Vedáñka*, and the latter, *Sauvidallaka*, and *antarvañs'ika*. None of these imply a eunuch necessarily. But whether a eunuch or not, it is certain that the meaning is not applicable here, for it is to be presumed that those who sat in consultation to decide upon appointing a foster-mother for the prince were men of higher rank than warders, whether male or female. Moreover, in a subsequent passage the warder of the palace announces to the king that a sage (*rishi*) old (*vṛiddha*) emaciated (*jírṇa*) and *mahallaka* had appeared at the gate. It cannot be assumed that he meant the sage to be a warder or a eunuch. Again, the sage describes himself as "old, emaciated, and mahallaka," and did not mean that he was a warder or a eunuch. It is evident then that the word has another meaning, and this occurs in Páli. In Childer's Páli Dictionary the equivalents given are "old, aged; spacious, large, broad, big," (p. 228), and Böhtlingk has given the meaning of old, derived from Buddhist works. As my text has old (*vṛiddha*) coupled with *mahallaka*, I infer that the latter means "very old," *i. e.*, not only old but "very old," an octogenarian or so, and these being the seniors or elders of the race, I take it that the idiomatic meaning is seniors or elders, who are in the preceding sentence described as *vṛiddha-vṛiddhá*.

41. *All these are inexperienced*, p. 138. The Sanskrit word is *Vadhúká*, which means a young wife but not a matron, *i. e.*, a married woman but not experienced in the duties of a mother.

42. *But here is the good matron Gautamí*, p. 138. The Sanskrit word which I render into matron is *prajávatí*, from *prajá* "offspring," and *vatí* "possessing," and it appears to be the most appropriate in contrast with the young wives (*vadhúkás*) who tendered their services, but were rejected on the grounds of their youth and inexperience. It should be noticed, however, that the reading in the Tibetan, the Chinese, the Ceylonese, the Páli, the Burmese and the Siamese texts is

Prajápati, which means Brahmá himself, or his ten divine sons or a king, a father, a son-in-law, or the sun. The word is of the masculine gender, and not applicable to a woman. Translators have all taken the term to be the proper personal name of the lady, making Gautamí her tribal name. It is doubtful, however, if in India in former times a masculine term was used for a female, and I suspect, therefore, that the difficulty of managing the liquid letter *v* has led to the conversion of *Prajávatí* into *Prajápati*. Women seldom received a tribal or gotra name in India. They lost their father's gotra on marriage, and their husband's gotra would not be distinctive enough for use; every woman in the family having the same gotra. In the case of Gautamí, her father's gotra, was Vaśishṭha, not Gautama. To European translators, who are so familiar with double names the two names appeared to be the most appropriate, but I have no reason to doubt that we have in the text an epithet and a proper name to deal with, and not a personal and a race name. It is possible, however, for an epithet to crystalise into a nickname.

43. *Then king S'uddhodana invited the S'ákyas to a meeting*, p. 138. This meeting to consider whether the prince would remain at home or become a hermit is quite unnatural and out of place here. In the Chinese text, the meeting is appropriately held for astrologers to expound the horoscope of the child. In the Sanskrit text no mention is made of casting a horoscope.

44. *A great sage (maharshi) named Asita*, p. 138. In Hindu works sages are classed into *Brahmarshis*, or sages of the region of Brahmá; *Maharshis* or those of the region called Mahar; *Devarshis* or those of the region of the Devas; *Rájarshis* or those of the caste of Kshatriyas, and simply *Ṛishis*, the last two being of the region of the mortals. The author of the Lalita-Vistara evidently does not bear in mind this classification, for he has called the sage in some places a Maharshi and in others Devarshi: his idea of a Maharshi was that of a great (*mahá*) ṛishi, nor is it peculiar to him.

The name of Asita has been changed in the southern texts (Páli, Burmese and the Siamese) into Kaladewila. This is, however, merely the result of a translation; Asita means black and *kála* is its synonym, the affix *dewila* being a corruption of *devala* a priest whose vocation is to worship idols in private houses.

The story of Asita, though substantially the same, is varied very much in detail in the southern and the Chinese texts. It is not worth while, however, to notice the differences at length. The following account is given of the sage in the Siamese text: "In those times lived a holy man named Kaladewila, who was a member of a religious body whose doctrine differed from those of Buddha; and he was the teacher of the king S'uddhodana. He was the master of the five supernatural arts, and of the eight perfections of meditative abstraction, and had the power of flying through the air, &c., &c. This day he had transported himself to the Davadungsa heavens, and, sitting there, heard the rejoicings of the angels, and was told by them of the birth of king S'uddhodana's son." (Alsbaster, p. 107.)

45. *He addressed his pupil Naradatta*, p. 139. As in the case of Prajávatí Gautamí so here, European translators have converted an epithet into a proper name. The Sanskrit text has *Naradattam mánavakam*, and *mánavaka* means a pupil, and is not a proper name. In the Chinese and the southern versions the name is changed into Nárada.

46. *There the divine sage* (*Devarshi*,) p. 139. See note 43.

47. *The king, taking up with his two hands the Prince*, p. 180. According to the Chinese version Asita and Nárada went to the nursery where the child lay. "Then Máya, taking the child in her arms with her hands, gently raised, attempted to make him bow his head in reverence towards the feet of Asita. But the child by his spiritual power turned himself round his mother's arms, and presented his feet towards the Ṛishi. On which the king, taking the babe, made the same attempt three successive times, with the same result.

"Now, when Asita came to look at the child, a brightness like that of the sun shone from his body, and illuminated the great earth, and his perfectly beautiful and graceful body sparkled like gold, his head like a precious covering, his nose straight, his shoulders round, his limbs perfectly proportioned.

"Then Asita rose from his seat and addressed the king: 'O king! make not the child bow his head to me! but let me rather worship his feet!' And again he recited this hymn of praise: 'O rare event! Oh! seldom seen! A great being has been born! a very great being has been born! The tidings I heard in heaven are indeed true, respecting this beautiful babe!'

"Then Asita, unbaring his right shoulder and bending his right knee to the ground, took the child in his arms, and, returning to his seat, rested on his knees.

"Then the queen said, 'Venerable one! surely you will let the babe reverence you by saluting your feet!' To whom the Ṛishi replied, 'Say not so, O queen; for, on the contrary, both I and Devas and men should rather worship him!"' (Beal, pp. 57-58.)

48. *Even as the fig blossoms rarely*, p. 142. The species of fig here referred to is the *Ficus glomerata*. The belief is universal among the Hindus that the fig never blossoms, except on very rare occasions, and that whoever is fortunate enough to behold the blossom becomes a king. The fact is, the floral envelopes of the fig keep the sexual organs completely enclosed, and those envelopes along with the organs gradually become the fruit without the envelopes ever opening. They are, besides, of a green colour, and, therefore, the inference is easily drawn that the fig does not blossom. The junction of the envelopes are well indicated on the top, and it is possible, in abnormal cases, for the junction to remain unclosed for a time, and then the flowering is visible; but whether such an abnormal case ever happens or not, I do not know. It is very common among Bengalis, when they a meet a friend whom they had not seen for a long time, to say "you are become a fig flower:" *tumi ḍumur phul haiyáchha.* The saying stands for the English "angel's visits."

49. *Coil of curly hair*, p. 142. The word in Sanskrit is *úshṇishas'írsha*, literally 'turban-headed;' *Ushṇísha*, however, is also used for the curly matted hair coiled round the head of a Buddha, and that is what is here referred to. See note 26, page 17. The Chinese version has "an excresence of (? on) the top of the head;" the French version of the Tibetan text has "Une excroissance qui couronne sa tête."

50. *His shoulders are raised like the saptachhada flower*, p. 142. This is the literal meaning; but in Foucaux's translation of the Tibetan text we have, "il a sept protuberances," (p. 107), and the Chinese make "the seven places full and round" (Beal, p. 55). The confusion has arisen from the attempt to translate *saptachhada*, "seven-folded." It is, however, also the name of the *Alstonia scholaris*, and I take the comparison to be with the flower of that plant, which is rounded, and the shoulders are made like it. A

synonym of *saptachadda* is *saptaparṇa* "or seven-leaved," which shows the flower to have seven leaves or petals and not folds.

51. *His radiance is delicate*, p. 143. The Sanskrit phrase is *sukshma-suvarṇa-varṇachhavi*. In French we have "la peau fine et de la couleur d'or," and in the Chinese version "the body pure, and of a golden yellow colour."

52. *The body of Sarvárthasiddha is as long as his fathom*, p. 143. The Sanskrit *nyagrodha*, which means both a fathom and a banyan tree, has been taken in the latter sense by the Chinese translator. A perfect human figure measures as long as the fathom, and in the Sámudrika this is reckoned to be an auspicious sign. The Tibetans take it to imply the simious peculiarity of the hands reaching below the knee.

53. *His fingers and toes are joined with webs*, p. 143. The web is noticed only at the root of the toes and the fingers, the skin between them rising slightly in a thin web.

54. *By these thirty-two signs*, p. 143. Following the punctuation in my text I can count only 30. The Chinese text has 32, and the Tibetan 37. The Mahávastu Avadána gives quite a different series of signs. See my 'Sanskrit Buddhist Literature of Nepal,' p. 125.

55. *Like a needle*, p. 144. I can make nothing of this comparison : the word in Sanskrit is *śuchyácháraḥ*.

57. *Your gratification will be long protracted*, p. 145. The conversation between the sage and his pupil is differently given in the southern texts, but it is not worth while to take any note of it.

58. *The mighty Náráyaṇa born*, p. 146. The comparison with Náráyaṇa here and elsewhere is worthy of note. The divinity and greatness of Náráyaṇa were so well established at the time, that the poet thought they afforded the highest comparisons that was available to him.

59. *Charioteer, quickly inform the king*, p. 146. The prose more appropriately names the warder. It was never the duty of a charioteer to carry messages from the gate to the audience chamber of a king. I cannot make out how the charioteer is named here.

60. *Wilderness*, p. 148. The Sanskrit prose text brings the

sage from the side of the Himavat mountain, but the Chinese version makes him the dweller of Tsang-chang grove, the locale of which is not mentioned. The Burmese version places him in the neighbourhood of Kapilavastu, for he is described to have been "in the habit of resorting daily to the Prince's palace for his food." (Bigandet, I, p. 40.) The Siamese version, in common with the preceding two, makes him present in the Trayastrinśa heaven, (*Davadungsa*, Siamese; *Tuwadeintha*, Burmese) on a visit, at the time of the birth, and thence to descend on earth, to appear before S'uddhodana (Alabaster, p. 107). The *Mahávastu Avadána* makes him a Bráhman of Ujjainí, in Dakshinápatha, who was well versed in the Vedas, and, having renounced the world, had practised austerities as a hermit on the Vindhyan mountain, whence he retired to the Himálaya. All the different versions make him the beau-ideal of a Hindu saint of profound erudition.

61. *Who has acquired the neutral knowledge*, p. 148. The Sanskrit term is *upekshá-samudgata-buddhi*, which implies that knowledge which, having rejected every thing as unreal, remains confined in itself. It is the same with the samádhi of the Yogís. M. Foucaux renders it into "qui est en progression d'une grande joie et d'une intelligence élevée par l'indifférence (mystique)." (p. 111.)

62. The *royal dynasty of Ikshháku*, p. 149. According to the Kuśa-játaka Ikshháku was so named because he was born in a sugarcane. Cf. my "Sanskrit Buddhist Literature of Nepal," p. 142.

63. *The shadow of these beings cannot any where possibly be seen*, p. 150. The belief is universal among the Hindus that the body of a Deva never casts its shadow on earth, nor in motion produces any sound, and celestial beings when on earth appearing before men may be easily made out by these tests. S'rí Harsha, in his Naishadha, makes use of this belief with great effect. When Damayantí, at her second Svayamvara, appeared before the assembled princes to select her lord, Indra, Agni, Yama, and Varuṇa* stood before her along

* इन्द्राग्निदण्डिदिगीश्वरपाशिभिस्तां
बाह्यं गते नरविशाथ समां प्रसाद ।
सा स्निग्धवैष्टिरिव काव्यकीनिवेश
च्छायमभूः कमपि शीनहुताप नाथं ॥ नै० १३ । ५५ ॥

with Nala, and all the five appeared exactly alike. This puzzled the lady much, and she was at a loss whom to select. She felt certain that some gods or aerial spirits had come forward to delude her and cause mischief, but she knew not how to make them out. At last it struck her that no god or spirit could have a shadow, and seeing that four out of the five of her suitors cast no shadow on the ground, she selected the one who had cast a shadow, and thereby got back her long-lost consort.*

94. *Silken vestments*, p. 151. The Sanskrit word is *paṭṭa-dámám*, which, literally translated, would mean *jute cords*, from *paṭṭa* 'jute' or 'flax', and *dáman*, a cord or rope. *Paṭṭa*, however, is also used to imply silk, and the translation may be silk cords; but neither jute cords nor silk cords are fit objects of offering, and I take *dáman* to mean by metonymy cloth. In the Hindi language it means the skirt of a coat, which must have proceeded from *dáman* having once meant cloth. I cannot, however, just now appeal to any ancient authority on the subject.

* श्रियं भजन्तां कियदस्य देवा-
श्छाया नलस्यास्ति तथापि नैषाम् ।
इतीरयन्तीव तया निरैक्षि
सा नैषधे न त्रिदशेषु तेषु ॥ स० १४ । २४ ॥

CHAPTER VIII.

VISIT TO THE TEMPLE.

Presents of maidens for the service of the Bodhisattva. Proposal to visit the family temple. Preparations for the visit. Prince's remarks to his aunt. Procession. Effect of the Prince's entrance into the Temple. The salutation of the gods.

Now, Bhikshus, on that very night[1] on which the Bodhisattva took his birth, there were born twenty thousand girls in the houses of merchants, Kshatriyas, Bráhmaṇas and householders of the great S'ákya race. They were all presented by their parents to the Bodhisattva for his service and attendance on him. Twenty thousand girls were given by king S'uddhodana for service and attendance on the Bodhisattva. Twenty thousand girls were given for the same purposes by friends, counsellers, relatives, cognates, brothers-in-law and wellwishers.[2] A like number of girls were given for the same purposes by ministers and courtiers.

Now, Bhikshus, the S'ákyas with their elders, both male and female, came together to king S'uddhodana, and thus addressed him: "May it please your majesty, the Prince should be taken to the house of the Devas."

The king said, "That is proper. Take the Prince to see it. Let the city be duly embellished along with all the roads, squares, crossings, market-places and highways. Remove therefrom all inauspicious objects, such as monocules, hunchbacks, deaf, blind, dead and deformed persons. Drive away all persons with imperfect organs. Let pleasant sounds be raised. Let auspicious trumpets be blown. Let propitious bells be rung everywhere. Decorate the gates of the city. Let there be sweet music of clarions and táḍavas. Let all commanders of castles and forts assemble together. Let all bankers, householders, officials, warders and courtiers come together. Harness horses to chariots for females. Set in array pitchers full of water. Bring together all learned Bráhmaṇs. Decorate all temples."

Bhikshus, all these arrangements were completed as ordered.

Then king S'uddhodana entered his chamber, sent for the great matron Gautamí, and said to her, "Dress the Prince so that he may be taken to the temple."

"Please your majesty," said the great matron Gautamí, and dressed the Prince. When the Prince was properly dressed, he innocently and with a smiling face and sweet accent thus addressed his aunt,[3] "Mamma, where will you take me to?"

"To the temple, my son," said she. Then the Prince, with a pleasant face and an arch smile, addressed these verses to his aunt:

"On my birth all these three thousand regions trembled; and S'akra, Brahmá, Suras, Mahoragas, Chandra, Súrya, Vais'-ravaṇa, and Kumára saluted me by lowering their heads to the ground. (1)

"Which are the gods then which are so much greater and nobler than me to whom you wish, mamma, to send me? I am the god of gods, nobler than all gods. There is no god equal to me; how can there be one greater than me? (2)

"For the gratification of the people, mamma, I shall go. By beholding me the crowd will be greatly exhilarated; even those who can exhibit wonders will respect me highly, and men and gods will know that I am the greatest god." (3)

Then, Bhikshus, king S'uddhodana, surrounded and attended by Bráhmaṇs, merchants, bankers, householders, ministers, provincial chiefs, warders, courtiers, friends, and cognates, took the Prince in a chariot well-embellished in the inner apartments, and proceeded along most sumptuously decorated roads, squares, crossings, and markets, redolent with the aroma of burning pastiles, and bestrewed with buds and flowers, amidst joyous greetings and auspicious music, followed by a grand retinue of elephants, horses, chariots and foot soldiers, carrying umbrellas, flags, pennons and standards. Hundreds of thousands of Devas bore the chariot of the Bodhisattva. Many hundreds of thousands of millions of tens of millions of Devaputras and Apsarases came under the sky, and showered flowers, and played divine music.

Thus did king S'uddhodana, amidst a mighty host of kings, with royal magnificence and kingly majesty, take the Prince to the temple, and enter it. Now, when the Bodhisattva set his right foot on the floor of that temple, all the inert images of the Devas, such as S'iva, Skanda, Náráyaṇa, Kuvera, Chandra, Súrya, Vais'ravaṇa, S'akra, Brahmá, and the guardians of the quarters, rose from their respective places, and fell at the feet of the Bodhisattva. Thereupon, men and gods by hundreds of thousands burst into derisive laughter, and covered their faces with their clothes. The whole of Kapilavastu shook in six different ways. Celestial flowers fell in showers. Thousands of clarions resounded without a cause. And the gods whose images were in the temple made manifest their respective shapes, and recited these Gáthás :

"Never does the great mountain Meru, the king of mountains, salute a mustard seed ; nor does the great ocean, the abode of the king of Nágas, salute the footprint of a cow. The sun, the moon and other luminaries, never salute fireflies. How can then the great master of merit, one born in the race of knowledge and virtue, salute the Devas? (1)

"Even as the mustard seed, or water in the footprint of a cow, or fireflies, so are the gods (compared to him). Men and gods of the three thousand regions, all those on the earth who claim greatness, like the Meru, the ocean, the sun, or the moon, obtain every desirable object and salvation by praying to him who is self-born and the noblest." (2)

Now, Bhikshus, on the entrance of the Bodhisattva into the temple thirty-two hundreds of thousands of Devaputras had their mind directed to the sequenceless perfect Sambodhi. This, Bhikshus, is the reason, this the result of the indifferent Bodhisattva entering the temple.[4]

NOTES.

1. *On the very night*, p. 173. The word in the Sanskrit text is *rátrim*, night, but the description at the beginning of chapter VII clearly implies that Máyá Deví went to the garden of Lumbiní during the day time, and the delivery took place during the day and not at night. The word *rátri*, however, was often used very much in the same way in which 'a day' is used in English, meaning a day and a night. There is a parallel of this in the English 'se'nnight,' which means seven nights and seven days. This form of expression suggests the idea that the Hindus, at one time, had, like the Greeks, Babylonians, Persians, Syrians, and Jews, the custom of beginning the day at sunset. In Genesis i. the evening always precedes the morning.

2. *Brothers-in-law and wellwishers*, p. 173. The Sanskrit text has *śyálahita*. M. Foucaux renders the corresponding Tibetan words into "Les parents du côté du père, ceux du côté de la mère,"(p. 113).

3. *Addressed his aunt*, p. 174. The lady was both aunt (mother's sister) as well as stepmother, (father's second wife), of the prince. Subhúti or Suprabuddha, king of Devadaha, had seven daughters, namely, Máyá, Mahámáyá, Atimáyá, Anantamáyá, Chúlímáyá, Kálisábá, and Mahâprajavatí, of whom the eldest and the youngest were married to Súddhodana, and the others to his brothers. The lady had two children, a son named Nanda, and a daughter named Gaṇapadakalyání.

4. *Bodhisattva entering the temple*, p. 175. The story of the visit to the temple does not occur in the Burmese and the Siamese versions of the life of the saint. In the Chinese version, the procession from the Lumbiní garden to Kapilavastu passes by the temple, and the opportunity is seized to present the infant before the gods. The story runs thus :—

"At this time, not far from Kapilavastu, there was a Deva temple, the Deva's name being "Tsan Chang" (Dirghávardana ?) at whose shrine the S'âkyas paid unwonted honours ; then S'uddhôdana forthwith took the infant in his arms to this temple and addressed his ministers in these words, 'Now my child may pay worship to this Deva.' Then his mother (or, nurse), took the child to pay the customary honours, at which time a certain Deva, called 'Abhaya' (wou wee), took the image of the Deva in the temple, and made it come down and bow before Bodhisatwa with closed hands and prostrate head, and addressed the nurse thus, 'This Prince of mortals is not called on to worship, but is deserving of all worship; let me adore him, for to whom he bows down, instant destruction would follow.'" (Beal's Romantic History of Buddha, p. 52.)

CHAPTER IX.

ORNAMENTATION.

Request of S'ákyas to present ornaments. Ornaments prepared. Effect of ornaments put on the Prince. Address of a sylvan goddess on the worthlessness of ornaments for the Prince.

Now, Bhikshus, Udáyana, a Bráhmaṇ, father of Udáyí,[1] and the family-priest of the king, came along with five hundred Bráhmaṇas when the Chitrá constellation[2] had risen just after the Hastá constellation, and thus addressed him: "May it please your majesty that the Prince may have some ornaments made for him."

The king said, "Be it so. Let a good number of ornaments be prepared."

Thereupon five hundred ornaments were prepared under orders of king S'uddhodana, by five hundred S'ákyas. They included ornaments for the hands, ornaments for the feet, ornaments for the head, ornaments for the neck, seal rings, earrings, armlets, waist-chains, golden threads, nets mounted with bells, nets mounted with jewels, jewel-mounted shoes, necklaces of various kinds of jewels, bracelets, and delightful crowns. Having prepared these, the S'ákyas brought them to the S'ákya king when the Pushya constellation was on the ascendant, and thus addressed him; "May your majesty decorate the Prince with these ornaments."

The king said, "Let the Prince be ornamented and honoured by you. I, too, have got all ornaments prepared for him."

They replied: "It would do us great honour, if the Prince would wear our ornaments for seven days and seven nights."

Now, the night having expired[3] and the sun having risen, the Prince had been taken for an airing in the garden named Vimalavyúha. There the prince was in the lap of the great matron Gautamí. Eighty thousand ladies went there and beheld the face of the Prince. Ten thousand maidens went there and beheld his face. Five thousand Bráhmaṇas did the same. Then the ornaments which had been prepared by the noble S'ákya king were tied on the person of the Prince; but they were all eclipsed by the splendour of the Prince's body,—they did not sparkle, nor glow, nor look bright. Even as a lump of ink brought near a piece of gold from the Jámbunada,[4] does not sparkle, nor glow, nor look bright, so were the ornaments deprived of their lustre by the splendour of the Prince's person. Thus were other ornaments that were tied on his person put to disgrace like a lump of ink. Thereupon Vimalá, a sylvan goddess, impelled by her liberal nature, came forward, and addressed the following Gáthás to king S'uddhodana and the S'ákyas:

"'Were these three thousand regions along with all their towns and highways fully covered with showy stainless gold, and were then the gold from Jámbu brought near, the lustre of the other gold would cease to glow, overpowered by the light of Jámbu gold, and the whole of these regions would be lustreless. (1)

"'Even that (Jámbu) gold placed beside the light issuing from the pores of the leader,—full of light, modesty and beauty—would cease to glow, to sparkle, and to radiate. By the light of Sugata's body it would become lustreless like ink. He is ornamented fully by a hundred merits; no ornament can appear lustrous on him. The splendour of that stainless body burns out the light of the sun, the moon and the celestial luminaries. (2)

"'The glory of S akra and Brahmá pales before him of consolidated beauty, whose auspicious body is decorated with the fruit of noble works. Of what avail are to him common ornaments made by man? Remove those ornaments, O ye inconsiderate people; insult not the intelligent one by these. He desires no artificial ornaments—this being of noble object. Give away these nice looking ornaments to slaves.' (3)

"The well-adorned S'ákyas of the noble family of the king were pleased and wonder-struck by this speech. They were gratified to know that the prince of the S'ákya race would thrive so auspiciously." (4)

Having said this, the goddess sprinkled excellent flowers on the Bodhisattva, and then vanished from view.[5]

NOTES.

1. *Udáyana, father of Udáyí*, p. 178. In the Chinese version the names are Udáyana, father of the Bhikshu Udayí. Grammatically both versions are wrong. Udayí should be the father, and its regular derivative Audáyana the son.

2. *Chitrá constellation*, p. 178. The Chinese version fixes the time at the junction of the asterisms Chin and Koh.

3. *Now the night having expired*, p. 178. The asterism is said to have been Pushya which is an auspicious constellation for putting on ornaments.

4. *Gold from the Jámbunada*, p. 179. A river flowing from the mount Sumeru reputed to produce gold of a superior quality. I fancy it refers to some imaginary object which had attained fame from some mythical story. In current Sanskrit Jámbunada is used as a synonym for gold.

5. *Vanished from view*, p. 180. The Chinese version makes the goddess recite the verses from the sky where she was not visible. (Beal, p. 66.)

CHAPTER X.

EDUCATION.

Procession to the school-room. The school-master falls overpowered by the sight of the Prince. He is helped to rise from the ground by a Devaputra, who recites Gáthás in praise of the Prince. The Bodhisattva enquires what he is to be taught, and names 64 kinds of writing. The recitation of the alphabet.

Then, Bhikshus, when the Prince had duly grown up,[1] he was taken to the writing school under a hundred thousand auspicious arrangements. He was accompanied and followed by ten thousand boys. He was followed by ten thousand cars loaded with food of all kinds, and with gold in the forms of ingots and coins.[2] Whenever on the roads, squares, highways and market roads of the town of Kapilavastu, the procession stopped, or people descended from their cars, then eight hundred thousand clarions resounded in harmony. Great showers of flowers were rained everywhere. Hundreds of thousands of maidens stood by courtyards, doors, gateways, balconies, houses, towers, and palaces with dishevelled ornaments and dresses; or carrying vases of gold set with jewels to purify the roads, they proceeded towards the Bodhisattva. Eight thousand celestial maidens were strewing flowers to behold the Bodhisattva. Devas, Nágas, Yakshas, Gandharvas, Asuras, Garuḍas, Kinnaras and Mahoragas, in semiform shapes, held forth flowers, garlands and clothes from under the sky. All the S'ákyas, led by king S'uddhodana, proceeded in front of the Bodhisattva. With such a retinue did the Bodhisattva proceed to the school. Then he entered the school. Now Vis'uámitra, the school master, feeling the beauty and glory of the Bodhisattva to be insufferable, fell prostrate on the ground. Subháñga,[3] a Devaputra of the class Tushitakáyika, seeing him thus prostrate, held him by the right hand and raised him, and, having raised him, from under the sky addressed the following Gáthás to him, to king S'uddhodana, and to the large assembly :

" Whatever S'ástras are current in the regions of the Devas, all figures and writings and calculations, all roots, all arts[+] in their immensity current on earth, were learnt by him many millions of ages (*kalpas*) ago. (1)

" But to follow the usual practice of the world, to practice well what he has already learnt, to train numerous children in the foremost path, to bring other millions to the path of truth, he has come to the school. (2)

" What avails him the mere knowledge of writing who is thoroughly versed in the fourfold path of the future, who is proficient in the knowledge of the cause and the effect of creation, who knows how the circle of creation is stopped, and who has had his memory well polished ? (3)

" There is none in the three regions who can be greater than him in conduct ; he is the greatest among all gods and men. You know not even the names of the writings which he learnt many millions of ages ago. (4)

" This pure being, the receptacle of wonders, knows at once all the numerous wonders of the world. He knows, too, the movements of all invisible formless objects. What are visible forms of written letters to him ?" (5)

Having said this, the Devaputra worshipped the Bodhisattva with celestial flowers, and then disappeared.

Then the nurses and maids sat around him, and the S'ákyas headed by S'uddhodana retired.

Now Bodhisattva, taking up a tablet made of Uragasára sandal-wood and excellent ink with a golden pen mounted with jewels, thus addressed the tutor Vis'vámitra : " Which is the writing, sir, which you wish to teach me ? (1) Is it the Bráhmí writing ; (2) or the Kharoshṭí ; (3) or the Pushkarasárí ; (4) or the writing of Añga ; (5) or that of Bañga ; (6) or that of Magadha ; (7) or Máñgalya writing ; (8) or Manushya writing ;

(9) or finger writing (*añguli*); (10) or that of S'akári; (11) or that of Bráhmavallí; (12) or that of Drávida; (13) or that of Kinári; (14) or that of Dakshiṇa; (15) or that of Ugra; (16) or figure writing; (17) or cursive (*anuloma*) writing; (18) or the half-bow-shaped writing (*ardhadhanus*); (19) or that of Darada; (20) or that of Khásya; (21) or that of Chína; (22) or that of Húṇa; (23) or that in which the letters are most in the middle, (*madhyákshara-vistara*); (24) or flowery writing, (*pushpa*); (25) or the writing of the Devas; (26) or that of the Nágas; (27) or that of the Yakshas; (28) or that of the Gandharvas; (29) or that of the Kinnaras; (30) or that of the Mahoragas; (31) or that of the Asuras; (32) or that of the Garuḍas; (33) or that of Mrigachakra; (34) or circular (*chakra*) writing; (35) or that of the Váyumaruts; (36) or that of the Bhaumadevas; (37) or that of the Antarikshadevas; (38) or that of Uttarakuru; (39) or that of Púrvavideha; (40) or the perpendicular writing (*utkshepa*); (41) or the pendulous writing (*nikshepa*); (42) or the scattered writing (*vikshepa*); (43) or the disordered writing (*prakshepa*); (44) or the ocean writing (*ságara*); (45) or the thunderbolt writing (*vajra*); (46) or the cross-writing (*lekha-pratilekha*); (47) or the slow writing (*anudruta*); (48) or the S'ástrávarta writing; (49) or the Gaṇanávarta writing; (50) or the Utkshepávarta writing; (51) or the Nikshepávarta writing; (52) or the Pádalikhita writing; (53) or the Dviruttarapadasandhi writing; (54) or the Yávaddaśottarapadasandhi writing; (55) or the Adhyábháriṇí writing: (56) or the Sarvarutasañgrahaṇí writing; (57) or the Vidyánulomá writing; (58) or the Vimiśrita writing; (59) or the Ṛishitapastaptáñ writing; (60) or rochamánándharaṇí-prekshaṇa writing; (61) or the Gagaṇaprekshaṇí writing; (62) or the Sarvaushadhinisyandán writing; (63) or the Sarvasárasañgrahaṇí writing; (64) or the Sarvabhútarutagrahaṇí writing? Out of these sixty-four kinds[5] which is it, sir, that you wish to teach me?"

The schoolmaster Vis'vámitra, wonderstruck and deprived of all vanity and self-importance, recited these Gáthás with a cheerful face:

"Wonderful this is of the Bodhisattva, the leader of men, that he should have learnt every s'ástra immediately on coming to the school! (1)

"On coming to the school he has learned writings of which I do not know even the names. (2)

"I cannot see his face, nor even his head; how can I teach him who has already acquired every style of writing. (3)

"He is the god of gods, the great god, the noblest of all gods, the omnipresent. He is unrivalled, the chief, the unequalled soul of all in these regions. (4)

"Through his grace I shall thoroughly teach the means of that knowledge which is worthy of all to even those who have already been taught." (5)

Then, Bhikshus, the ten thousand boys along with the Bodhisattva began to learn writing. In the presence of the Bodhisattva the teacher began to teach the boys the alphabet. When they pronounced the letter *a*, then resounded the words—all sacraments are impermanent.[6] On *á* being pronounced there resounded the welfare of one's own and of others. By the letter *i*, the fulness of the organs. By the letter *í*, the earth is full of calamities. By the letter *u*, the world is full of accidents. By the letter *ú*, the lessening of vigour in the world. By the letter *e*, the sound of the evil of raising probes. By the letter *ai*, the propriety of the mundane course. By the letter *o*, the ultimatum of advice. By the letter *au*, the sound of peregrination. By the letter *am*, the origin of infallibility. By the letter *ah*, the sound of transition. By the letter *k*, the redemption of deserts. By the letter *kh*, the likeness of all religions to the sky. By the letter *g*, faith in the sound of religion. By the letter *gh*, the destruction of the darkness of dense ignorance and delusion. By the letter *ń*, the purification of the body. By the letter *ch*, the truthfulness of the four Árya paths. By the letter *chh*, the destruction of fancies and passions. By the letter *j*, the conquest of decay and death. By the letter *jh*, the overthrow of the fish-bannered chief. By the letter *ṇ*, knowledge. By the letter *ṭ*, the destruction of all screens. By the letter *ṭh*, the question of ṭhapaniya. By the letter *ḍ*, the overthrow of the unriotous Mára. By the letter *ḍh*, sexual matter. By the letter *ṇ*, the affliction from dust. By the letter *t*, the distinction of sameness. By the letter *th*, the fulness of vigour, power and ardour. By the letter *d*, the aroma of charity, self-controul and application. By the letter *dh*, the seven kinds of wealth of A'ryas. By the letter *n*, the knowledge of names and forms of things. By the letter *p*, the great object, or the *summum bonum*. By the letter *ph*, the visible attainment of fruition. By the letter *b*, the destruction of bonds. By the letter *bh*, the world exists. By the letter *m*, the suppression of pride and haughtiness. By the letter *y*, the suppression of ritual religion. By the letter *r*, abjurance of amour and love for the *summum bonum*. By the letter *l*, the removal of bonds. By the letter *v*, the noble path or the great translation (*varayána*). By the letter *ś*, the acquisition of tranquillity. By the letter *sh*, the suppression of the sixfold form and the attainment of the six understandings. By the letter *s*, the understanding of the knowledge of the omniscient. By the letter *h*, disaffection for afflictions destroyed. By the letter *ksh*, longing for the great religion by the overthrow of pride.

Thus, Bhikshus, in making the boys learn the alphabet innumerable thousands of initial words of religion were pronounced through the grace of the Bodhisattva. Thus, while the Bodhisattva was in the schoolroom, the minds of thirty-two thousand boys were imbued with the sequenceless perfect knowledge.

This was the reason this the cause why the Bodhisattva, though already thoroughly taught, came to the school room.[7]

NOTES.

1. *When the Prince had duly grown up*, p. 18. The Chinese version opens with a consultation held by the king when the Prince was

eight years old, to select a proper tutor. Viśvámitra is recommended as one "most perfectly acquainted with the Śástras, and in every respect the most suited to become teacher of the prince, in all and every kind of scholar-like erudition." (Beal, p. 67). The southern versions do not refer to the subject.

2. *Ten thousand carts loaded with all kinds of food &c.* p. 181. The food was given away in alms, according to some.

3. *Subháńga*, p. 181. Śuddhavara according to the Chinese text.

4. *All arts*, p. 182. The arts are called kalá in Hindu works, and usually reckoned at 64. I do not, however, know the names of all of them. In Vátsyáyana's Káma Sútra, we have the following list of 64 Arts which are appropriate for young ladies. They are called *Yogas*, and young ladies are recommended to practice them alone, or in the company of their tutors, fellow students, friends of the same age, &c. (*Chátuhshashṭhikán yogán kanyá rahasyekákinyabhyaset, &c*)

1. Vocal music. (G*íta*.)
2. Instrumental music. (*Vádya*.)
3. Dancing. (*Nṛitya*.)
4. Acting, or the union of the above three for public exhibitions. (*Náṭya*.)
5. Drawing. (*Álekhya*.)
6. Tattooing. (*Viśeshaka-chchhedya*.)
7. Making ornamental designs on the flour with rice-meal and flowers. (*Taṇḍula-kusumávali-vikára*.)
8. Making beds of flowers. (*Pushpástaraṇa*.)
9. Staining, dyeing, and colouring of the teeth, cloth and the body. (*Daśana-vasanáńgarága*.)
10. Setting jewels. (*Maṇibhumiká-karma*.)
11. Bed-making. (*Sayana-rachana*.)
12. Musical glasses, or playing on China cups containing varying quantities of water to regulate the tone. (*Udaka-vádya*.)
13. Making fountains. (*Udaka-gháta*.)
14. Pictorial art. (*Chitra-yoga*.)
15. Making of necklaces, garlands, wreaths, rosaries &c. (*Málya-granthana*.)
16. Making of ornaments of flowers for the head. (*Keśa-śekhara-rápíḍa-yoga*.)

17. Scenic representations. (*Nepathya-sañyoga.*)

18. Marking the cheeks before the ears with sandal and other pastes. (*Karṇapatra-bhaṅga.*)

19. Perfumery. (*Gandha-yukti.*)

20. Display of jewellery on the person. (*Bhúshana-yojana.*)

21. Jugglery. (*Aindrajálika.*)

22. Prestidigitation. (*Hasta-lághava.*)

23. Ornamental cookery. (*Chitra-sáka-púpa-bhaksha-vikára.*)

24. Preparation, of beverages (*Pánaka-rasa-rágásava-yojana.*)

25. Tailoring or sewing. (*S'úchikarma.*)

26. Making artificial flowers, &c., with thread. (*Sútrakriḍá.*)

27. Solution of riddles, charades, &c. (*Prahelikú.*)

28. Modelling, or making images. (*Pratimálá.*)

29. Mimicry. (*Durvachka-yoga.*)

30. Reading or elocution. (*Pustaka-váchana*)

31. Solution of verbal puzzles. (*Kávya-samasyá-púraṇa.*)

32. Making bows, sticks, canes, &c., with thread. (*Paṭṭikávetra-vána-vikalpa.*)

33. Making twist with a spindle or a distaff. (*Tarku.*)

34. Wood-carving. (*Takshana.*)

35. Decoration of houses. (*Vástu-vidyá.*)

36. Testing of silver and jewels. (*Rupya-ratna-paríkshá.*)

37. Knowledge of metals. (*Dhátu-váda.*)

38. Colouring of gems and beads. (*Maṇirágaka-ranjana.*)

39. Accertaining the existence of mines from external appearances. (*Ákarajṉána.*)

40. Gardening. (*Vrikshâyurveda.*)

41. Cock-fighting quail-fighting, ram-fighting, &c. (*Mesha-kukkuṭa-śávaka-yuddha-vidhi.*)

42. Teaching of parrots, &c., to speak. (*Suka-sáriká-pralápana.*)

43. Making use of unguents, pomades, &c., or shampooing. (*Utsádana kauśala.*)

44. Guessing unseen letters and things held in a closed fist. (*Akshara-mushṭiká-kathana.*)

45. Use of secret language—or modifying ordinary language so as to make it not ordinarily intelligible. (*Mlechchhitaka-vikalpa.*)

46. Knowledge of languages. (*Desabháshá-vijṉána.*)

47. Making of flower carriages. (*Pushpa-śakaṭiká.*)

48 Making of monograms, logographs and diagrams. (*Yantra-mátriká.*)

49. Exercises in enigmatic poetry. (*Dháraṇa-mátriká.*)

50. Lapidary art. (*Sañpáṭya.*)

51. Lexicography and versification. (*Abhidhána-kosha-chhandah-jnána.*)

52. Devising different expedients for making the same thing. (*Kriyá-vikalpa.*)

53. Tricks. (*Chhalitaka-yoga.*)

54. Dice-playing. (*Dyúta-viseshá.*)

55. Incantation to attract persons and things. (*A'karsaṇa-kṛiḍá.*)

56. Exhibiting Tableaux vivants, or assuming various forms. (*Náṭikákhyaka-yoga.*)

57. Tricks as taught by Kuchumára. (*Kuchumára-yoga.*)

58. Coiffure. (*Keśa-márjana-kauśala.*)

59. Filling up of stanzas of which a portion is told. (*Mánasa-kávya-kriyá.*)

60. Changing the appearance of fabrics, such as making cotton cloth appear like silk. (*Vastra-gopanáni.*)

61. Juvenile sports. (*Bála-kridakáni.*)

62. Etiquette. (*Vainâyiki.*)

63. Art of warfare? (*Vaijayiki.*)

64. Physical exercise. (*Vyáyámaki*)

The list as given by S'rídhara Svámí in his commentary on the Bhágavata Puráṇa is somewhat different from what I find in my MS. (a corrupt one) of Vátsyáyana, and some of the terms are doubtful. S'rídhara makes Baladeva and Kṛishṇa learn these accomplishments from their tutor Sándípani, but many of the accomplishments, sewing and cookery for instance, are obviously feminine, and would ill suit a man even in his youth. Vátsyáyana is therefore right in assigning them to young ladies. It might be said that these are the 64 arts, and some of them are for men, and others for women; but I do not think so.

5. *Of these sixty-four kinds*, p. 183. The 64 names may be classed under four heads; *viz.*, 1st referring to particular countries; 2nd, to particular tribes or classes; 3rd, implying peculiarities in the configu-

ration of the letters; 4th, cryptic or imaginative forms. Under the first head may be reckoned the writings of Aṅga, Baṅga, Kaliṅga, &c., and these probably imply certain then existing and current forms of writing. The second includes the Devas, Khasiyas, Húnas, Kinnaras, Daradas, &c., but there is nothing to show that some of the tribes named, such as the Khasiyas, the Daradas, and the Nágas, ever had any writing current among them. The Garuḍas and Mahoragas or mythical beings. No information is available to show the character of the other two heads; a good many of them are probably fanciful.

6. *All sacraments are impermanent*, p. 184. The attempt here is to indicate important specific dogmas by their initial letters. All the dogmas referred to are not known to me, and it is not worth while to attempt their explanation. We have here the archetype of the political alphabets which are now-a-days so often published as squibs. In the Chinese version a practical turn is given to the dogmatic terms, by making them illustrations of the sounds of the letters. Thus "by sounding the letter 'A' pronounce it as in the word 'anitya'." The Tibetan version, in common with the southern ones, omits this part of the text.

7. *Came to the school-room*, p. 185. The Chinese version adds to the instruction in writing and letters an account of the appointment of a separate teacher for instruction in martial accomplishments. (Beal, p 70.)

CHAPTER XI.

VISIT TO AN AGRICULTURAL VILLAGE.

Visit to an agricultural village. Repose under a tree. Four meditations. Adoration by five Ṛishis. Search for the Prince. Discovered under the tree. The miracle of the shadow of the tree. Corroborative Gáthás.

Thus, Bhikshus, did the Prince thrive in his youth. On one occasion he went, along with other boys, sons of ministers, to visit an agricultural village.[1] After seeing the agricultural works he entered a garden. There, rambling about, alone without a second, he beheld a pleasant, nice-looking Jambu tree. He sat under its shadow.[2] When he was seated his mind was absorbed into one point. Thus absorbed, he engaged himself with care and circumspection in a contemplation devoid of desires, sins, and inauspicious works. This was the first contemplation, the fruit of discrimination, and full of affectionate joy. Then came the second contemplation, which results from the purity of mind engendered by the argumentative and the deliberative states, and in which from the unalterability of the mind there results perfect non-argumutative and non-deliberative conditions.[3] In that state, from indifference to affection, he was indifferent, and, knowing that he was full of memory, he felt felicity in his body. When the proficient knew that the indifferent one, full of memory, and joyous, realised the objectless third contemplation. Then from the destruction of both pleasure and pain and from the isolation from lowness and exhileration of mind he realized the fourth contemplation, in which the memory, rejecting all ideas of pleasure and pain, is purified. At that time five foreign Ṛishis, who knew well the five (conditions of things) and were full of miraculous powers, were travelling in the air from the south towards the north. When they came over the noble grove they felt obstructed, and could not proceed. Feeling doubtful and horripilated, they recited the following Gáthás :

"We have travelled over this Meru mountain, hard as adamant, which has piercied up high through the atmosphere, and spread wide in the air like a herd of elephants rending asunder lines of many-branched trees of magnificent size. (1)

"We are able to go without fail, to the abodes of the gods, and high in the sky into the homes of Yakshas and Gandharvas, and yet, coming over this big forest, how and by whose miraculous power is it that we are restrained?" (2)

Then the forest god that was there thus addressed a Gáthá to the sages.

"Know that the son of the S'ákya king, born of the race of kings of kings, resplendent as the morning sun, of complexion bright as the new-blown lotus, of face beautiful as the moon, the noblest of men, the adored of Devas, Gandharvas, Nágendras, and Yakshas, greater than ten hundred thousands of worlds, has taken possession of this grove, and is engaged in meditation, and his majesty counteracts the power of miraculous force."

Then the Ṛishis looked downwards, and beheld the Prince radiant in his beauty and glory. The idea struck them thus; "Who can be the seated one? Is he Vais'ravaṇa, the lord of wealth? or Mára, the lord of desires? or the king of great serpents? or Indra, the wielder of the thunderbolt? or Rudra, the lord of Kumbháṇḍas?[4] or Krishṇa, the valiant? or the moon, son of a god? or the sun, the thousand-rayed? or a universal emperor?" Then they broke forth in verse:

"His beauty is greater than that of Vais'ravaṇa; is he verily, Kuvera manifest? or is he the image of the wielder of the thunderbolt? or is he the moon? or the sun? or Káma, god of love? or the image of Rudra? or of Kṛishṇa? or is the beautiful one, endowed with all auspicious signs, the pure Buddha?"

The forest god replied to the sages in verse.

"Whatever beauty there may be in Vais'ravaṇa, or in the thousand-eyed; whatever beauty there may be in the four guardians of regions, or in Brahmá, the lord of creation; whatever resplendence there may be in the planets,—were they all to acquire this S'ákya youth they would not in the least add to their radiance."

The Ṛishis, after hearing this verse from the god, descended on the earth, and beheld the Bodhisattva engaged in contemplation, and resplendent with an immensity of light around his body. They approached the Bodhisattva, and bepraised him in verses. Among them one said:

"In this world burning with afflictions he is born as a lake. He will acquire that religion wherewith he will quench the world."

Another said:

"In this world, immersed in the darkness of ignorance, he is born as a lamp. He will acquire that religion wherewith he will enlighten the world."

Another said:

On the highway of the ocean of grief, he is evidently the noblest vehicle. He will acquire that religion wherewith he will ferry mankind over the creation.

Another said:

"The redeemer of those who are enthralled by affliction is born. He will acquire that religion wherewith he will dis-enthral all creation."

Another said:

"There is born the great physician for those who are afflicted with disease and decay. He will acquire that religion where-with he will wipe off birth and death."

The Ṛishis, having gratified the Bodhisattva with these verses, circumambulated his person by the right side, and passed away through the sky.

King S'uddhodana, who was never at ease in the absence of, and without seeing, the Bodhisattva, enquired "where is the Prince gone? I do not see him here."

Then a large party went forth in search of the Prince. A minister saw the Prince seated on a couch under the Jambu tree, and engaged in contemplation. At that time the shadow of

20.	Gobhilíya Gṛihya Sútra, Fasc. I—XII @ /10/ each .. Rs.	7	8
21.	Hindu Astronomy, Fasc. I—III @ /10/ each	1	14
22.	Íṣá Kena Kaṭha Praṣna Muṇḍa Máṇḍukya Upanishads, Fasc. III—VI @ /10/ each	2	8
23.	Kátantra, Fasc. I—VI @ 1/ each	6	0
24.	Kathá Sarit Ságara, English, Fasc. I—IX @ 1/ each	9	0
25	Kaushitaki Bráhmaṇopanishad, Fasc. I and II @ /10/ each ..	1	4
26.	Kávyádarṣa of Ṣri Daṇḍin, Fasc. I—II (Fasc. III—V out of stock), @ /10/ each	1	4
27.	Lalita Vistara, Fasc. I—VI @ /10/ each	3	12
28.	Ditto English, Fasc. I—II	2	0
29.	Maitri Upanishad, Fasc. I—III @ /10/ each	1	14
30.	Mímáṃsá Darṣana, Fasc. I—XVI @ /10/ each	10	0
31.	Márkaṇḍeya Puráṇa, Fasc. III—VII @ /10/ each	3	2
32.	Nṛisiṃha Tápaní, Fasc. I—III @ /10/ each	1	14
33.	Nirukta, Fasc. I—IV @ /10/ each	2	8
34.	Nárada Pancharátra, Fasc. I—IV @ /10/ each	2	8
35.	Nyáya Darṣana, Fasc. I and III @ /10/ each	1	4
36.	Nítisára, or, The Elements of Polity, By Kámandaki, Fasc. II—IV (Fasc. I out of stock)	1	14
37.	Piñgala Chhandaḥ Sútra, Fasc. I—III @ /10/ each	1	14
38.	Prithiráj Rásau, Fasc. I—IV @ /10/ each	2	8
39.	Ditto English, Fasc. I	1	0
40.	Páli Grammar, English, Fasc. I and II @ /10/ each	1	4
41.	Prákṛita Lakshaṇam, Fasc. I	1	8
42.	Rig Veda, Vol. I, Fasc. I	0	10
43.	Ṣrauta Sutra of Ápastamba, Fasc. I—II @ /10/ each	1	4
44.	Ditto Áṣvaláyana, Fasc. I—XI @ /10/ each	6	14
45.	Ditto Láṭyáyana Fasc. I—IX @ /10/ each	5	10
46.	Sáma Veda Saṃhitá, Fasc. I—XXXVII @ /10/ each	23	2
47.	Sáhitya Darpaṇa, Fasc. I—IV @ /10/ each	2	8
48.	Sáñkhya Aphorisms of Kapila, Fasc. I and II @ /10/ each ..	1	4
49.	Súrya Siddhánta, Fasc. II—IV @ /10/ each	1	14
50.	Sarva Darṣana Sangraha, Fasc. I and II @ /10/ each	1	4
51.	Sañkara Vijaya, Fasc. II and III @ /10/ each	1	4
52.	Sáñkhya Pravachana Bháshya, English, Fasc. III	0	10
53.	Sáñkhya Sára, Fasc. I	0	10
54.	Taittiríya Áraṇyaka, Fasc. I—XI @ /10/ each	6	14
55.	Ditto Bráhmaṇa Fasc. I—XXIV @ /10/ each	15	0
56.	Ditto Saṃhitá, Fasc I—XXXII @ /10/ each	20	0
57.	Ditto Prátiṣákhya, Fasc. I—III @ /10/ each	1	14
58.	Ditto and Aitareya Upanishads, Fasc. II and III @ /10/ each ..	1	4
59.	Ditto Aitareya Ṣvetáṣvatara Kena Íṣá Upanishads, English, Fasc. I and II @ /10/ each	1	4
60.	Táṇḍyá Bráhmaṇa, Fasc. I—XIX @ /10/ each	11	14
61.	Uttara Naishadha, Fasc. I—XII @ /10/ each	7	8
62.	Váyu Puráṇa, Fasc. I—VII @ /10/ each	4	6
63.	Vaiṣeshika Darṣana, Fasc. I—IV @ /10/ each, (Fasc. V out of stock) ..	2	8
64.	Vásavadattá, Fasc. III	0	10
65.	Vishṇu Smṛiti, Fasc. I—II @ /10/ each	1	4
66.	Yoga Sútra of Patanjali, English, Fasc. I	0	14

Arabic and Persian Series.

1.	'Álamgírnámah, with Index, Fasc. I—XIII @ /10/ each	8	2
2.	Áín-i-Akbarí, Persian text, Fasc. I—XXII @ 1/4 each	27	8
3.	Ditto English Translation, Vol. I (Fasc. I—VII)	12	4
4.	Akbarnámah, with Index, Fasc. I—XX @ 1/4 each ..	25	0	Vol. I, III
5.	Bádsháhnámah with Index, Fasc. I—XIX @ /10/ each	11	14
6.	Dictionary of Arabic Technical Terms and Appendix, Fasc. I—XXI @ 1/4 each	26	4
7.	Farhang-i-Rashídí (complete), Fasc. I—XIV @ 1/4 each	17	8
8.	Fihrist Ṭúsí, or, Ṭúsy's list of Shy'ah Books, Fasc. I—IV @ /12/ each ..	3	0
9.	Futúḥ-ul-Shám Waqídí, Fasc. I—IX @ /10/ each	5	10
10.	Ditto Ázádí, Fasc. I—IV @ /10/ each	2	8
11.	Haft Ásmán, History of the Persian Masnawi, Fasc. I	1	4
12.	History of the Caliphs, English, Fasc. I—VI @ 1/ each	6	0

		Rs.	As.
13.	Iqbálnámah-i-Jahángírí, Fasc. I—III @ /10/ each ..	Rs. 1	14
14.	Iṣabáh, with Supplement, Fasc. I—XXIX @ /12/ each	21	12
15.	Maghází of Wáqidí, Fasc. I—V @ /10/ each	3	2
16.	Muntakhab-ul-Tawáríkh, Fasc. I—XV @ /10/ each	9	6
17.	Muntakhab-ul-Lubáb, Fasc. I—XVIII @ /10/ each, and Fasc. XIX with Index @ /12/	12	0
18.	Mu'áṣir-i-'Álamgírí (complete), Fasc. I—VI @ /10/ each	3	12
19.	Nukhbat-ul-Fikr, Fasc. I	0	10
20.	Niẓámí's Khiradnámah-i-Iskandarí, Fasc. I and II @ 1/ each ..	2	0
21.	Suyúṭy's Itqán, on the Exegetic Sciences of the Koran, with Supplement, Fasc. I—X @ 1/4 each	12	8
22.	Ṭabaqát-i-Náṣirí, Fasc. I—V @ /10/ each	3	2
23.	Ditto English, Fasç. I—XIV @ 1/ each	14	0
24.	Táríkh-i-Fírúz Sháhi, Fasc. I—VII @ /10/ each	4	6
25.	Táríkh-i-Baihaqí, Fasc. I—IX @ /10/ each	5	10
26.	Wís o Rámín, Fasc. I—V @ /10/ each	3	2
	Notices of Sanskrit Manuscripts, Fasc. I—XV @ 1/ each	15	0

ASIATIC SOCIETY'S PUBLICATIONS.

		Rs.	As.
1.	ASIATIC RESEARCHES. Vols. VII—XI; Vols. XIII and XVII, and Vols. XIX and XX @ 10/ each	90	0
	Ditto Index to Vols. I—XVIII	5	0
2.	PROCEEDINGS of the Asiatic Society from 1865 to 1869 (incl.) @ /4/ per No.; and from 1870 to date @ /8/ per No.		
3.	JOURNAL of the Asiatic Society for 1843 (12), 1844 (12), 1845 (12), 1846 (5), 1847 (12), 1848 (12), 1849 (10), 1850 (7), @ 1/ per No. to Subscribers and @ 1/8 per No. to Non-Subscribers; and for 1851 (7), 1857 (6), 1858 (5), 1861 (4), 1864 (5), 1865 (8), 1866 (7), 1867 (6), 1868 (6), 1869 (8), 1870 (8), 1871 (7), 1872 (8), 1873 (8), 1874 (8), 1875 (7), 1876 (7), 1877 (8), 1878 (8), 1879 (7), 1880 (8), @ 1/8 per No. to Subscribers and @ 2/ per No. to Non-Subscribers.		
	N. B. The figures enclosed in brackets give the number of Nos. in each Volume.		
	General Cunningham's Archæological Survey Report for 1863-64 (Extra No., J. A. S. B., 1864)	2	0
	Ethnology of India (Extra No., J. A. S. B., 1866)	2	0
	Theobald's Catalogue of Reptiles in the Museum of the Asiatic Society (Extra No., J. A. S. B., 1868)	2	0
	Catalogue of Mammals and Birds of Burmah, by E. Blyth (Extra No., J. A. S. B., 1875)	4	0
	Sketch of the Turki Language as spoken in Eastern Turkestan, Part II, Vocabulary, by R. B. Shaw (Extra No., J. A. S. B., 1878) ..	4	0
	A Grammar and Vocabulary of the Northern Balochí Language, by M. L. Dames (Extra No., J. A. S. B., 1880)	4	0
4.	Aborigines of India, by B. H. Hodgson	3	0
5.	Analysis of the Sher Chin, by Alexander Csoma de Körös	1	0
6.	Anis-ul-Musharrihin	3	0
7.	Catalogue of Fossil Vertebrata	2	0
8.	Ditto of Arabic and Persian Manuscripts	1	0
9.	Examination and Analysis of the Mackenzie Manuscripts by the Rev. W. Taylor	2	0
10.	Han Koong Tsew, or the Sorrows of Han, by J. Francis Davis ..	1	8
11.	Iṣṭiláhát-uṣ-Ṣúfíyah, edited by Dr. A. Sprenger, 8vo.	1	0
12.	Ináyah, a Commentary on the Hidayah, Vols. II and IV @ 16/ each ..	32	0
13.	Jawámi-ul-'ilm ir-riyáẓí, 168 pages with 17 plates, 4to.	2	0
14.	Khizánat-ul-'ilm	4	0
15.	Mahábhárata, Vols. III and IV @ 20/ each	40	0
16.	Moore and Hewitson's Descriptions of New Indian Lepidoptera, Part I, with 3 coloured Plates, 4to.	6	0
17.	Puráṇa Sangraha	1	0
18.	Sharí'at-ul-Islám	4	0
19.	Tibetan Dictionary	10	0
20.	Ditto Grammar	8	0
21.	Vuttodaya, edited by Lt.-Col. G. E. Fryer	2	0

BIBLIOTHECA INDICA;

A

COLLECTION OF ORIENTAL WORKS

PUBLISHED BY THE

ASIATIC SOCIETY OF BENGAL.

New Series, No. 575.

THE

LALITA-VISTARA,

OR

MEMOIRS OF THE EARLY LIFE OF ŚÁKYA SIÑHA.

TRANSLATED FROM THE ORIGINAL SANSKRIT.

BY

RÁJENDRALÁLA MITRA, LL. D., C. I. E.,

FASCICULUS III.

CALCUTTA:

PRINTED BY J. W. THOMAS, AT THE BAPTIST MISSION PRESS.

AND PUBLISHED BY THE

ASIATIC SOCIETY, 57, PARK STREET.

1886.

LIST OF BOOKS FOR SALE

AT THE LIBRARY OF THE

Asiatic Society of Bengal,

No. 57, PARK STREET, CALCUTTA.

AND OBTAINABLE FROM

THE SOCIETY'S LONDON AGENTS, MESSRS. TRÜBNER & CO.

57 and 59, Ludgate Hill, London, E. C.

BIBLIOTHECA INDICA.

Sanskrit Series.

Atharvaṇa Upanishad, (Sanskrit) Fasc. I—V @ /6/ each ..	Rs.	1	14
Agni Puráṇa, (Sans.) Fasc. I—XIV @ /6/ each		5	4
Aitareya Áraṇyaka of the Rig Veda, (Sans.) Fasc. I—V @ /6/ each ..		1	14
Aphorisms of Sáṇḍilya, (English) Fasc. I		0	6
Aphorisms of the Vedánta, (Sans.) Fasc. III—XIII @ /6/ each ..		4	2
The Asvavaidyaka, Fasc. I		0	6
Brahma Sútra, (English) Fasc. I		0	12
Bhámatí, (Sans.) Fasc. I—VIII @ /6/ each		3	0
Bṛihad Áraṇyaka Upanishad, (Sans.) Fasc. VI, VII & IX @ /6/ each ..		1	2
Ditto (English) Fasc. II—III @ /6/ each		0	12
Bṛihat Saṃhitá, (Sans.) Fasc. I—III, V—VII @ /6/ each		2	4
Chaitanya-Chandrodaya Náṭaka, (Sans.) Fasc. II—III @ /6/ each ..		0	12
Chaturvarga Chintámaṇi, (Sans.) Vols. I, Fasc. 1—11; II, 1—25; III, 1—13, @ /6/ each Fasc.		18	6
Chhándogya Upanishad, (English) Fasc. II		0	6
Gopatha Bráhmaṇa, (Sans. & Eng.) Fasc. I and II @ /6/ each ..		0	12
Gobhilíya Gṛihya Sútra, (Sans.) Fasc. I—XII @ /6/ each		4	8
Hindu Astronomy, (English) Fasc. I—III @ /6/ each		1	2
Kálamádhaba, Fasc. I and II @ /6/		0	12
Kátantra, (Sans.) Fasc. I—VI @ /12/ each		4	8
Kathá Sarit Ságara, (English) Fasc. I—XIII @ /12/ each		9	12
Kúrma Purana, Fasc. I		0	6
Lalita-Vistara, (English) Fasc. I—III @ /12/ each		2	4
Manutiká Sangraha, Fasc. I.		0	6
Mímáṃsá Darṣana, (Sans.) Fasc. II—XVIII @ /6/ each		6	6
Márkaṇḍeya Puráṇa, (Sans.) Fasc. IV—VII @ /6/ each		1	8
Nṛisiṃha Tápaní, (Sans.) Fasc. I—III @ /6/ each		1	2
Nirukta, (Sans.) Vol. I, Fasc. 1—6; Vol. II, Fasc. 1—6, Vol. III, Fasc. 1—4, @ /6/ each Fasc.		6	0
Nárada Smṛiti, Fasc. I and II @ /6/		0	12
Nyáya Darśana, (Sans.) Fasc. III		0	6
Nítisára, or The Elements of Polity, By Kámandaki, (Sans.) Fasc. II—V @ /6/ each		1	8

(Continued on third page of cover.)

other trees had turned away, but that of the Jambu tree had not forsaken the body of the Bodhisattva. Struck with amazement, exhilaration, delight, joy and satisfaction he hastily repaired to king S'uddhodana, and thus reported in verse the circumstance: "Please your majesty, behold the Prince in meditation under the shadow of the Jambu tree. In his beauty and glory he is as resplendent as S'akra or Brahmá. (1)

The tree under which the nobly endowed is seated, does not remove its shadow from the noble being in meditation." (2)

King S'uddhodana went to the Jambu tree, and, seeing the Bodhisattva resplendent in his beauty and glory, recited this verse:

"Is it a fire issuing from the crest of a mountain? or is it the moon surrounded by its stellar host? My body is overpowered by the sight of him meditating in his glory like a lamp."

Then saluting the feet of the Bodhisattva he recited this distich:

"Since thou art born a sage, since thou meditatest on the being of light, O preceptor, I salute thy feet once and again."

At this time some lads carrying sessamum seed made a noise. To them said the ministers, "Make no noise."

They enquired, "why?"

The ministers replied, "although surrounded by the darkness of the world, Siddhártha, the auspiciously emblazoned, the son of the great king, the luminous as the sky, is engaged in meditation, firm as the mountain, and the shadow of the tree does not forsake him."

On this subject (the following Gáthás) may be quoted:

"In midsummer when the spring had returned, in the month of Jyaishṭha, when leaves and flowers had bloomed in profusion, when herons and peacocks, parrots and mainas, were cackling, many were the S'ákya maidens who had issued forth to ramble about. (1)

"Said the Prince, 'Chhanda, we shall proceed with all the boys to behold the country. What is the good of remaining at home like anchorites? we should go with exhilarating maidens in our company.' (2)

"At midday the pure being, the Buddha, surrounded by fifty boys and a retinue of servants, without informing either his father or his mother, issued forth, and repaired to an agricultural village. (3)

"In that agricultural village of the king there existed a Jambu tree with numerous large branches. Seeing the village and knowing the trouble of its people, the Prince said, 'alas! that the agriculturists have to undergo so much labour in their profession!' (4)

"Then going under the shadow of the Jambu tree, in a humble spirit, he collected some grass and spread it to form a smooth cushion; and seated thereon he, the Bodhisattva, performed in calm repose the four meditations. (5)

"Five sages, travelling through the air, came over the place but could not pass over the Jambu tree. Surprised at this, with humbled pride they looked about. (6)

"'We travel with irrepressible velocity over the Meru, the noblest of mountains, and across the Chakravála mountains but we have not been able to pass over that Jambu tree. What can be the cause of this? There must be something here to-day!' (7)

"Descending on the earth, they beheld under the Jambu tree the S'ákya prince, resplendent as the gold from the Jambu river, seated on a couch and engaged in meditation. (8)

"Wonder-struck, they touched their heads with their ten nails brought together with joined hands; they fell on his feet, and saluted the noble asylum of mercy. 'With ease wilt thou enliven with nectar all fallen mortals.' (9)

"The sun travelled on, but the tree did not withdraw its shadow, refreshing as that of the lotus leaf, from the Sugata, but held it on. Devas by thousands, standing with joined hands, did homage to the feet of the firmly resolved one. (10)

"S'uddhodana, looking everywhere in his house, enquired, 'where is my son gone to?' The aunt said, 'I have searched for him, but cannot find him. Please your majesty, enquire where is the Prince gone to.' (11)

"In haste S'uddhodana enquired of the warder, the porters, and every one of the household, 'Have you seen my son? where is he gone to?' 'We have heard, your majesty, he is gone to the village of the agriculturists.' (12)

"Attended by many S'ákyas, the king quickly repaired to the farmers' village, and, entering it, beheld the auspicious one resplendent in his beauty, exceeding in radiance the light of millions of suns. (13)

"Leaving aside his crown, his sword, and his shoes, and joining in salutation his ten fingers to his head, he said, 'noble is thy conduct. The noble sages of goodly speech foresaw that you had come down for Bodhi knowledge.' (14)

"Full twelve hundred well-disposed Devas and five hundred S'ákyas, who had come to the place, beheld the miracle of the Sugata, the ocean of merit, and acquired firm faith in the Sambodhi. (15)

"He, the Prince, caused the three thousand endless regions to quake, and, knowing by the virtue of his transcendental memory, acquired by his meditation, that they had come to him, he, the Lord of Brahmá, talked with his father, rose from his seat, and started homewards. (16)

"'O king, if gold be required I shall (said he) shower gold; if cloth be wanted I shall bestow cloth. Whatever else is required, I shall shower the same, so that everything may be abundant on this earth.' (17)

"Having thus addressed his father and his courtiers and companions, that pure being returned home, intent upon doing all the good he could to the world following him." (18)

NOTES.

1. *To visit an agricultural village*, p. 190. The description here seems to imply, and the Mahávastu Avadána says definitely, that the visit was casual—a ramble in the spring season. The Chinese version makes the occasion to be a ploughing match to which the father took the son. It says: "Now at another time it happened that S'uddhodana Rájá assembled all the S'ákya princes, and took with him the Prince Royal to go to see a ploughing match (or field cultivation or sowing). Then in the enclosed space were assembled the half-stripped men, each labouring hard in the ploughing contest, driving the oxen and urging them on if they lagged in their speed, and from time to time goading them to their work. And now, when the sun increased in his strength, and the sweat ran down both from men and oxen, then for a few moments they ceased from their labours. In the meantime, various insects came forth from the ground, and flocks of birds, in the interval of the plowing exercises, came down in multitudes and devoured them. The Royal Prince, seeing the tired oxen, their necks bleeding from the goad, and the men toiling in the midday sun, and the birds devouring the helpless insects, his heart was filled with grief, as a man would feel who saw his own household bound in fetters, and, being thus affected with sorrow on behalf of the whole family of sentient creatures, he dismounted from his horse Kanṭaka and, having done so, he walked about in deep reflection." (Beal, pp. 73*f.*) For the insects and birds the Mahávastu substitutes a frog and a serpent. The Southern versions make this the festival of the ploughing season, an annual festival still faithfully observed in Burmah and Siam, and not unknown in India.

2. *He sat under its shadow*, p. 190. The Chinese version, in common with the Sanskrit, makes the Prince ramble about till he comes to the tree under which he sits down, but instead of making him go there alone, sends with him all his attendants, who are subsequently sent away. In the Southern versions the Prince is taken to the place when he was a child. The Burmese text says, "The royal infant was brought out by the nurses on this joyful occasion. A splendid

jambu tree (*Eugenia*), loaded with thick and luxuriant green foliage, offered on that spot, a refreshing place under the shade of its far-spreading branches. Here the bed of the child was deposited. A gilt canopy was immediately raised above it, and curtains, embroidered with gold, were disposed round it. Guardians having been appointed to watch over the infant, the king, attended by all his courtiers, directed his steps towards the place where all the ploughs were held in readiness. He instantly put his own plough; eight hundred noblemen, less one, and the country people followed his example. Pressing forward his bullocks, the king ploughed to and fro through the extent of the fields. All the ploughmen, emulating their royal lord, drove their ploughs in a uniform direction. The scene presented a most animated and stirring spectacle on an immense scale. The applauding multitude filled the air with cries of joy and exultation. The nurses, who kept watch by the side of the infant's cradle, excited by the animated scene, forgot the prince's orders, and ran near to the spot to enjoy the soul-stirring sight displayed before their admiring eyes. Phralaong, casting a glance all round, and seeing no one close by him rose up instantly, and, sitting in a cross-legged position, remained absorbed as it were in a profound meditation." (Bigandet, I, pp. 50*f*.).

3. *Non-argumentative and non-deliberative condition*, p. 190. Here, as elsewhere, the Buddhists have borrowed the detail of the Hindu Yoga to the very letter. Yogís describe four kinds of meditation; 1st, the argumentative; 2nd, the deliberative; 3rd, the joyous; and 4th, the egoistic. When meditation is confined to crude matter, it is argumentative. When subtile matter is made the theme of thought, it is deliberative. When all ideas of argument and deliberation have passed away and the thinking principle is immersed in a sense of absolute happiness, it is joyous. And when that sense of joy has passed and a mere consciousness is all that is left behind, it is egoistic. These ideas have been worked out in a roundabout way in the text. For the details of these conditions the reader is referred to my translation of the Yoga Aphorisms of Patanjali, pp. 17 *et infra*. The Chinese and the Southern authors have discarded all mention of these as too abstruse for the temper of their worldly-minded people.

CHAPTER XII.

DISPLAY OF ACCOMPLISHMENTS.

Consultation for the selection of a bride. The Prince's choice. Search for a bride. Gopá discovered. A reception held by the Prince. Daṇḍapáṇi's condition. Preparations for a grand convocation. The elephant of the Prince killed by Devadatta and cast aside by the Prince. Display of accomplishments. Caligraphy. Arithmetic. Gymnastic exercises. Archery. The monster bow. Other accomplishments. Bestowal of Gopá by her father. Gopá's reasons for not remaining veiled in her new home, and the S'ákya's assent to her wish.

Now, Bhikshus, the Prince having grown up,[1] king S'uddhodana was one day seated in his council chamber amidst a number of S'ákyas when some elders of the race, both male and female, thus addressed him[2]: "It is known to your majesty what has been foretold by competent Bráhmaṇas and astrologers, what will happen to Prince Sarvárthasiddha. It has been said that should the Prince retire from the world, he will become a Tathágata, an Arhat, a perfect Buddha. On the other hand, should he not retire, he will become a king, sovereign over all, victorious, virtuous, master of religion, and lord of the seven jewels, and these are the seven jewels, *viz.*, the wheel, the elephant, the horse, the jewel, the wife, the master of the household, and the commander. He would have, moreover, a thousand sons, the noblest among heroes, mighty ones, handsome ones, and overthrowers of inimical armies. He will by his virtue rule the circle of the earth without the aid of arms and without punishments. It behoves, therefore, that your majesty should cause him to be married, so that, surrounded by women, he may enjoy life, and not retire from the world, and our imperial race may not be brought to an end, and we may be respected and obeyed by all minor chiefs."

King S'uddhodana then thus replied to them—"If that be

your wish, what maiden do you think would be worthy of the Prince?"

Thereupon each out of the five hundred S'ákyas there assembled, said: "My daughter is beautiful and worthy of the Prince."

The king said, "The Prince is hard to please, and so I must enquire of him what sort of a maiden will be most agreeable to him."

Thereupon the S'ákyas waited upon the Prince and desired to know his wishes.

The Prince said, "You will have a reply on the seventh day."

He then reflected,[3] 'Well known are to me the endless evils of lust; lust is the root of all enmities, confusion, grief, and pain; it is dreadful as the venomous serpent, burning as a fire, keen as the sword; I have no longing or desire for lust, nor can I rejoice in a female apartment, for I should dwell in silence in a grove, with a peaceful mind, immured in the joys of contemplation and meditation.' Then arguing the subject in his mind, taking into consideration the facility of the means (for attaining perfection), and maturing the end of truth, in great compassion recited the following Gáthás:

"Lotuses in sacred tanks sprouting from mire[4] and spreading on water in their radiance, are admired by all. Should the Bodhisattva acquire the experience of domestic life, he will be able to place millions and millions of beings in immortality. (1)

"Bodhisattvas, who in former times acquired true knowledge, had all acquired the experience of wives, sons and gynacea; they were not affected by lust, nor deprived of the joys of contemplation, and verily I shall learn their merits. (2)

"The maiden who would be worthy of me should not be a common one. She, who has no envy, who is ever truthful, ever vigilant, and thoroughly pure in beauty, birth, lineage and race, is the person to gratify my mind. (3)

"I shall need the maiden who is accomplished in writing and in composing poetry, who is endowed with good qualities. No common, unaccomplished person should be fit for me; I shall wed her only who is as perfect as I describe. (4)

"The noble one should be endowed with beauty and youth, but not proud of her beauty; such a benevolent one should have her mother and sister living; she should be benevolent, and disposed to give alms to S'ramaṇas and Bráhmaṇas. Father, wed me to such a maiden. (5)

"She who has no ill-repute, no fault, no wickedness, no envy, no affectation, no evil eyes; who evinces no affection for a stranger even in her dream; who is always satisfied with her own husband, always self-controlled and careful; (6)

"who is never proud, nor ill-behaved, nor impudent; who, though devoid of vanity, is never slavish; nor addicted to drink, lust, food, sound and smell; never begging; always content with her own; (7)

"abiding in truth; never fidgety, nor blundering, nor impudent, nor remaining demure in her veil; not eager to attend public shows; always devoted to religion; ever pure in body, speech and mind; (8)

"never given to langour; full of prosperity; not deluded by vanity; considerate, engaged in good works; always attentive to religious duties; dutifully respectful to her father-in-law and her mother-in-law; loving her maids and dependants like herself; (9)

"well versed in the rules of the S'ástras; expert as a public woman; retiring to bed and rising therefrom before her lord; devoted to her friends; without deception like a mother;—such should be the maiden, O king, whom I should marry."[5] (10)

Now, Bhikshus, king S'uddhodana, having read these verses, thus addressed the family priest[6]: "Do you, great Bráhmaṇa, proceed to the great city of Kapilavastu, and, entering every house, examine all the maidens. Whosoever has these qualities,[7] whether she be a Kshatríya, or a Bráhmaṇa, or a Vais'ya, or a S'údra's daughter, report her to me."

"But why this latitude?"

"Because the Prince is not anxious about race, or lineage, but about quality."

At this time the following Gáthás were recited:

"Inform me of the maiden who possesses these qualities, whether she be the daughter of a Bráhmaṇa, a Kshatriya, a Vais'ya, or a S'údra; for my son is not particular about family or lineage; his mind delights in merit, in truth, and in virtue."

Now, Bhikshus, that priest, having taken a copy of those verses, roamed about from house to house in the great city of Kapilavastu, searching for a bride. Finding nowhere a maiden according to the acquirements of the verses, he came, in course of his search, to the residence of Daṇḍapáṇi, a S'ákya.[8] Arriving thereat, he entered it, and beheld a maiden like what he sought—a graceful, handsome maiden, of exquisitely beautiful complexion, neither very tall nor short, neither very corpulent nor very thin, neither very fair nor very dark, of budding youth, a jewel of a maiden, beyond compare.

The maiden touched the feet of the priest in welcome, and enquired, "What may be your mission, O great Bráhmaṇ?"

The priest said, "The son of S'uddhodana, a prince of great beauty, bearing the 32 marks of greatness on his person, and, endowed with virtues and valour, has written these verses describing the qualities of his bride. Whoever possesses these qualities, will be his wife."

He then handed to her the written verses. The maiden read them, and then, displaying a gentle smile on her face, thus answered him in verse.

"All the qualities as you describe, O Bráhmaṇ, abide in me. May that benign and handsome one be my lord. Go and report this to the prince, and tarry not. He will not have to associate with a common person."

Now, the priest approached the king, and thus reported to him: "Sire, the maiden I have seen will be worthy of the Prince."

The king asked, "Who is she?"

The priest replied, "Sire, the daughter of Daṇḍapáṇi, a S'ákya."

King S'uddhodana then thought within himself, "the Prince is of lofty aspirations, and difficult to please. He has in him all the qualities of his mother, and desires to acquire other merits. I shall therefore cause to be prepared As'oka bouquets[9] which the Prince may offer to all the maidens, and on whomsoever he will cast his eyes, her I shall bestow on him."

Now, king S'uddhodana caused to be made a great number of As'oka bouquets decorated with gold, silver, lapislazuli, and many other kinds of jewels. Having got them ready, he proclaimed by the ringing of bells all over the city of Kapilavastu that on the seventh day the Prince will hold a reception, and present As'oka bouquets to all the maidens of the town, and all the maidens should, therefore, attend the reception hall.

Now, Bhikshus, on the seventh day the Bodhisattva repaired to the reception hall,[10] and took his seat on a throne. The king had placed spies who, unseen, watched on what maiden the eyes of the Prince would rest.

All the maidens of Kapilavastu came to the reception hall of the Bodhisattva in order to have his audience, and receive the As'oka bouquets.

The Prince handed the As'oka bouquets to his guests, who, unable to bear the refulgence of the Prince, received the presents and quickly retired. Gopá, the daughter of Daṇḍapáṇi,[11] the S'ákya, now came to the reception, attended and beserved by her maids, took her place on a side, and watched the Prince with untwinkling eyes. When all the bouquets had been given away, she advanced before the Prince, and said with a smiling face, "what harm have I done, Prince, that you should deny me the usual courtesy?"

The Prince replied, "No, I have not been wanting in courtesy, but you were the last to come." Saying this, he took off from his finger a ring worth many hundred thousands,[12] and offered it to her.

She remarked, "Am I, Prince, worthy of this from you?"

The Prince responded, "Pray, accept all these ornaments of mine."

She rejoined, "No, we shall not disadorn the Prince, for we will disadorn Mára."[13] Saying this she retired.

Now the spies repaired to the king and said, "Sire, the eyes of the Prince fell on Gopá, a S'ákya maiden, daughter of Daṇḍapáṇi, and he had a short conversation with her."

On hearing this, the king sent the priest to Daṇḍapáṇi with the message that he may bestow his daughter on the Prince.

Daṇḍapáṇi said, "The noble Prince is thriving in his home. But we have a family custom not to give our daughter on any who is not an expert in art. We always select those who are experts in art. The Prince is not so, nor is he proficient in the use of swords, bows, elephant driving, and wrestling. I shall give my daughter to one who is proficient in art. Please, report this to the king."

The king reflected, "Now, twice has this reproach been cast on me. When I said, why don't the S'ákya youths come and pay their respects to the Prince, then I was told, 'why should we pay our respects to the Prince;' and now again. What should I do about this?" Thinking this, he sat still in sorrow.

The Bodhisattva heard the news, and then, coming to the king, thus addressed him, "Why are you, Sire, in this sorrowful mood?"

The king said, "Enough, it concerns you, my son."

The Prince said, "Sire, it is meet that you should relate the particulars to me." When the Prince had thrice said this, king S'uddhodana related to him all the particulars.

Hearing them the Bodhisattva said, "Sire, is there any youth in this city, who can rival me in displaying art accomplishments?"

The king smiled and said, "Are you able, my son, to display any art accomplishments?"

The Prince replied, "Yes, Sire, I am able. Do you invite all persons, experts in art, in whose presence I may display my accomplishments."

The king, thereupon, caused a proclamation to be published by the ringing of bells[14] in the town of Kapilavastu, to the effect that on the seventh day the Prince will display his art accomplishments, and all experts should assemble on the occasion to behold them.

On the seventh day five hundred S'ákya youths assembled in the arena, and Gopá, the daughter of Daṇḍapáṇi, the S'ákya, planted a flag of victory[15] therein, saying, whoever will be able to display the highest accomplishment in swordmanship, archery, elephant guiding, and wrestling, to him this shall be awarded.

Foremost issued from the town Prince Devadatta.[16] At the time a majestic white elephant was entering the town for the use of the Bhodhisattva. Seeing it Devadatta, proud of his S'ákya prowess, and envious of the Prince, seized the trunk of the elephant with his left hand, and gave the animal such a slap with his right hand that it at once fell dead. Then came there Prince Sundarananda, who, seeing the elephant at the city gate and finding it was dead, enquired, " who has killed this animal?"

The crowd of people there said, " Devadatta."

He said, " Devadatta has not done a becoming act."[17] Then seizing the carcass by the tail, he dragged it aside from the city gate.

Then issued forth the Bodhisattva mounted on a car. He saw the elephant, and seeing it was dead, enquired, " who has killed this animal?"

The people said, " Devadatta."

He remarked, " this act is unbecoming of Devadatta." He then enquired, " by whom has this been removed from the passage?"

The people replied, " by Sundarananda."

He observed, " It was good of Sundarananda. But this is a large carcass, and its rotting will cause serious nuisance in the town." Saying this, he put forth one foot from the car and, seizing the tail of the animal by the great toe only, whirled the carcass across the seven walls and seven moats of the city, and cast it two miles away in the outskirts. The spot where the carcass fell was depressed into a deep hollow which, to this day, is called the " Elephant hollow"[18] (*Hastigarta*). Gods and men by hundreds and thousands, seeing this, burst forth into loud shouts of joy and laughter, and waved their clothes.[19] Some Devaputras, coming below the sky, sang the following Gáthás:

"Since taking the mighty elephant of infuriated noble gait by the great toe[20] he has cast it in the outskirts across the seven walls and seven moats of the city, he, the wise one, will for certain cast away from the world by the force of his wisdom, those who are inflated by the power of vanity."

Now, five hundred S'ákya youths proceeded to the place where other youths had gone to exhibit their art accomplishments. King S'uddhodana, surrounded by the elders of the race (both male and female) and attended by a large retinue, proceeded to the same place, wishful to behold the encounter of the Bodhisattva with other S'ákya youths.

The first object of display was writing, and those who were most expert in it came forward: they appointed the tutor Vis'vámitra as the judge. He, the schoolmaster, examined the exercises to ascertain which youth had excelled in the knowledge of writing, either in the finish of caligraphy, or in the capacity of writing many kinds of alphabets. He then, smiling with approval on the superiority of the Bodhisattva in the knowledge, gave his award by reciting the two following verses:—

"Whatever writings exist in the region of man, or in that of the Devas, in the region of the Gandharvas, or in that of Surendra, in all of them the pure being is thoroughly proficient. (1)

"Nether you nor I have ever seen the letters, nor heard the names of those writings in which this moon among men is learned. I declare, therefore, that he has distinguished himself the most." (2)

The S'ákyas said, "Well, let it be that he is successful in writing; he must now prove his knowledge of arithmetic, and should be examined in it."

Thereupon Arjuna, a S'ákya astrologer and councilor,[21] who was thoroughly proficient in the calculation of numbers, was appointed judge. He was then told, "Do you decide who amongst these youths acquits himself best in arithmetic."

Now, the Bodhisattva set a sum to a S'ákya youth, but that youth could not work it, and was defeated.

The Bodhisattva then said, "Let you put the sum, and I shall work it."

Then a S'ákya youth set a sum, but could not defeat the Bodhisattva. Then two, three, five, ten, twenty, thirty, forty, fifty and even all the five hundred simultaneously set questions to him, but could not confound the Bodhisattva, for he solved them all.

The Bodhisattva then said, "Enough, enough of this dispute; now all of you five hundred should together frame your question, and I shall solve it."

Thereupon all the five hundred S'ákya youths set a question with an illustration, but the Bodhisattva immediately and easily solved it. Thus were all the S'ákya youths overcome by the Bodhisattva. The astrologer councilor Arjuna was struck with wonder by this, and recited these verses:—

"In calculation he has established himself foremost among these five hundred youths; he is sure soon to acquire perfect proficiency in Boddhi knowledge. (1)

"Such is his learning and understanding, such his wisdom, memory and intellegence, that even I, who am thoroughly proficient in learning, should still learn from him." (2)

All the S'ákyas stared with wonder and astonishment, and in one voice burst forth "Victory! Victory attends this Prince Sarvárthasiddha!" All of them then rose from their seats and, having with folded hands saluted the Boddhisattva, thus addressed king S'uddhodana; "Thou hast, Mahárája, attained the highest blessing, since your son has so quickly, so readily and so smartly solved all the questions."

Then king S'uddhodana enquired of the Bodhisattva, "Can you, my boy, enter into competition in calculation and order of reckoning with Arjuna, the astrologer councilor?"

The Prince replied, "Let him proceed."

Then Arjuna, the astrologer councilor, asked the prince, "Do you, Prince, know the order of reckoning after a koṭis'ata?" (Numeration table).

"I do," replied the Prince.

Arjuna asked, "how should the order of reckoning proceed after a koṭiśata ?"

The Bodhisattva replied:

"A hundred Koṭis'atas make an *Ayuta ;*[22]
A hundred Ayutas make a *Niyuta ;*
A hundred Niyutas make a *Kaṅkara ;*
A hundred Kaṅkaras make a *Vivara ;*
A hundred Vivaras make an *Akshobhya ;*
A hundred Akshobhyas make a *Vivāha ;*
A hundred Vivāhas make an *Utsaṅga ;*
A hundred Utsaṅgas make a *Bahula ;*
A hundred Bahulas make a *Nágabala ;*
A hundred Nágabalas make a *Tiṭilambha ;*
A hundred Tiṭilambhas make a *Vyavasthána-prajṇapti ;*
A hundred Vyavasthána-prajṇaptis make a *Hetuhila ;*
A hundred Hetuhilas make a *Karahu ;*[23]
A hundred Karahus make a *Hetvindriya ;*
A hundred Hetvindriyas make a *Samáptalambha ;*
A hundred Samáptalambhas make a *Gaṇanágati ;*[24]
A hundred Gaṇanágatis make a *Niravadya ;*
A hundred Niravadyas make a *Mudrábala ;*[25]
A hundred Mudrábalas make a *Sarvabala ;*
A hundred Sarvabalas make a *Visaṇjṇágati ;*
A hundred Visaṇjṇágatis make a *Sarvasaṇjṇá ;*
A hundred Sarvasaṇjṇás make a *Vibhútaṅgamá ;*[26]
A hundred Vibhútaṅgamás make a *Tallakshaṇa.*[27]

"Were atoms cast off to the number of a Tallakshaṇa, the mountain king Sumeru would be exhausted. After this comes the reckoning called *Dhvajágravatí,* and in reckoning it all the sand of the Ganges river, thrown grain by grain would be exhausted. After this comes the sum of *Dhvajágraniśámaṇi,* next to it *Váhanaprajṇapti,* and next *Kurutá ;* next to it comes *Sarvanikshepá,* in counting which, grain by grain, the grains of sand in ten river Ganges would be exhausted. After this comes *Agrasárá,* which numbers as many as the grains of sand in a hundred millions of

Ganges river. Even after this comes *Paramáṇurajaḥpraveśánugata.*" Of this no comparison can be made with anything that exists in the world, except with the Tathágata Bodhisattva when having established himself on the top of the noble Bodhimaṇḍa, he is about to face the sanctification of all religion."

Arjuna enquired, "how is the table beginning with *Paramáṇurajas* reckoned, Prince?" (Long measure.)

The Bodhisattva replied:

"Seven Paramáṇurajases (subtile atoms) make a *Reṇu;*

Seven Reṇus make a *Truṭi,* (a visible atom);

Seven Truṭis a *Vátáyanarajas* (a mote that blows in through a window);

Seven Vátáyanarajases a *S'aśarajas* (a mote that is seen in a moon-beam, or that which is raised by the motion of a hare);

Seven S'aśarajases an *Eḍakarajas* (dust-grain on a ram);

Seven Eḍakarajases a *Gorajas* (dust grain on a cow);

Seven Gorajases, a *Likshá* (egg of a louse—a nit);

Seven Likshás a *Sarshapa* (mustard seed);

Seven Sarshapas a *Yava,* (a barleycorn);

Seven Yavas an *Aṅguliparva* (an inch—width of the thumb);

Twelve Aṅguliparvas a *Vitasti* (a span);

Two Vitastis a *Hasta* (cubit);

Four Hastas a *Dhanus* (a bow);

One thousand Dhanuses a *Kros'a* as current in the Mágadha country (Indian mile);

Four Kros'as, a *Yojana* (an Indian league).

Who amongst us knows how many Paramáṇurajases go to form a *Yojanapiṇḍa* (a cube of one Yojana)?[28]

Arjuna said, "Even I, Prince, am bewildered; what shall I say of people of limited understanding? Will you, Prince, define of how many atoms a Yojanapiṇḍa is made?"

The Bodhisattva replied, "In a Yojanapiṇḍa there are atoms which have to be reckoned at a full Niyutas of Akshobhya, thirty hundred thousands of Niyutas, sixty hundred thousand Koṭis'atas, twenty-two Koṭis, five millions, and twelve thousands. These added together make a Yojanapiṇḍa. At this rate the continent of Jambu includes seven thousand yojanas; Goḍáníya[28] includes eight thousand yojanas; Púrvavideha nine thousand yojanas; the island of Uttarakuru ten thousand yojanas. Calculating in this way the four continents of this region would amount to a full hundred koṭis. The great oceans of these four continents also number a hundred koṭis. The Chakravála and the Maháchakravála mountains[29] each include a hundred koṭis. So does each of the following;[30] *viz.*, the kingdoms of the four Mahárájika Devas, the region of the Trayastriñśa Devas, that of the Yámas, that of the Tushitas, that of the Nirmáṇaratis, that of the Paranirmitavasavartis, that of the Brahmakáyikas, that of the Brahmapurohitas, that of the Brahmapársadyas, that of the Mahábrahmas, that of the Parittábhas, that of the Apramáṇábhas, that of the A'bhás'varas, that of the Parittaśubhas, that of the Apramáṇaśubhas, that of the S'ubhakṛitsnas, that of the Anabhrakas, that of the Puṇyaprasavas, that of the Vṛihatphalas, that of the Asañgisattvas, that of the Avṛihas, that of the Sudṛiśas, that of the Sudarśanas, and that of the Akanishṭha Devas. What is said is this. The three thousand great thousand regions are immense and extensive. Whatever hundred yojanas of atoms are included in these three thousand great thousand regions, and whatever thousand yojanas to koṭis of yojanas, whatever niyutas of yojanas, and yojana-agrasáras are calculated, are all computed on the basis of atoms, so there are countless numbers of atoms in these three thousand great thousand regions."

Thus, on the rules of numbers having been explained by the Bodhisattva, Arjuna, the astrologer-councillor, and the whole host of the S'ákyas were pleased, exhilarated, delighted and wonder-struck. Each of these remained garbed in a single piece of cloth, and covered the Bodhisattva with all their other clothes and ornaments. The astrologer-councillor Arjuna recited these two Gáthás:—

"Such wonderful knowledge in reckoning koṭis'ata, ayuta,

niyuta, niyutáni, kañkara, vimbara, akshobhya and beyond them exceeds my power. (1)

"But behold, O S'ákyas, he has alone, by a single effort, given us the reckoning of all the atoms in the three thousand regions, of grass, of herbs and of drops in water. What more wonderful can be effected by the five hundred (S'ákyas) ?" (2)

Now gods and men by hundreds of thousands raised shouts of cheers and laughter by hundreds of thousands. Some Devaputras, coming under the sky, recited this Gáthá :

"Whatever knowledge has been acquired by the mind of the whole of the animated creation of the three orders, has been derogated, for has not all knowledge of calculation been stored in one being who knows everything?"

Thus, Bhikshus, were all the S'ákya youths discomfitted, and thus did the Bodhisattva excel them all.

Subsequently in leaping, jumping, and running the Bodhisattva excelled all. Thereupon the Devaputras, coming under the sky, recited the following Gáthás :

"By fasts, austerity and restrictions; by mercy, control of the passions, and benevolence practised for ten million kalpas; by making light his body and mind, he has become the leader. Listen to his excellences. (1)

"Do ye behold in this being, now abiding as a householder, the noblest of beings. He can travel over all the ten quarters of the globe in a moment. He has worshipped with gold and jewels Jinas without number, and in regions without limit. (2)

"You cannot know his advent and his departure, which proceed from his miraculous powers. What is there in this earth that cannot be performed by him, or which exalt him not in merit?" (3)

Thus did the Bodhisattva excel all.

Then the S'ákyas said, "Let the Prince now excel in wrestling. He should be examined about it."[31]

The Bodhisattva was then standing aside. All the five hundred S'ákya youths at once rushed forward to wrestle with him.

Thirty-two S'ákya youths stood forward ready to fight. Then Nanda and A'nanda went forward, but, on being touched by the hand of the Bodhisattva, fell on the ground, unable to withstand his might and vigour. Then Prince Devadatta, vain, proud, mighty, full of S'ákya prowess, anxious to encounter the Bodhisattva, strutting round the arena under the sky, in playfulness fell on the Bodhisattva. The Bodhisattva, unceremoniously but without any excitement, easily seized him with his right hand, wheeled him round three times in mid air for his punishment, and then, without feeling any enmity, with a benevolent mind, cast him on the ground without hurting his body.

Then the Bodhisattva said, "Enough, enough of this. Let all of you come united to wrestle with me."

Then all the youths in a body fell upon the Bodhisattva; but, touching him, they felt his majesty, vigour, prowess and firmness to be intolerable, and touched by him they tumbled on the ground. Thereupon hundreds of thousands of gods and men burst forth in hilarious cheers. The Devaputras, coming under the sky, cast heavy showers of flowers, and in one voice recited the following Gáthás:—

"All the wicked wrestlers in the ten quarters of the globe become as nothing before him. They are instantly overcome by the bull among men. They fall on the ground the moment they are touched. (1)

"He can pound into dust[32] with his bare hands the Meru, the Sumeru, the Vajraka,[33] the Chakravála, and whatever other mountains there exist in the ten sides of the earth. What wonder is there that sons of mortals should drop before him? (2)

"He will, when about to attain the absolute knowledge under the noble tree, through his benevolence, destroy the wicked veteran Mára, the friend of darkness, with all his army, his horse and war-chariots." (3)

Having done this the Bodhisattva excelled all.

Then Daṇḍapáṇi thus addressed the S'ákya youths: "All this has been seen and examined. Let him show now his power in archery."[34]

Then an iron drum was set up as a target at a distance of two kros'as, for Ánanda. The target for Devadatta was set up at a distance of four kros'as. The target for Sundarananda was set up at a distance of six kros'as. A target was set up at a distance of two yojanas for Daṇḍapáṇi. For the Bodhisattva the iron target was set up at a distance of ten kros'as; and beyond it were ranged seven palm trees and a mechanical image of a boar, made of iron. Ánanda hit his target at the distance of two miles, but could not send his arrow further. The drum at the fourth kros'a was hit by Devadatta, but he could shoot his arrow no further. The drum at the sixth kros'a was hit by Sundarananda, but he could not send his arrow any further. Daṇḍapáṇi hit his target at the distance of two yojanas, and the arrow remained fixed in it, but could go no further. Then the Bodhisattva stepped forward, but every bow he took up snapped on the attempt to string it.

Thereupon he said: "Is there any bow in this city which will withstand my stringing it, and my bodily force and vigour?"

The king replied, "Yes, my son."

The Prince said, "Which is it, sire?"

The king. "Your grandfather, my son, was named Siñhahanu, (having the jaws of a lion). His bow is now worshipped with garlands and aromatics in the temple of the gods. None has been as yet able to string it, much less to draw it."

The Bodhisattva. "May it please your majesty to send for it from the temple; I shall try it, until I have stringed it."

Now, all the S'ákya youths tried their utmost, but failed to string that bow, much less to draw it. At last it was stringed by Daṇḍapáṇi, the S'ákya; but even with his utmost might and main he failed to draw it. The Bodhisattva then stringed it. Then without rising from his seat, but assuming the half bedstead position, (*i. e.*, leaning on one knee) he took it with his left hand, and drew it with a single finger of his right hand. The sound of the twang of that bow resounded all over the city of Kapilavastu. The citizens were all bewildered, and enquired of each other, "Whence is this sound?" The reply was, "Prince

Siddhártha has twanged his grandfather's bow, and thence the sound."

Thereupon all men and gods, in great delight, burst forth in hundreds of thousands of hilarious cheers and laughter. Devaputras, coming under the sky, thus addressed the king and the multitude:

"Since the saint has stringed the bow without rising from his seat and the ground, he will doubtless soon fully attain his object after overthrowing the army of Mára."

Now, Bhikshus, the Bodhisattva, having stringed the bow, took an arrow, and, with great force and vigour, shot it. That arrow successively pierced the targets of Ánanda, Devadatta, Sundarananda and Daṇḍapáṇi, and, passing on to the iron drum at the tenth kros'a, pierced it through, as also the seven palm trees and the mechanical boar made of iron, and disappeared within the earth. The spot where the arrow touched the earth was so pierced as to appear like a well. To this day that spot is called *Sarakúpa*, "the arrow well."[85] Hundreds of thousands of men and gods burst forth in loud and repeated shouts and cheers. All the S'ákyas became joyous and struck with wonder. But this feat and these accomplishments in art are not particularly wonderful. Devaputras, coming under the sky, thus addressed the king and the multitude:

"Why this wonder and wherefore?

"This being, who will assume the seat of former Buddhas on this earth, assuming the bow of might and the arrow of nihility and soullessness, will kill the master of evil, pierce through the network of darkness which envelopes the eye (of reason), and attain the prosperous, stainless, griefless ultimatum of Bodhi."

Saying this, the Devaputras showered flowers on the Bodhisattva, and then disappeared.

In this way he excelled in all arts and accomplishments current among men, exceeding all in human and celestial regions—in leaping; in running foremost; in writing, printing and arithmetic; in wrestling and archery; in quick walking, jumping, and swimming; in the use of arrows; in riding on the neck of the elephant, on the back of the horse, and on the chariot; in fighting with bows; in firmness, vigour, and veteranship; in wrestling; in the use of the goad and the lasso; in vehicles for going upwards, forwards and on water; in boxing; in hair-dressing; in cropping, piercing, swimming, and high jump; in guessing; in divining others' thoughts; in explaining enigmas; in hard beating; in dice-playing; in poetry and grammar; in book-writing; in assuming shapes (pantomime); in the art of decoration; in reading; in pyrotechnics; in playing on the Víná; in music and dancing; in reciting songs; in story-telling; in dances; in symphony; in dramatic exhibition; in masquerade; in making flower garlands; in shampooing; in tinting jewels; in dyeing cloth; in jugglery; in explaining dreams; in divining from the cries of birds; in the knowledge of the characteristics of women, men, horses, cattle, goats, and eunuchs; in demonology; in the Vedic glossary; in the Nigamas, Puráṇas, Itihásas, Vedas, grammar, Nirukta, (lexicography), S'ikshá, (phonology), Chhandas (versification), yajna rituals (kalpa), and astronomy; in the S'áñkhya, the Yoga and the Vaiśeshika doctrines; in ceremonials; in dress; in political economy *(arthavidyá)*; in ethics, legerdemain (Áścharya), and surgery (Ásura); in the knowledge of the cries of mammals and birds; in disputation *(hetuvidyá)*; in lac ornaments; in wax-works; in needle-work; in basket-work; in leaf-cutting; in perfumery.[36]

Now, at that time Daṇḍapáṇi, the S'ákya, bestowed his daughter, the S'ákya maiden Gopá, on the Bodhisattva. She was caused by king S'uddhodana to be duly married to the Bodhisattva. Having obtained her from amidst eighty-four thousand maidens, the Bodhisattva, according to human practice, gratified himself by enjoying and associating with her. Gopá was installed the chief queen amidst the eighty four thousand maidens, and she did not cover her face in the presence of any person, neither before her mother-in-law, nor before her father-in-law, nor before other persons of the house. They all advised her and argued with her.

A bride should not remain unhidden, but she (Gupá) was always manifest before all. Now, she, the Sákya daughter, hearing these words,[37] recited the following verses in the presence of all the people of the house:

"Venerable sirs, the uncovered state shows the best, whether when seated or when walking, even as jewels are seen most resplendent when mounted on a flagstaff.[38] (1)

"It is showy when going forward, and it is showy when coming back. Standing or sitting it is, venerable sirs, showy everywhere. (2)

"It is showy when speaking, as it is when one is silent, even as the sparrow (*kalavinka*)[39] is beautiful both in its appearance and in its voice. (3)

"A clever man endowed with learning, whether robed in kus'a grass, or in no clothes, or in miserable apparel, or lean, displays his beauty by his own merit. (4)

"He is ever resplendent, venerable sirs, who is free from sin, like an unadorned child. The sinner is never beautiful. (5)

"Those who have sin at heart but are sweet of speech, are like a pitcher smeared with nectar but full of poison. They are hard of heart, like the rough rock on the top of a mountain peak. They are unworthy of sight to all. (6)

"They appear pleasant like a child to all; they are, like sacred pools, beneficial to all; they are, venerable sirs, always like pitchers, full of curds and cream—pure, agreeable, and auspicious,—(7)

"who, avoiding the association of sin, have accepted the friendship of prosperity and the Three Jewels. Those, who rejecting sin accept the religion of Buddha, are always successful, alway auspicious, always beautiful. (8)

"Of what avail is hiding the face for them who have control over their person; who have overcome the evil tendencies of the organs; who have control over their speech, and are always of beautiful speech; whose secret organs have been pacified, and whose minds are always cheerful? (9)

"A thousand folds of cloth cannot hide the nature and mind of him who has not modesty and sense of propriety manifest in him, but he who has those qualities and is ever truthful—he may roam about everywhere in nudity, like a jewel unadorned. (10)

"What avails the hiding of the face to her whose mind is well nourished, whose organs are always under command, who is always satisfied with her husband, and never dreams of a stranger? She may always remain manifest like the sun or the moon. (11)

"Ṛishis, noble-minded persons, those who can divine the secrets in the hearts of others, the assemblage of gods, know well my motives. So long as my behaviour, my qualities, my prudence remains undisturbed, what need is there for me to cover my face with a veil?" (12)

King S'uddhodana heard these Gáthás pregnant with the wisdom and good sense of Gopá, the S'ákya maiden, and hearing them he was transported with joy, delight, and gratification. He bestowed on the lady a necklace made of brilliant rose-coloured pearls, valued at many hundreds and thousands of millions, and a gold necklace set off with many jewels and flowers, and then joyously exclaimed—

"Even as my son is adorned with many traits, so is my daughter resplendent with noble qualities. The two are noble beings who have come to me, each a piece of fresh butter like unto the other."

Then they returned home with the Bodhisattva at the head, in the order in which they had come out.

NOTES.

1. *The Prince having grown up*, p. 198. The Chinese version fixes the age at the nineteenth year, when the king provided the Prince with three palaces for the three principal seasons of the year, and a large retinue of attendants and handmaids. Separate servants were engaged to rub his person, to smooth it, to anoint it with aromatic oils, and to bathe it. There were among them hair-dressers, looking-glass holders, custodians of essences, of hair chaplets, and of the wardrobe. Every garment for the prince was made of Kásiká material, *i. e.*, silken, silk being used by the king and others for outer garments only. The Burmese version brings the age to the sixteenth year, when the palaces were provided and the marriage took place. The Siamese text follows the Burmese record.

2. *Some elders of the race, both male and female, thus addressed him*, p. 198. In the Chinese version the proposition comes from the king himself, who, adverting to the prophecy of Aśita, asks his councillors to devise means for preventing the Prince from becoming a hermit. The Siamese text says, "when the palaces were finished, the king announced his intention of raising his son to the sovereignty (making him vice king), and called upon the Śákya Princes to offer their daughters as his wives," (p. 120). The Burmese text summarily disposes of the subject by saying the Prince was married.

3. *He then reflected*, p. 199. This enquiry of the king about the Prince's choice and the latter's cogitations and reply are not noticed in the southern versions.

4. *Lotuses in sacred tanks, sprouting from mire*, p. 199. The purport is that good may proceed from evil, even as lotuses thrive in the mire at the bottoms of old tanks. This maxim convinces the Prince that marriage, though *in se* bad, would lead to good, and therefore it was proper for him to marry.

5. *Such should be the maiden, O king, whom I should marry*, p. 200. Although the cogitation is held in private, the verses, being designed for the information of the king, are directly addressed to the king.

6. *Thus addressed the family priest*, p. 200. This search for a bride is unnoticed in the southern versions. According to the Chinese the bride was discovered by the conversation which the Prince had with Yaśodhará in a drawing-room.

7. *Whosoever has these qualities*, p. 200. The theory of giving prominence to good qualities at the expense of caste could be appreciated only in the caste-ridden country of India, and therefore it finds no place in the Chinese and the southern versions. The author tries to take credit for liberality on this score, though the sequel does not bear him out. A S'ákya is selected at last. Perhaps his object was indirectly to extol the S'ákya race, which alone was the repository of all merit.

8. *The residence of Daṇḍapáṇi, a S'ákya*, p. 201. The Chinese version, following the Mahávastu Avadána, gives Mahánáma as the name of the father of Yaśodhará. He was a minister of state, and a member of the Vasita gotra. The Lalita-Vistara does not assign to Daṇḍpáṇi any ministerial office.

9. *Aśoka bouquets*, p. 202. The word in the Sanskrit text is *Aśoka-bháṇḍa*, *Aśoka* meaning the flower of the tree so named (*Jonesia aśoka*) or "griefless," *i. e.*, joyous, and *bháṇḍa*, an ornament,—an ornament of aśoka flowers, or an auspicious ornament. Rev. S. Beal makes the Chinese version have "every kind of jewelled ornament and delightful trifle (un lung)." The Tibetan text has been rendered by M. Foucaux into "ornements agréables." The word aśoka is seldom used in the sense of joyous or auspicious, and the flower of that name being a great favourite with Indian ladies even to this day, I think the flower is meant, and with it bouquets are the most appropriate trifles that could be made. The flowers are never strung into garlands, nor worn in any other way. On the 8th of the waxing moon in the month of Chaitra a fast is observed by Hindu women; and of that fast the most important parts are the embracing of the tree which is then in full bloom, and the eating of the blossoms thereof. According to the Rámáyaṇa, Sítá was confined by Rávaṇa in an aśoka grove, and the exemplary constancy which the lady evinced while so confined has associated the tree with constancy, and every young lady who wants to acquire that virtue courts the tree. Bouquets made of the blossoms of that tree are, therefore, very fitting presents to give to maidens.

10. *Repaired to the reception hall*, p. 202. The Chinese make the gate of the palace the place of reception. (Beal, p. 80.)

11. *Gopá, the daughter of Daṇḍapáṇi*, p. 202. Gopá is an *alias* of Yaśodhará. The Lalita-Vistara always uses Gopá, but the Mahávastu Avadána prefers Yaśodhará. The Chinese text follows the latter work.

12. *A ring worth many hundred thousands*, p. 202. The Chinese text has a hundred thousand, but like our text does not say whether they were pieces of silver or gold. Mr. Beal supplies the word gold. A very valuable ring is what the text means, its respect for figures being of the slenderest.

13. *No, we shall not disadorn the Prince for we will disadorn Mára*, p. 202. The young lady, by anticipation, identifies herself here with the Prince. The plural "we" cannot be honorific here. The reply in the Chinese text is much more natural and becoming. It runs thus—"It would be a pity for me to do that, and so deprive the prince of that which so much becomes him." (Beal, p. 81.) The Mahávastu Avadána assigns as a reason for her refusal some slights which the Prince had shown to Yaśodhará in two former existences; *cf.* my 'Sanskrit Buddhist Literature of Nepal,' pp. 126 & 129, and Beal's 'Legendary Life of Buddha,' p. 93.

14. *The king, thereupon, caused a proclamation to be published by the ringing of bells*, p. 203. The word in the Sanskrit text is *ghaṇṭá-ghosha*, "the sound of ghaṇṭá." Ghaṇṭá ordinarily means a bell, but it may also mean a gong, but for the latter the common term is *káñsya*, and I prefer, therefore, the first meaning, though I have nowhere seen any mention in Sanskrit books of the use of bells for giving publicity to proclamations. Bells seem to have been the archetype of the modern tomtom and the English auctioneer's bell. According to the Burmese text the instrument used was a drum.

15. *Planted a flag of victory*, p. 204. The lady takes a more forward place in the tournament than what is usual among Indian maidens. She assumes the position of *La Royne de la beauté et des amours* in a Norman tournament, and her flag occupies the place of the prize which the noblest lady offers the victor at a European tournament. In the Chinese text it is her father who places her at a conspicuous place and proclaims—"Whoever the victor may

be in this contest of skill and of arms, he shall carry off this my daughter as his prize." This is in accord with the reproach of Daṇḍapáṇi as given in the Chinese text. It runs thus: "Our S'ákya rules are these—if a man excel all others in martial exercises, then he is crowned victor, and carries off the prize of the fairest maiden; but if he fail, then no such prize can be his. I fear the Prince Royal has been brought up delicately, and has learned none of the arts and practices of chivalry, either in tilting, or wrestling, or boxing; but how can I wed my child to one so utterly void of skill in these arts, as I fear the prince to be?" (Beal, p. 84.) The Siamese reproach is—"O king! thy son is of proper birth, and his appearance is admirable; but so far as we know he has never learned anything, and has no knowledge or accomplishments. Therefore we hesitate to offer our daughters to him." (Alabaster, p. 120.)

In the Burmese text the tournament is brought on after the marriage. "The prince was devoting all his time to the pleasures of his harem, and his relatives strongly remonstrated against his mode of living which precluded him from applying himself to the acquisition of these attainments befitting his exalted position." (Bigandet, p. 52.) The Prince, in reply, comes forward to prove his fitness.

The idea of the tournament has been borrowed from Hindu legends, with such alterations of details as were thought necessary to cover its borrowed character. Everything connected with the Prince was miraculous, and a miracle had to be designed for each event, and the rich mine of the Hindu legends yielded the materials for the miracles. Even the miraculous character of his birth is based on a Hindu legend. The idea of bringing forth S'ákya from the left side of his mother's womb has obviously been borrowed from the Hindus with whom it prevailed from a very remote period of antiquity. In the Sañhitá of the Ṛig Veda (IV, 18) there occurs a hymn in which it is given at length. The story runs that Vámadeva, while in his mother's womb, thought of signalising his birth, by being born in an uncommon way. His mother, perceiving this, invited Aditi and her son Indra to come and expostulate with him, whereupon the following conversation takes place:

1. [" Indra speaks.] 'This is the old and recognised path by

which all the gods are born, so, when fullgrown, let him be born in the same manner; let him not cause the loss of this his mother.'

2. [" Vámadeva speaks.] 'Let me not come forth by this path, for it is difficult (of issue): let me come forth obliquely from the side: many acts unperformed by others are to be accomplished by me: let me contend (in war) with one (enemy) in controversy with one opponent.

3. 'He (Indra) has asserted (that it will) cause the death of my mother: let me not proceed by the usual way, but proceed quickly, according (to my will)."'—*Wilson's Ṛig Veda*, III, pp. 153*f.*

The idea of perfect knowledge of learning in early boyhood is not confined to the Buddhists. The Jains have a similar story about the last of their great saints. According to them: " When Mahávíra—so the story goes, and it is with slight variations repeated over and over again—was about eight years old, his parents thought it time that he should learn to read and write. With great pomp they accordingly took him to school and introduced him to the Guru. Then Indra, by the shaking of his throne advised of what was going on here below, came down from heaven, assumed the form of an old Bráhman, and asked the child to solve the grammatical difficulties by which the mind of the Guru had long been disturbed, and which nobody had been able to explain before. Mahávíra not only answered all the questions put to him, but he also propounded various kinds of grammatical rules, and his utterances became the Jainendra grammar. The Guru, delighted with what he had heard, made Mahávíra a Guru too, and saluted by Indra, the child returned home with his parents." (*Indian Antiquary* for March, 1881.) In the Bhágavata, the story occurs in connexion with Kṛishṇa.

The wrestling feats are obviously revised versions of the gymnastic exercises of the Páṇḍus and the Kurus, and the archery follows the story of Arjuna's feat at the court of Drupada, who had promised to give away his daughter Draupadí to whoever would hit a target (a fish) from its shadow in a saucer of water. The bow incident comes from the Rámáyaṇa, and in Europe it has its counterpart in Homer.

16. *Prince Devadatta*, p. 204. A cousin and rival of Prince Siddhártha. He had been ever at war with his relative, and often tried to bring disgrace on him during his monastic life. *Cf.* My 'Sanskrit Buddhist Literature of Nepal.' The incidence of killing the elephant occurs in the Chinese text after the tournament, in the journey home.

17. *He has not done a becoming act*, p. 204. The negative particle is wanting in my Sanskrit texts; but it occurs in the Tibetan version, and is obviously required by the context.

18. *Elephant hollow*, p. 204. Mr. Carlyle has identified this with a circular tank at Bhuila, between the southern ditch of Bhuila Dih and village of Jaitpur. It is called *Háthi Gaḍhe* or *Háthi kund*. *Cf.* Arch. Survey Report, vol. XII, p. 159.

19. *And waved their clothes*, p. 204. The ancient Indian counterpart of the modern English waving of handkerchiefs.

20. *By the great toe*, p. 205. How an elephant can be seized by a person with his great toe only is a mechanical problem which the Buddhist faithful alone can solve. A kick is what is meant.

21. *Arjuna, the astrologer-councillor*, p. 205. In the Chinese text the ministerial position of this worthy is not adverted to. He is simply "a very eminent master of arithmetic." (Beal, p. 85.)

22. *Karahu*, p. 207. Kalahu in Tibetan.

23. *Gaṇanágati*, p. 207. Gaṇagati in Tibetan.

24. *Mudrábala*, p. 207. Mudrabala in Tibetan.

25. *Vibhútaṅgama*, p. 207. Vibhutágama in Tibetan.

26. *Tallakshaṇa*, p. 207. The names are mostly new to Hindu Sanskrit arithmetic. The table does not correspond with one given by Burnouf in his *Lotus de la bonne loi*.

27. *Yojanapiṇḍa*, p. 208. The Hindu table of weights begins with *Trisareṇu*, 28 of which make a *likshá*. According to Hindu physicians the Trisareṇu is made up of 30 Paramáṇus. Neither mode of calculation corresponds with the Buddhist scheme. *Cf.* Colebrooke's 'Essays' I, p. 529, and Thomas' 'Initial Coinage of Bengal,' and 'Pathan Kings of Delhi.'

28. *Goḍániya*, p. 209. Following M. Foucaux, I take this to be Gauḍa, or northern Bengal.

29. *Chakravála and Maháchakravála mountains*, p. 209. The Chakravála is a range of mountains which encircles the earth; and Maháchakravála is situated beyond that chain.

30. *So does each of the following*, p. 209. In the Sanskrit text the phrase "hundred koṭis" is repeated before every name. To obviate this frequent repetition I have introduced this line to cover all.

31. *He should be examined about it*, p. 209. The Chinese text does not refer to this wrestling.

32. *He can pound into dust*, p. 211. The word in the Sanskrit text is *masichúrṇa* "powdered lampblack," *i. e.*, so pounded as to be without grit, like lampblack.

33. *Vajraka*, p. 211. I have read of no account of this mountain.

34. *Let him show his skill in archery*, p. 211. The Chinese text here describes the appointment of one Sahadeva as the umpire.

35. *In perfumery*, p. 215. Some of the terms are not of clear import. They are obviously technical, but I know not the nature of the arts to which they were applied. The translations given are purely mechanical. The arts named, it will be seen, are in some respects different from the 64 kalás named in the Bhágavata Puráṇa (*ante*, p. 187). Negative evidence is not often of much value, but it is worthy of note that the text notices by name the Sáñkhya, the Yoga and the Vaiśeshika doctrines, but does not name the Mímáñsá and the Vedánta systems. The Nyáya is probably included in the *Hetuvidyá*. It is possible that *Kriyákalpa*, as distinct from *Yajnakalpa*, stands for the Mímáñsá. Its position between the Yoga and Vaiśeshika would suggest the idea. I have dislocated it and translated it into ceremonials.

37. *Mounted on a flagstaff*, p. 215. A jewel of great excellence mounted on a pole and held up high, sheds its lustre so as to appear like a lamp, hence the simile. (*Cf. ante*, p. 35.)

38. *Sparrow*, p. 215. I suspect the word *kalaviṅka* stands here for some other bird than a sparrow; but I know of no such. The plumage and voice of a sparrow are not such as to be worthy of the comparison here made.

CHAPTER XIII.

THE IMPLORATION.

The celestial consultation. The Bodhisattva's knowledge of time. Exhortatory verses. Description of the palace. Celestial implorations.

Now, Bhikshus, when the Bodhisattva was passing his time in the gynaceum, many Devas, Nágas, Yakshas, Gandharvas, Asuras, Garuḍas, Kinnaras, Mahoragas, Brahmás, and Lokapálas, proclaiming their delight, came to the place, eager to offer worship to the saint. At another time this idea struck those beings: Verily, for long is the noble being tarrying in the gynaceum. These people matured for a long period with the fourfold blessings of charity, sweet speech, good service, and sense of equality, are urging him to impart religious instruction, so that the four religious vessels may disappear, and the Bodhisattva, subsequently issuing forth from his home, may acquire the absolute and thorough Bodhi knowledge. Thereupon they respectfully and cheerfully joined their hands and saluted him. Then they stood aside with an anxious desire to know when it will be that they will have the felicity of beholding the noble and pure being renounce his home, and, renouncing it, take his seat at the root of the great and supereminent tree, and, overthrowing Mára, attain the sequenceless and thorough Bodhi knowledge,—that he may be endowed with the ten powers of Tathágatas,[1] the four Tathágata accomplishments,[2] the eighteen sections of Buddha religion,[3]—turning the twelve-formed wheel of religion with its three transitions,[4] and by his Bauddha duties and auspicious emancipatory speech gratify men, gods and Asuras.

Now, Bhikshus, the Bodhisattva had for a long period, extending over innumerable kalpas, been agreeable to all. He was the great teacher of all worldly and superworldly duties. He was for long acquainted with the proper season, the proper moment, and the proper time for the performance of all duties which has auspiciousness for their root. He was infallible, well knowing, and thoroughly versed in the five realities.[5] He had attained mastery over the chapter on occult powers, over the organs of his body, over the knowledge of proper and improper times. He pervades all time, and does not exceed the limit like the great ocean after it has reached the height of the tide.[6] Endowed with the power of his intellect and understanding, he had himself learnt everything. He knew this is the proper time for this; this is the proper time for acceptance, and this for refusal; this is the proper time for collecting, and this for dispensing; this is the proper time for negligence, this for speaking, this for silence; this is the time to go out, this for accepting asceticism; this is the time for reading, this for pleasure, and this for deliberation; this is the time for mixing with Kshatríyas, this with Bráhmaṇas, householders, and courtiers, this for Devas, Nágas, Yakshas, Gandharvas, Asuras, Garuḍas, Kinnaras, Mahoragas, S'akra, Brahmá, Lokapálas, Bhikshus, Bhikshukís, Upásakas, Upásikás; this is the time for preaching religion; this is the time for the final dissolution. Everywhere and at all times a Bodhisattva is proficient in the knowledge of time, he is the pervader of time.

Now, again, Bhikshus, this is the rule with reference to all Bodhisattvas at their last existence, that when they are dwelling in the female apartment they should for certain be inspired by the Buddhas inhabiting the ten quarters of the earth, with such religious hymns as these, accompanied by the harmony of musical instruments.

On that subject this is said:

"The best among all those foremost men who dwell in the ten quarters of the earth, inspire the noblest of beings with these delightful Gáthá songs, with the accompaniment of sweet music. (1)

"Beholding living creatures groaning under a hundred evils, thou, oh Lord, our well-doer, didst, in former times, resolve that thou wouldst redeem those of this world who would seek thy asylum. (2)

"O pure one, O hero, recall to mind thy resolution for the good of the earth. This is the time, this is the moment, this is the opportunity; issue forth from this noble mansion, O noble Ṛishi. (3)

"For them, of yore, thou didst reject thy head, thy hands, thy feet and many magnificent treasures in order that thou mayst encounter Bodhi knowledge; thou art the controller of men and gods, the noblest in creation, the endowed with a hundred merits. (4)

"Thou hast performed fasts and penances through thy good conduct. Through thy forbearance thou hast done good to the earth. By thy vigour thou hast acquired all noble qualities. In meditation and knowledge there is none equal to thee in the three regions. (5)

"Through thy benevolence many immersed in passion and filth of innumerable kinds have been translated to manifest redemption. Thy mercy has purged many of their evil qualities and falsehood, and made them wise. (6)

"Through thy knowledge of virtue, through thy auspicious soul, through thy knowledge of meditation, through thy immaculate fasts and penances, thou showest resplendent in the ten quarters, even as the pure moon without a cloud. (7)

"These and many such musical sounds reverberating from the voice of Jinas and calculated to overpower men and gods, inspire thee. This is thy time; renounce and come forth." (8)

Now, Bhikshus, the palace in which the Bodhisattva resided was replete with every requisite for enjoyment, rivalling the abode of gods. It was a noble palace, furnished with covered terraces, balconies, gateways, windows, halls, and pavilions. It was decorated with all kinds of jewels and beautiful ornaments tastefully set off. Uplifted on it were parasols, flags and pennants, ornamented with numerous strings of jewelled bells. Hundreds of thousands of silken fabrics streamed all about it. Innumerable jewels were set on it. Garlands of pearls were suspended from it. It was provided with stairs decorated with silken carpets and jewels. It was begirt with silken draperies and garlands. It was redolent with the fumes of aromatic pills and pastilles. It had awnings of rich stuffs spread everywhere. Pleasant, sweet-scented flowers of all seasons and well-blown tank lillies and fresh lotuses were enjoyable everywhere in it. It resounded with the sweet voice of patraguptas, parrots, mainas, koels, geese, peacocks, bráhmini geese, kuṇálas, sparrows, partridges and birds of various other kinds. It was provided with delightful floors, blue as the lapis-lazuli. Every form about it was pleasant to the sight. It was the delighter of undelighted eyes. It was the exciter of gratification and enjoyment. It was in this noble mansion that the Bodhisattva then resided. He was dwelling in this house with wide and excellent corridors. His person was stainless, dirtless, and free from foulness. He had not laid aside his garlands and ornaments. His body was anointed with unguents, fragrant as the surabhi flower.[7] His body was draped in auspicious, pure, white, stainless vestments. He was lying on an exquisitely formed bed, soft as the down on the pod of the káchilindika, and decorated with numorous bouquets of excellent flowers. He was constantly beserved with unobjectionable, agreeable, beneficient objects of enjoyment, even as the wives of the immortals. He was being entertained by the music of conch-shells, trumpets, drums, *paṇasa, tunuva, víná, vallaki, táḍáva,* and damsels were enlivening him with the soft, pleasing, sweet, gratifying music of the flute. At that time issued forth, with the voice of the clarion, the following exhortative verses from the Lord Buddhas residing in the ten quarters of the globe:

"Whatever the joyous and well-disposed damsels charmingly sounded with their flutes, through the influence of the noblest Jinas in the ten quarters of the globe, the same manifested themselves in diverse and beautiful Gáthás. (1)

"Beholding these crowds without a protector, thou didst resolve of yore, hero, to deliver them, after acquiring the rank devoid of disease and grief, (*i. e.*, of a Buddha,) from disease, death and other pains. (2)

"That resolve was noble. Now quickly issue forth from this house; betake to the surface of the earth on which dwell many Ṛishis, and acquire the unrivalled Jina wisdom. (3)

"In former times thou didst abandon precious wealth and jewels—thy hands and thy feet, and thy life; this is now thy time, great sage, do overflow the earth with the perennial stream of religion. (4)

"In former times thy conduct was noble and pure and perfect. Thou didst then bestow a hundred blessings by thy speech. Thy conduct is unrivalled; O great sage, redeem the world from its diverse pains. (5)

"Through thy forbearance thou hast accomplished a hundred noble acts; through thy forbearance thou hast cheerfully borne many hard things said against thee; through thy forbearance thy soul is fixed on mercy and self-control. O king of the bipeds, turn thy mind to renunciation. (6)

"In former times thy firm, immovable, unshaken vigour had spread wide, overcoming a hundred Namuchis with their armies; do dispel the three-fold pain.[8] (7)

"For that thou didst undergo fasts and penances. Bearing in mind the sins and pains of the Kali age, do thou rain the unfailing water of immortality, and sooth those who are ever thirsty and helpless. (8)

"Calling to mind thy former noble resolve, and quickly issuing forth from this excellent house, do soothe the thirsty with the waters of immortality, after thyself acquiring the immortal and griefless state. (9)

"By the acquisition of wisdom thy virtuous knowledge has become wide and extended and endless; do thou shed the auspicious and grateful light of wisdom for the ignorant and those who follow the wrong path. (10)

"Thou hast practised a hundred acts of benevolence for the development of the blessing of mercy; whatever thou hast practised, do practise the same for the good of the world. (11)

"Such Gáthás formed of beautiful flowers strung together

without a thread, and full of the vigour of the Jinas of the ten quarters of the globe, and resounding through diverse musical instruments, exhorted the prince reposing on his couch. (12)

"And again, while the delightful and enticing charmers pleasingly and sweetly sang with the aid of musical instruments, the Jinas of the ten quarters, the controllers of gods and men, so resounded these musical notes as to echo forth from mountains. (13)

"Thou hast acquired many virtues for the good of creation. Thou hast mastered the merits of Jinas in thy career. Oh, recall to mind, do recall to mind, thy former fasts and penances; do quickly repair to the noble tree and attain the immortal rank. (14)

"Thirsty are mortal men devoid of the merits of Jinas. In thee are reposited the merits of intelligence, cheerfulness, and power. Thou art the bestower of the nectar of immortality. Thou art endowed with the ten occult powers. O adored of wise men, O prince, do thou swiftly distribute the nectar. (15)

"Forsaking, in former times, wealth, jewels and gold in this earth; forsaking friends and sons, the earth with its cities and fairs; forsaking even thy race, thy hands, thy feet, and thy eyes and even thy head, thou didst bless the world by thy devotion to Jina merits. (16)

"In former times, when thou wast born a son to a mortal,[9] a man, standing in front, addressed thee in these words, "Pray, bestow on me this earth with all its towns and fairs," and, in reply, thou didst grant the gift most cheerfully, and without the least uneasiness of mind. (17)

"In former times, when thou wast born sovereign of men in the family of a Bráhmaṇ, thou didst do service to thy seniors, and injured no one. Thou didst place, O noble Bráhmaṇ, numbers in benignity, and thou didst then, lord, retire to thy place. (18)

"In former times, O prince, when thou wast born a noble Ṛishi, an irate king of the Kali age[10] tore asunder the members of thy body. After performing the duties of thy race without any disturbance of mind, thou didst depart for thy home with thy hands and feet entire. (19)

"Remember, again, that when in former times thou wast born the son of a Ṛishi[11] and dwelt in penance in a mountain home, thou wast destroyed by a poisoned arrow shot by a king, thou didst show thy mercy to the king, and didst not feel disturbed in mind. (20),

"In former times when thou, greatly endowed with merit, didst live as the lord of deer[12] and ramble over hills, rivers and marshes, according to thy list, a barbarian entrapped thee, and thou didst follow him without being afflicted in heart on that account. (21)

"In former times when thou wast born a Bráhmaṇ, a precious jewel of thine fell into the depths of the ocean and by thy superior powers thou didst recover it therefrom. (22)

"In former times when thou wast a noble Ṛishi, a bird approached thee[13] and said, "be thou my asylum." Thou didst reply, "you are safe here," and, for his sake, thou didst give up thy own person, but never forsook the bird. (23)

"Remember, again, that when formerly a Ṛishi asked thee to count the leaves of a tree under which he dwelt, thou didst count the leaves on the tree and never made a mistake. (24)

"O, thou of white qualities, when thou didst live as a parrot on a tree,[14] thou didst not, when the tree withered and died, forsake it, knowing it to be thy home. When the king of the gods came to know of it, he recalled with delight thy qualities, and produced a worthy tree for thy home. (25)

"Thus, unrivalled are thy fasts and penances. Thou hast, owner of merits, achieved many good deeds. This is the time for thee to renounce the earth with all its towns, and quickly to place the creation in the exercise of the virtues of Jinas. (26)

"When the charming damsels with their persons decorated with ornaments and rich vestments, were singing in harmony with the accompaniment of excellent music, there arose, through Jina merit, from the ten quarters of space, these Gáthás of varied and mellifluous sounds in harmony with the cadence of music. (27)

"From many millions of kalpas this was, O lamp of the universe, thy resolve, "I shall be born here for the redemption of the creation subject to disease and death." Do thou, lion among men, call to mind that former resolve. The time has come for thy renunciation, king of the bipeds. (28)

"As a mortal son on earth innumerable have been the benefactions that have been given away by thee; thou hast given away wealth, gold, precious stones, rare vestments, beautiful jewels, thy own hands and feet and eyes; dear sons and thriving kingdoms have been given away by thee; and never hast thou, devoid of the defects of the dwellers of hell, ever denied a prayer. (29)

"O thou auspicious king, thou of the rabbit mark, (*i. e.*, beautiful as the moon bearing the mark of the hare on its breast,) with a mouth set with handsome teeth, with mind embued with mercy and benevolence, crowned with jewels, refulgent as the moon; beginning with these, O hero of the royal race, thou hast done many noble acts for the guidance of many royal personages. (30)

"Thou hast, O Sugata, for many kalpas practised good conduct—conduct flawless as the mani jewel[15]—conduct which has purified good conduct. Thou hast practised it with the same assiduity with which the yak preserves its hair.[16] Thou hast practised good conduct for the good of this world. (31)

"By thy devotion to good conduct, O noble elephant,[17] thou didst, when pierced by the arrow of thy enemy, covetousness, show him mercy and favour, and overshadow the heat of the day by such noble acts as giving up thy excellent tusks; but thou didst never abandon thy good conduct. (32)

"In the exercise of thy good conduct thou hast suffered from numerous travails—a thousand pains, many injurious speeches, and imprisonment. By thy patience thou hast, O king, preserved all in ease. And those who sought to kill thee have been pardoned. (33)

"When thou didst dwell in thy mountain abode as a bear thou didst carry on thy shoulders a man[18] benumbed with icy cold, and shivering through fear. Living in peace on fruits and roots, thou didst abstain from injuring him through thy forbearance. (34)

"Firm, fixed, immovable, unshaken was thy vigour. Thou hadst acquired Bodhi knowledge by thy fasts and penances, virtues and learning. Thy well-practised purity has become obedient to thee by the might of thy vigour. Lion among men, this is the time for the renunciation of thy home. (35)

"Formerly thou wast born on this earth as a noble horse of a golden colour.[19] Thou didst travel through the air to the island of the cannibals (Rákshasas). Relieving men there from a hundred pains thou didst place them in salvation. Beginning with such works, many noble deeds were accomplished by thy vigour. (36)

"O thou who hast overcome all pain by thy self-control, thou chief among meditationists, thou didst overcome the feeble, fickle mind bent on pleasing worldly objects, by thy merits, for the good of creation. By devotion to meditation do thou make men attached to meditation. (37)

"When formerly thou wast a Ṛishi immersed in calm meditation, without thyself being a king, thou didst instal men in the rank of royalty. By the aid of the tenfold blessings thou didst place them in the way to Brahmá. Thereby lost men, through the ten blessings, attained the home of Brahmá. (38)

"By thy knowledge of the ten quarters and their intermediaries and that of motion, thou art the knower of the true law; by thy knowledge of the conduct and the language of others and of the nature of the senses, as well as of civility, humility, and thought, thou art proficient. This is the time, prince, for renunciation. (39)

"In former times, beholding mankind suffering from perverted vision resulting from disease, death and diverse pains, thy mercy was moved in favour of the sufferers, and for the good of this region, thou, bereft of darkness, didst place them on the straight path. (40)

"Thus did numerous divers Gáthás of attractive merit, refulgent with the glory of Jinas, exhort the hero, saying, 'beholding the multitude of this earth groaning under pain, tarry not, oh noble Buddha! this is the time for renunciation.' (41)

"For the foremost being for whom delightful damsels bedecked with beautiful raiment, jewelled necklaces, and fragrant garlands, with loving earnestness exhilarated with divers music, Gáthás endowed with the ardour of Jinas thus burst forth in music: (42)

"For that for which thou didst for many kalpas renounce things hard to give up, for which thou didst assiduously cultivate good conduct, patience, vigour, meditation, and knowledge a hundred times over, for the welfare of creation—the time for that has now arrived. Think, leader, the thought of renunciation, and tarry not. (43)

"In former times thou didst abandon treasures of jewels, and ornaments of gold and silver, and perform rites of various kinds during different births; thou didst abandon dear wives and sons, extensive kingdoms and life. For the sake of Bodhi knowledge innumerable were the renunciations made by thee, of things the most difficult to renounce. (44)

"Thou wast Adinapunya, a king of renowned beauty; (thou wast) Nimindhara, Nimi, Kṛishṇabandhu, Bahmadatta, and Kes'arí; [20] thou wast Sahasrayayṇa, Dharmachinti, Archimat, and Driḍhadhana. For the sake of poor creatures thou didst abandon hard-earned wealth and sons, difficult to give up. (45)

"Thou didst, as Soma (Suta-soma), Diptavírya and Puṇyarasmi,[21] abandon the earth and vigour to uphold thy gratitude. A royal saint (*Rájarshi*), beautiful as the moon, a hero, an upholder of truth, a profound thinker, an unfailing reasoner, well disposed, and compassionate thou wast, O king. (46)

"Even as the kings Chandraprabha, Viśeshagámí, Renu, even as Kás'írája, the hero of charity, the son of Ratnachúḍa, and other royal personages gave away things difficult to part with, so do thou shower in a mighty downpour the rain of religion. (47)

"In former times thou didst behold noble beings, (numerous) as the grains of sand in the Ganges, and worship them as Buddhas with boundless devotion; thy desire was to be the foremost Buddha, the redeemer of mankind; the time for that has now arrived; do quickly issue forth from the excellent house. (48)

"First didst thou worship Amoghadarśi with a sála flower. After that thou didst devotedly look at Vairochana. Then didst thou offer Dundubhis'vara a myrobalan. Holding up a flambeau of hay thou didst visit the abode of Chandana (49)

"Beholding Reṇu entering a town thou didst throw on him a handful of gold dust; with religious zeal thou didst address Dharmes'vara, who sympathised with his worshippers. Beholding Sumantadars'í thou didst exclaim 'salutation, salutation.' With delight thou didst cast a golden necklace on the shoulders of Mahárchi. (50)

"Thou didst offer Dharmadhvaja a fringe; Nírodha a handful of munga seed; Jṇánketu an as'oka flower; Jogayána a driver;* Ratnaśikhi a lamp; Padmayoni herbs; Sarvábhibhu a pearl necklace; Ságara a lotus; (51).

"Padmagarbha an awning; Siñha a tent for protection from rain; Sárendraraája a beverage (or many things); Pushpita milk; Yasodatta Barleria flower (*kuruṇṭha*); Satyadarsi utensils; Jṇánameru prostration with body; Nágadatta vestment; (52)

"Atyuchchagámí agaru sandal; Vikshu a handful of salt; Mahaviyúha a lotus; Rasmirája jewels; S'ákya Muni† a handful of gold; Indraketu hymns; Súryánana a head ornament; Sumati a handful of gold and a tiara; (53)

* The passage may mean an asoka flower and a vehicle with a pair and a driver to Jagayan.

† There must be some mistake, the Siddhártha addressed is S'ákya, and he could not have made the offering to himself.

"Nágávibhu a mani jewel; Pushpa a white tent; Bhaishajyarája a jewelled umbrella; Siñhaketu a chair (or rug); Guṇágradhárí a jewelled net; Káśyapa musical instruments; Archiketu incense and powdered Agallochum; Chaitya flowers. (54)

"Thou hast given Akshobhyarája a temple; Lokapújita a garland; Tagaraśikhi a kingdom; Durjaya all kinds of essences; Maháپradípa self; Padmottara ornaments; Dharmaketu beautiful flowers; Dípakári a blue lotus. (55)

"These and other great men didst thou of yore worship; and thou didst other great deeds. Pray, think of those past Buddhas, their worship, and their ordinances. Helpless beings are now full of pain; issue forth from this noble mansion, and tarry not. (56)

"Thou didst obtain perfect forbearance by the very sight of Dipañkara, as also the fivefold imperishable science in due order.[22] Then didst thou introduce the worship with proper attention of the succeeding Buddhas in all regions for innumerable kalpas. (57)

"During the lapse of unnumbered ages many are the Buddhas that have come to an end. Even among these whereto are thy own various natures and names gone? All conditions are naturally mutable; there is nothing eternal in productions.[23] Inconstant are the passions and enjoyment of regal powers. Issue forth from the noble house. (58)

"Age, suffering, disease and death are coming on apace, so is the horrible, dreadful, fierce, mighty fire at the end of the kalpa.[24] All conditions are naturally perishable; there is nothing eternal in productions. Beings are immersed in great misery. Do ye, owner of merit, issue forth. (59)

"When the ladies with the diverse music of the lute and the flute were entertaining the supreme lord of men resting on his couch, the sound of the consort thus broke forth: (60)

"The threefold world is ablaze, burning with the fire of age, disease, suffering and death; it is without a protector. Without an asylum; the inert world is turning about like a bee confined in a jar. (61)

"Inconstant is the threefold world, even as an autumnal cloud, or the acting in a theatre. Birth on this earth is ever followed by fall, like a mountain stream. Life on this earth passes away lightly, quickly and rapidly, like the lightning in the sky. (62)

"On earth and in the region of the gods, in the three perishable paths,[25] are ignorant beings turning round and round under the influence of worldly desires and ignorance in the five conditions, like the wheel of a potter. (63)

"Overcome by dear beautiful forms, by constant sweet sounds, by pleasing smells and flavours, by the pleasures of touch, the world is held in the lasso of the evil genius (*Kali*),[26] even as a haltered deer in the hands of a fowler. (64)

"The effects of passion are always attended with fear and death; they are always injurious, full of grief and accidents; they are keen as the sharpened edge of the sword, smeared with poison. For the good of creation abandon them like a pitcher of urine. (65)

"The effects of passion always trouble the memory* and heighten the quality of darkness; they produce causes of fear, and are invariably the roots of misery; they promote the growth of the vine of worldly thirst, dreadful and destructive. (66)

"Even as a spark of fire is calculated to produce a dreadful conflagration, so are these passions known to be by sensible people; they are like great quagmires; they are keen as a forest of swords,† as a razor dipped in honey.‡ (67)

* *Tamaskarana* from *tamas* the quality of darkness, but I am doubtful about the correctness of my rendering.

† From *asi* "sword" and *sindhu* "an ocean" = an ocean of swords. Had the word *sindhu* preceded *asi*, I would have rendered the compound "the sword of the Sindhu country," that country having been noted for blades of a superior quality. Rhetorically, this meaning would be better.

‡ The sense may be that the sharpness is so keen that it cuts without causing any sensation of pain, or a sensation of soothing; or that the razor is tempered in honey and therefore very sharp. I am not aware of any process

"Even as is a lake full of serpents, or a pitcher full of urine, so are the passions known to be by wise men. They are troublesome and inimical like spikes, like the falchions of warriors,* like the nails of dogs,† like the enmity of monkeys. (68)

"The qualities of the passions are (unsteady) like the (image of the) moon in water; (unreal) as a reflection, as the echo in a mountain, as a shadow, as a scene on the stage, as a dream—so are they known to be by men of experience. (69)

"The qualities of the passions last only for a moment; they are (delusive) as the mirage; (hollow) as the froth and bubbles on water; they are evolved from false imaginings: so say all wise men. (70)

"In the dawn of youth when the body is in its perfect beauty, it is the occupation of youth to love, to long, to cherish. When it is undone by age, disease, and pain it is abandoned even as a deer forsakes a dried up river. (71)

"To care for, love, and hold dear wealth, corn and goods of diverse kinds is the occupation of youth; but when wealth is wasted, and distress supervenes, men forsake them as an empty wilderness. (72)

"Like a plant in blossom or a tree bearing fruits, a man in wealth is engaged in acts of beneficence and gratifications for others; but when he has lost his wealth, and is decayed and reduced to the necessity of begging, he becomes unwelcome like a vulture. (73)

of tempering in which honey is used; but all viscid fluids cause slow cooling, and are therefore more or less adapted for tempering. The comparison is common enough in the former sense.

* *Dvija-peśisamá* in the original, literally like the "flesh" *peś'i*, of the twice-born *dvija*. or the flesh of birds. *Peś'i* also means a scabbard, and I take it to be equivalent to a sword. *Dvija* or twice-born may well stand for Kshatriyas or the warrior caste. *Dvija* is also used to imply a serpent and *peś'i* may stand for eggs, *i. e.*, they are serpents' eggs, pregnant with mischief.

† I am doubtful about this rendering, the word in the original, is *svánakara* 'the hand of a dog.'

"When one has authority and effects and power and is handsome in body, he is a welcome companion, gratifying both to the mind and the senses; but when he is overcome by decay, disease, distress and loss of wealth then he is as repulsive as death. (74)

"On the expiry of youth and in the decay of age one becomes like a tree struck by lightning, or a house dilapidated by age; promptly say, O sage, when is the time for the extinction of that decay? (75)

"Age dries up both men and women, even as the Málu creeper[27] destroys a dense Sála forest; age is the robber of vigour, power, and energy; a man in decay is (as helpless) as one caught in a quagmire. (76)

"Age is the deformer of beauty and handsomeness; it is always the robber of vigour and of enjoyment; it is the cause of overthrow and of death; it destroys radiance, power, and strength. (77)

"The world is aggrieved by a hundred diseases; by innumerable ailments and suffering; (it is restless,) like a deer in a burning forest. Behold the world immersed in age and disease; pray, quickly direct the means of putting an end to suffering. (78)

"Even as coldness in winter deprives trees, grass, tubers, and herbs of their vigour, so do disease and age destroy the vigour (of man); they take away beauty, might and organic powers. (79)

"Disease and age are always the causers of waste and destruction of wealth and corn and treasures; of anguish and obstruction; of pain as regards dear ones, and of burning like the sun in the heaven. (80)

"Death, transition, and fall are the works of time; they always cause separation from dear objects and persons; they never return, they never restore union; (they float away) like trees, leaves and fruits on the current of a river. (81)

"All are subject to death; none can control it; death takes

away all like a river carrying away wood that has fallen into it; helpless man passes on to the second (region) governed by the fruit of his own actions. (82)

"Death swallows men by hundreds, like even as the Makara destroys creatures living in water; or the Garuḍa, serpents; or the lion, the elephant; or fire, grass and herbs and other objects. (83)

"From these and other evils by hundreds thou didst resolve to free the world. Call to mind that former resolve of thine. This is the time for thy departure.' (84)

"When the cheerful damsels were entertaining the great sage with music, diversified Gáthás issued forth from the sounds of the music through the grace of Sugata. (85)

"All things proceeding from the residua of former acts[28] are known to be sapless and impermanent like the lightning in the sky. Thy time has come, the time for thy proceeding forth, O Suvrata! (86)

"All residua of works are impermanent, unlasting, fragile like an unbaked water-jar; like a play on a stage; like a town built of dust—all lasting for a short while only. (87)

"Residua are by nature subject to destruction, they are transitory and moving like the cloud of autumn, like the sand on the banks of a river, subject to cause and essentially weak. (88)

"Residua are like the flame of a lamp, by nature produced and destroyed suddenly; in unsteadiness they are comparable to the passing wind; unsubstantial and feeble like froth. (89)

Residua are inert and hollow; they appear like the stem of a plantain tree; they are delusive to the mind like jugglery; (worthless) as the babble of infants; (transient) as the (flame of) a handful of hay. (90)

"Through cause and consciousness proceed all the products of residua; all this (creation) therefore is due to the mutual reaction of causes; ignorant people do not understand this. (91)

Even as a rope is made by power employed in uniting muṇja

and valvaja bark,[*9] and a water lift must rest on a wheel; neither can result by itself, (92)

so all worldly objects are produced by the co-operation of one material with another. They are never found singly in *esse* or *posse*. (93)

Even as a seed produces a sprout, but the sprout is not identical with the seed, nor does the sprout abide in it, owing to all things being transitory but continuous in nature, (94)

they have residua and ignorance for their cause, and in residua there is no permanence: Both residua and ignorance are verily substanceless; by nature they are inert. (95)

One may see an impression from a seal, but there is no transference into the impression of that seal; nor does the one abide in the other, and therefore there is no permanency in either; there is unbrokenness of the chain of residua, but no constancy. (96)

By the union of the image, the eye, and consciousness, vision is product; form does not proceed from the eye, nor is there an entrance of the form into the eye. (97)

The qualified are agreeable because soulless, and not because there is a soul; and the reverse (*i. e.*, the admission of soul) is untrue and imaginary; the sensation of vision is produced therein (*i. e.*, in that imaginary soul). (98)

He knows (that soul) is produced on the destruction of knowledge, and it disappears on the origin of knowledge, who knows the present, the past, and the future to be void and delusive. (99)

The triple contact of a stick with another and the force of the hand is the cause of the production of fire, and the action may be easily created. (100)

When a Paṇḍit enquires whence is a thing come, and whereto does it go, he hunts everywhere in foreign lands and his own land, but never can he make out whence the coming and whereto is the going. (101)

The causes of works *(karma)*, are skandhas, field (*lit.* matter receptacle, *dhátváyatana)*, will, and ignorance; materials explain the origin of existence; they do not subserve the noblest end. (102)

"Letters are produced through the instrumentality of the larynx and the lips acting on the palate and the tongue; but not a letter can be found in the larynx, nor in the palate. (103)

"Speech proceeds from a union of causes under the influence of the mind and the intellect; but both the mind and the speech are invisible in form, and can be grasped neither internally nor externally. (104)

"A wise man perceives the production and disappearance of speech, as also the sound and pitch of the voice, and that they exist only for a moment; thus are all speeches comparable to an echo. (105)

"Even as by the threefold instrumentality of cord, wood, and manual exertion music is produced in the *túna, víná* and other sweet-sounding instruments, (106)

"and a wise man, enquiring everywhere on this side and that side to know whence it comes and whereto it goes, fails to ascertain the cause of the appearance and disappearance of a sound, (107)

"so do all products of residua proceed from instrumental and material causes, and the Yogi, conscient of the truth, knows all residua to be void and perishable. (108)

"The Skandhas, space, and materials are void, both essentially and apparently; properly understood, they have no substratum, and are of the same nature as ether. (109)

"This character of attributes was understood by thee on thy seeing (the Buddha) Dípañkara; having understood it for thyself, do ye explain it to men and gods. (110)

"The creation is being burnt by discordant and falsely-assumed wrath and enmity; O, do ye shower the nectariferous rain of cool water from thy cloud of mercy! (111)

"For obtaining it thou hast bestowed benevolences on paṇdits for innumerable millions of kalpas; and having obtained it, the noblest Bodhi, revered sir, thou shalt have acquired the most highly prized wealth for (the well-being of) living beings. (112)

"Call to mind thy former career; neglect not, charioteer of living beings, the disrespectable, the wealthless, the poor, and the afflicted; do collect for them the desiderated wealth. (113)

"Thou hast always cherished good conduct, for the salvation of perishable regions, and in order that thou wouldst show the immortal door of heaven, for the good of millions of beings. (114)

"Call to mind thy former career; closing the doors of the lower regions, do unbar the immortal gate of heaven; accomplish thy generous wishes. (115)

"Thou hast well cherished forbearance, for the suppression of enmity and anger among the embodied; ferrying them over the ocean of worldliness, establish them in peace, prosperity and diseaselessness. (116)

"Call to mind thy former career; neglect not those who are inimical, quarrelsome and destructive; establish the creation disposed to injury on the land of forbearance. (117)

"The object with which heroism was cultivated by thee was to acquire the ship of virtue, and, rescuing the world from all oceans (of evil), to establish it on a region devoid of enmity and disease. (118)

"Call to mind thy former career; the world is deluded by fourfold evil; O leader, do ye promptly save living beings by the might of thy vigour and strength. (119)

"Thou hast undergone the labour of meditation and prayer; this was not done for heroism, but with this resolve,—'I shall place those whose senses are in delusion or in a primitive state of rudeness on the right path.' (120)

"Call to mind thy former career; the world is groaning, enveloped in a net-work of pain; neglect not; place the people oppressed with pain in the bliss of concentrated meditation. (121)

"In former times, knowledge was well cultivated by thee, with this resolve that thou wilt bestow on the world enveloped in the blinding darkness of delusion and error the eye for the microscopic vision of many hundred virtues. (122)

"Call to mind thy former career; bestow on the world enveloped in the blinding darkness of delusion and error the superior knowledge of excellent refulgence, and the clear and stainless eye of virtue. (123)

"These and such-like Gáthás issued forth from the sound of the music of the damsels, and thou, hearing them made up thy mind to forsake the world, in order that thou mayst be infused with devotion, and able to appreciate the noble and chief wisdom." (124)

Thus, Bhikshus, the Bodhisattva, dwelling in the female apartments, became dispassionate,—dispassionate in hearing the voice of religion, by accepting it in his mind. How so? It was because, O Bhikshus, the Bodhisattva, for a long time, had cultivated respect for religion, the history of religion, and by exertion had become the searcher of religion, the lover of religion, and the devotee of religion. He established religion by argument; he was a promulgator of the traditional religion; the bestower of the unrivalled great religion; the disinterested teacher of religion; unmiserly in dispensing religion; devoid of the desire of recompense for teaching fully; possessed of religion and its subsidiaries; a hero in the acquisition of religion; a destroyer of irreligion; a protector of religion; an asylum of religion; a superior asylum of religion; devoted to religion; the recipient of the jewel of religion; thoroughly practised in forbearance; accomplished in the transcendental knowledge *(prajnápáramitá)* experienced in the easy means of salvation *(upáya-kauśalya)*.

Now, Bhikshus, the Bodhisattva, by the exercise of the great and easy means, showed to the whole of the dwellers of the zenana the enviable path of salvation. He did this after having shown the dwellers of the zenana the path of salvation by the practice of great merit; after having followed the career of virtue for the reformation of mankind of former Bodhisattvas of surpassing worldly merit; after having known for a long time the evils of passion; after having, for maturing the minds of beings, enjoyed all objects of desire; after having exhibited his unrivalled supremacy in accumulating the treasures of special virtue and power resulting from the root of immeasurable good; after having tasted the sensuous pleasures resulting from the enjoyment of diverse objects of gratification relating to form, sound, smell, and touch—all most charming and of superhuman and super-celestial character; after having exhibited the entire and unlimited control he possessed over his mind in all matters regarding objects of desire; after having discussed with men who had acquired the root of good through their previously acquired power of reflection; after having evinced a feeling of sympathy for afflicted persons. Perceiving then that the time for maturing the mind of the self-willed dwellers of the zenana had arrived, the Bodhisattva repeatedly called to mind his former resolves. He brought face to face the Buddha religion; he spread out his powers of reflection; he revived his unbounded mercy for living beings; he thought of the salvation of beings; he beheld the overthrow of all wealth and misfortune; he examined the nature of all accidents and fears of the world; he tore asunder the lasso of Mára and of Kali; he exerted himself to free himself from the trammels of the world; he wholly devoted his mind to Nirváṇa.

In this respect Bhikshus, the Bodhisattva was thoroughly cognizant of the defects of the world from beginning to end; he was by purification and discrimination undesiring; he was by an act of renunciation free from desire; he was facing the Buddha Nirváṇa; he was diverted from the world; he was forward for the domain of Tathágata; he was averse to the domain of Mára; he was acquainted with the blazing evils of the world; he was desirous to extricate himself from the three elements; he was proficient in escaping from the evils of the world; he was desirous of mendicancy; he was intent upon going away from home; he was bent on discrimination (between the real and the unreal); he was prompted by discrimination; he was bent forward by the weight of discrimination; he was disposed to go to the wilderness and wild places; he was longing for thorough discrimination; he was accomplished in effecting his own and other's welfare; he was a hero in the knowledge of the hereafter; he was desirous of wealth for the world; he longed for the good of the world, the enjoyment of the world, and the Yoga and mercy for the world; he was kind to the world; he derived benefit for the world; he rejoiced in benevolence; he was highly merciful; he was proficient in matters worthy of collection; he was always self-controlled; he was of wide grasping mind; he was proficient in the moral law *(Vinaya)* which improves mankind; he cherished the feeling of affection for all beings as if they were his only son; he abjured all things with perfect disinterestedness; he was engaged in the distribution of charity; he was open-handed; he was a hero in beneficence; he had performed all sacrifices; he was rich in virtue; he had well collected virtue; he had well disciplined his mind about pride and vanity, and was perfectly free from them; he was unrivalled; he was the giver of the great gift, and had given it; he desiderated not the fruition of work; he was a hero in great gifts; he was born for the oppression of the host of evils arising from desires, ardent desires, covetousness, faults, pride, vanity, delusion, envy and the like; he had practised the art of preparing the mind for omniscience; his mind was bent on the great renunciation; he was invested in mail; he was kind to creation; he was well-wishing; he was protected by armour; he was possessed of the power and vigour of mercy for the emancipation of beings; he was the master of abnegation of self, equally and unchangeably kind to all beings; he satisfied the desires of every one according to his wish; he was the receptacle (*lit.* vase) of Bodhi; he was the measurer of virtue, undeterred by time; he had Bodhi knowledge for the object of his meditation; his standard had never been lowered; he had bestowed gifts for the purification of the three circles; he struck with the adamantine thunder of knowledge; he was for well-controlled pain; his character was replete with the quality of good behaviour; his object was to direct well the actions of the body, speech, and mind; he always looked with fear at even the minutest vileness; pure was his conduct; defectless and stainless was his mind; his mind abhorred all evil discourse, harsh words, raillery, scandal, chastisement, reprimands, killing, imprisonment, restraint and pain; he was endowed with the aroma of forbearance; his mind was unbroken, unstruck and unagitated; he had, for the good of all beings, adopted the support of burning rigour; he was the root of all blessings; his memory was unfailing in the cause of religion; he was thoroughly learned; he had thorough self-control; he was of undisturbed mind; he had fixed his mind on concentrated meditation; he was an adept in spreading religion widely; he had attained the true light; he was free from cloud and darkness; his soul was untouched by unstayable pain; his heart dwelt on the picture of well-being; memory, understanding, thorough renunciation, occult powers, control of the organs, the stores of knowledge, the path, the most revered truths, all the conditions of the Bodhi knowledge were under his controul; his mind was invulnerable in the feeling of equality and fraternity; he believed in the principle of production from cause; knowing the truth he did not attribute the cause to a wrong source; he delighted in the three passages to complete deliverance; he knew the following of all laws to be unreal as a delusion, a mirage, a dream, a moon in water, an echo, a reflection.

Now Bhikshus, this happened to the Bodhisattva. Thus exhilarated by the innumerable Gáthás issuing from the music through the influence of the Buddhas of the ten quarters of the globe, he at the time realised before him the four preliminaries of the former Bodhisattvas when they had matured their career in their zenana, and were about to attain their final stage. What were these four? They were 1st, charity, sweet speech, acquisition of wealth, and equality; this is called the duty of the application and purification of the fourfold acquired property which he brought face to face. The second was called the duty of reflection on the race of the three jewels and the destruction, universal knowledge, the knowing of the mind, the acquisition of the occult powers, and change, which he brought face to face. The third was called the duty of not forsaking all living beings, and the spread of mercy, which he brought face to face. The fourth was called the duty of non-recognition of differences, and firm belief in the religion of all the former Buddhas, which he brought face to face.

Having thus brought face to face these four preliminaries of religion, the Bodhisattva, with a view to train the mind of his zenana (*lit.* to mature), at that moment effected the purification of his occult powers. This was effected by these and such like Gáthás by hundreds of thousands through the sound of music influenced by the grace of the Bodhisattva.

Thus :—

"To enliven mercy for living beings, and to prepare the mind for the great knowledge, words issued forth through the music in exquisite metres with an object, with a noble object. (1)

"Faith, contentment, final emancipation, respect, pridelessness, submission to teachers, enquiry about what is good, research, remembrance, reflection,—these were the words which issued forth. (2)

"Charity, suppression of the passions, control of the mind, and discipline were the words, forbearance was the word, vigour was the word, meditation, renunciation, and ecstacy were the words, the means of knowledge was the word—which issued forth. (3)

"Benevolence was the word, mercy was the word, contentment, indifference, and knowledge were the words, the amelioration of beings through the ascertainment of the four objects to be collected was the word—which issued forth. (4)

"Memory and special understanding were the words, the thorough suppression (of the passions), the occult powers, the five organs of sense, the five different kinds of powers, the components of the Bodhi, were the words—which issued forth in music. (5)

"The distinction of the force of the eightfold path, and capacity were the words, the perception of the evanescent character of pain and disease, and the knowledge of there being no (immortal) soul were the words, the pain of misfortune was the word,—which issued forth in music. (6)

"Dispassion was the word, discrimination was the word, knowledge of decay was the word, absence of a (first) creation was the word, non-destruction and non-habitation were the words, nihilation (Nirváṇa) was the word—which issued forth in music. (7)

"These and such like words in music issued forth through the influence of the word Sambodhi; on hearing which all beings were affectionately taught to incite the noble being in favour of knowledge." (8)

Thus, Bhikshus, were the eighty-four thousand damsels purified by the Bodhisattva dwelling in his zenana. Innumerable were the hundreds of thousands of Devas, who happened to be there, who benefitted thereby in the knowledge of the sequenceless Bodhi.

Now at the time of the Bodhisattva's renunciation of his home, a Devaputra of the region of Tushitakáyika, named Hrídeva, who had acquired the thorough sequenceless Bodhi, at about the close of night, approached, with a retinue of 32,000 Devaputras, the place where the Bodhisattva resided, and from under the sky addressed him these Gáthás:

"O lion among men! thou hast shown to the world thy glorious descent, thy birth, and thy career in the inner apartments, in which thou hast followed precedents. (1)

"Thou hast purified many in the world of humanity, having thyself acquired the true religion; this day is the time for thy departure; pray reflect on it. (2)

"The manacled cannot effect ransom, nor can the blind point out the right path; the unmanacled can emancipate the fettered, and he who has eyes can point out the right path to the blind. (3)

"Those beings who are the slaves of their desires, who are attached to their homes, their wealth, their offspring and their wives,—even they, taught by thee, may direct their mind to renunciation. (4)

"Knowing that forsaking sovereignty, sensuous gratifications, the four continents, and the seven jewels, thou wouldst issue forth, the world of men and gods eagerly anticipates it. (5)

"Further, thou delightest in the pleasures of meditation and religion, and art not addicted to sensuous gratifications; do ye therefore, awaken gods and men by hundreds who are sleeping for ever so long. (6)

"Quickly pass away youth, even as do unsteady and rapidly moving mountain torrents. The desire to renounce home after youth has departed is not very praiseworthy. (7)

"It would be most appropriate, therefore, that the renunciation should take place in the pride of youth. Redeem thy promise, and subserve the good of the celestial host. (8)

"No more is satisfaction derived by the gratification of sensuous desires, than is (thirst) allayed by the water of the salt sea. Thy satisfaction rests in the adorable, super-celestial, stainless knowledge. (9)

"Thou art dear to king S'uddhodana and his country, and lovely of countenance like a hundred-petalled lotus; do ye reflect on the disposition for renunciation. (10)

"Oh matchless hero, do quickly place on the road to salvation and peace those who are burning in the fire of pain, who are shelterless, and who are bound in oppressive fetters. (11)

"Thou art proficient in the profession of the physician; do ye, by the administration of the medicament of religion, quickly place in the felicity of Nirváṇa those beings who are diseased and ever in pain. (12)

"Quickly bestow the blessings of the eye of knowledge on men and gods who are stone-blind, eyeless, or whose sight is overcast by the net-work of deep delusion. (13)

"Numerous are the Devas, Asuras, Nágas, Yakshas and Gandharvas who are cherishing this anticipation, 'we shall see him attain the Bodhi; we shall listen to the matchless religion.' (14)

"The king of serpents beholds his mansion illuminated by thy splendour; his desire is that he will offer thee endless worship in his home. (15)

"The four guardians of the quarters with their armies are anticipating thee, with the desire 'we shall persent him four vases and the standard of Bodhi.' Fulfil their desires. (16)

"Brahmá of the peaceful career longs to attain benevolence, speech, and mercy, (saying), 'I shall adore the king of men, turning the matchless wheel.' (17)

"The goddess purified by the Bodhi is chanting in the Bodhimaṇḍa, 'I shall behold him coming here and thoroughly acquiring the Bodhi.' (18)

"And men and gods who had beheld thy career in the inner apartments, (say) 'be ye moving forward; there will be no career after that.' (19)

"Call to mind the sweet sound, the sweet faultless speech of Dípañkara, and proclaim the unfailing sound of a Jina." (20)

NOTES.

1. *The ten powers of the Tathágata*, p. 224. The word Daśabala is a specific name of Buddha, and Dr. Wilson, following a Hindu etymologist, explains it to mean "powerful in the ten worlds;" but this passage shows clearly that the interpretation is not correct. The powers meant are (1) charity, (2) good conduct, (3) forbearance, (4) vigour, or determination, (5) meditation, (6) intelligence, (7) power, (8) knowledge of means, (9) contemplation, and (10) transcendental knowledge. दान-शील-क्षमा-वीर्य्ये-ध्यान-प्रज्ञा-बलानि च । उपायः प्रणिधिर्ज्ञानं दश बुद्धबलानि वै ॥ The 7th includes supernatural or occult powers obtainable by the exercise of Yoga. Patañjali, in his Yoga aphorisms, (see my translation, chapter 3) describes a great number of these; but Hindu writers generally reduce them to eight, including

(1) *Animá* or molecularity; (2) *Laghimá* or extreme levity; (3) *Prápti* or accessibility; (4) *Prákámya* or wilfulness; (5) *Garimá* or ponderosity; (6) *I's'itá* or sovereignty; (7) *Vas'itá* or subjugation; and (8) *Kámávasáyitá* or self-control. These are known by the names of *vibhuti*, *ṛiddhi*, *siddhi*, *bhúti*, *ais'varya* and *bala*. The Buddhists generally use the last term, and I have frequently rendered it into "occult powers."

2. *The four Tathágata accomplishments*, p. 224. These include firm determination, earnest meditation, persevering exertion, and close investigation. These are the means of obtaining the occult powers.

3. *The eighteen sections of the Buddha religion*, p. 225. These refer to the different courses of life that Buddhists may follow.

4. *Turning the twelve-formed wheel of religion and its three transitions.* The wheel of law is represented as having 12 radii, emblematic of the twelve *nidánas* or primary causes of all things and its three transitions are the three *Yánas*, or schools.

5. *The five realities*, p. 225. These are—(1) that pain is inseparable from mundane existence; (2) that the cause of pain resides in desires; (3) that the pain subsides on the cessation of desires; (4) that the desires can be extinguished by knowledge; (5) that the knowledge consists in full appreciation of the truth.

6. *Like the great ocean after it has reached the height of the tide*, p. 225, *i. e.*, after the greatest tribulations have been surmounted. Even as after the high tide is over, there follows an ebb, so after the tribulations of life are over, there is a calm.

7. *Surabhi flower*, p. 227. This is the poetical celestial flower of the Hindus—the *Párijáta*. The Hindus use the word surabhi too. Commonly, the name is applied to the *Erethrena fulgens*, a tree bearing very bright red blossoms.

8. *Threefold pain*, p. 228. Pain proceeding—(1) from internal causes, (2) from natural and extrinsic causes, (3) from superhuman causes. See Wilson's S'áṅkhya-káriká, p. 2.

9. *When thou wast born a son to a mortal*, p. 229. The story occurs in the *Bodhisattvávadána-kalpalatá*. All the stories referred to here occur in the Játakas and Avadánas, and a good many have been preserved in stone on the rails and gates of the Sánchi and the Bhárut Topes. Buddhists are greatly attached to the stories, and various recensions are current among them. Some of them have been unquestionably borrowed by the Hindus; others are of Hindu origin.

10. *An irate king of the Kali age*, p. 229. I remember the story, but cannot now find out the work in which it occurs.

11. *Thou wast born the son of a Ṛishi*, p. 230. This refers to the *Das'aratha Játaka*—to the king who killed the son of a blind hermit. It occurs in the Sánchi gateway. See Fergusson's Sánchi Tope, p. 208, and my Antiquities of Orissa, I, p. 89.

12. *The lord of deer*, p. 230. The story occurs in the *Mahávastu Avadána*. See my Sanskrit-Buddhist Literature of Nepal, p. 123.

13. *A bird approached thee*, p. 23. The story occurs repeatedly in both Buddhist and Hindu legends; the latest English version occurs in Lord Lytton's 'Glenaveril.'

14. *Thou didst live as a parrot on a tree*, p. 230. The story occurs in the *Avadána S'ataka*.

15. *The Mani jewel*, p. 231. Described in Chapter V, *vide ante*, p. 33.

16. *The yak preserves its hair*, p. 231. The shaggy coat of long hair which covers the yak is its protection from the icy cold of the Tibetan plateau, and the animal is believed to be particularly careful in its preservation.

17. *O noble elephant!* p. 231. This refers to the story of Buddha's entering his mother's womb in the form of an elephant, *vide ante*, p. 94.

18. *Thou didst carry on thy shoulders a man*, p. 232. The story occurs in the *Avadána S'ataka*.

19. *A noble horse of a golden colour*, p. 232. The Lord was born as a horse four times, and there are four different stories current. The one referred to here occurs in the *Mahávastu Avadána*, and an abstract of it is given in my Sanskrit-Buddhist Literature of Nepal, p. 155.

20. *Thou wast Nimindhara, Nimi, Kṛishṇabandhu, Brahmadatta and Kes'ari*, p. 233. These occupy a prominent part in Buddhist birth stories, and are described as princes of ancient times.

21. *Thou didst as Soma (Sutasoma) Díptavírya, and Puṇyarasmi*, p. 233. I am not certain whether the text means three persons, or one person (the first) having for his epithet the second and the third words. The story of Sutasoma occurs repeatedly in the Játakas and the Avadánas. Cf. Sanskrit-Buddhist Literature of Nepal, pp. 47—56.

22. *The fivefold imperishable science in due order*, p. 235. The true knowledge of the five realities. See Note 5, *ante*, p. 251.

23. *There is nothing eternal in productions*, p. 235 The philosophy inculcated here is that everything in nature is evanescent. It is founded on the doctrine of Nihility or *Sunyaváda*, which is recognized by all the works of the Maháyánasútra class of which the Lalita-vistara is one.

24. *The horrible, dreadful, fierce, mighty fire at the end of the Kalpa*, p. 235. This refers to the Hindu belief that at the end of each Kalpa, there is a mighty conflagration which reduces the world to ashes. The Buddhists borrow such cosmical doctrines very freely from their neighbours.

25. *In the three perishable paths*, p. 235. The Sanskrit word used is *patha* a road, and is a synonym of *adhman* which in philosophical writings stands for condition. The three conditions are the antecedent, the postcedent, and the present conditions, and all things must pass through these conditions in course of time. See my translation of the Yoga Aphorisms of Patanjali, p. 129.

26. *In the lasso of the evil genius (Kali)*, p. 236. This is another instance of belief in the cosmological vagaries of the Puráṇas. Kali is the ruler of the present age, and everything follows the course in which he guides it.

27. *Age dries up both men and women, even as the Málu creeper destroys dense sál forests*, p. 236. The Málu is a large vine which thrives best in the sub-Himalayan sála forests, where it so envelops the tree on which it ascends, as to destroy it soon. Those who are familiar with the plant cannot fail to appreciate the appropriateness of the simile.

Mr. Atkinson, in his N. W. Gazetteer, Vol. X, p. 723, says, "it is the Bauhinia Vahlii, W. *et* A.—*Máljau, málu*. It is a large creeper that occurs rather commonly in the lower hills and upper Bhábar from the Jumna to Sardá, especially at the bottom of hot valleys and along the sides of precipices. The leaves are used for making umbrellas, and, sewn together with twigs, form baskets for holding pepper, turmeric, and ginger. They are also used as a substitute for plates at meals, and by the petty shop-keepers to wrap up the goods that they sell. This creeper often attains a length of 40 to 50 feet, and is generally cut down in July—August, though it may be cut at all seasons. In its natural state it is used for making rope-bridges, but to manufacture rope from it, the outer bark is peeled off and thrown away, and the inner coating is steeped in water and twisted when wet. A large creeper will produce a maund of this fibre known as *selu*. Before being used, the bark is boiled and beaten with wooden mallets, which renders it soft and pliable enough for being made into rope and twine used in the erection of rope-bridges, for thatching, stringing cots, and the like. These ropes, though strong, are not very durable, and require occasional soaking, though, if constantly kept in the water, they rot quickly and altogether do not last more than eighteen months. The broad flat seed of the pod is eaten fried in clarified butter. Hooker, II, p. 279."

Voigt gives the following botanical account of the plant; "Tull Ghauts. Ravines at Kandalla. Morung Mountains. Kheree Pass. Deyra-Dhoon. Kemaon. Fl. largish, white, gradually becoming cream-coloured, March and April, for C. S. *Leaves*, often a foot each way, firm, tough, durable, collected in the N. Circars, and sold in the bazars for plates, lining baskets, covering packets, thatching houses, &c. *Seeds* eaten raw; when ripe tasting like cashew-nuts. (Roxb.). *Bark* employed in making rope." Hortus Suburbanus Calcuttensis, page 254.

28. *All things proceed from the residua of former acts*, p. 239. This is an allusion to the Yoga theory about instinct. Life being admitted as eternal and transmigration being an accepted doctrine of the faith, it is believed that every act leaves an impression, or residuum on the field of the mind, which lies dormant until revived, and as every work, good, bad or indifferent, leaves an impression, and the impression remains, the sum of them lead to repeated actions under given conditions. This is the doctrine of Karma or every work leading to a fruit, and nothing is produced which is not the fruit of a former work. Cf. my translation of the Yoga Aphorisms of Patanjali, pp. 176, 178, 179.

29. *Even as rope is made by power employed in uniting munja and valvaja bark*, p. 240. In the present day rope is usually made with the munja bark alone, and it is common all over Northern India. I have nowhere seen the valvaja used as a conjunct. The text probably refers to some ancient local practice.

CHAPTER XIV.

THE DREAM.

King S'uddhodana's dream. His enquiry about the Prince. He causes three palaces to be built for constant enjoyment, and sets guards. The Prince proposes to go to the garden. The charioteer reports the circumstance to the king. He issues a proclamation, and makes arrangement for the procession. The Prince sees an old man in the way. The second procession, in course of which he sees a diseased person. The third procession, in course of which he sees a corpse. The fourth procession, in course of which he sees a hermit. Hearing of this account the king further strengthens the fortifications, sets guards, and directs constant jubilation in the palace. Confirmatory Gáthás.

Now, Bhikshus, the Bodhisattva, having been thus exhorted by the Devaputra, revealed this dream[1] to the king S'uddhodana. When the king S'uddhodana was asleep, he saw in his dream that at the end of the night the Bodhisattva, surrounded by a large following of Devas, was issuing forth from the palace, and that, after coming out, he had accepted the condition of an ascetic and had put on an ochre-coloured garb. Waking up, he quickly enquired of the warder in attendance, "Is the Prince in the zenana?"

The warder replied, "Yes, sire."

The spear of anguish pierced the heart of the king dwelling in the inner apartment. He saw this and other premonitory signs that the Prince for certain will depart.

Now it occurred to him, surely the Prince should no longer be permitted to visit the garden; he should always entertain himself here amidst the ladies.

Then three palaces fitted for use in different seasons were erected[2] by the king S'uddhodana for the entertainment of the Prince; the summer palace, the autumn palace, and the winter palace. The summer palace was delightfully cool; the autumn one was temperate, and the winter one was warm by nature. The ladders of each of these palaces could not be raised or lowered by (less than) five hundred persons; and the sound of their raising and lowering could be heard from a distance of half a yojana. Orders were issued that the Prince should never be permitted to go out of his own accord.

It had been predicted by astrologers and soothsayers that the Prince would depart through the 'Lucky Gate' (or the Gate of Mars, *Mańgaladvára*); so the king caused very heavy doors to be fitted to that gate. Each door could be opened or shut by the labour of (not less than) five hundred men, and the sound of the opening and the shutting would extend to a distance of half a yojana. The means for the gratification of the five senses were also collected, and damsels were always kept in attendance for singing, music and dancing.

Now, Bhikshus, the Bodhisattva ordered the charioteer, "quickly get the chariot ready; I propose to go to the garden."[3]

Thereupon the charioteer repaired to the king S'uddhodana, and said, "Sire, the Prince desires to proceed to the garden."

The king reflected. The Prince has never been to the pleasure-garden to behold its well-laid parterres except in my company; now, if the Prince should go there surrounded by ladies, he will be disposed to sport in dalliance and not think of renouncing his home. So, out of profuse affection for the Bodhisattva, he caused the news to be published by the ringing of bells throughout the town that on the seventh day the Prince would proceed to the pleasure-garden to behold the grounds; therefore the people should hide all offensive sights, so that the Prince may not see anything repulsive. All pleasant objects and auspicious sights should be put forth.

Now, on the seventh day the whole town was decorated.[4] The garden was set off and spread over with flowers of various colours; and parasols, standards, and flags were set up everywhere. The road by which the Bodhisattva would proceed was watered, smoothed, sprinkled with aromatic waters, scattered with loose flowers, made redolent with the incense of pills and pastilles, set off with pitchers full of water and plantain trees arranged in rows; many-coloured awnings were hung up everywhere, and net-works decorated with jewelled bells and garlands were hung up. The fourfold army was set in array, and attendants were ready for the decoration of the Prince's apartments.

The Prince started for the garden by the eastern gate, attended by a large retinue. Now, through the grace of the Bodhisattva and the devise of the Devaputras of the class S'uddhávásakáyika, there appeared in front, in that road, an emaciated, old, decrepit person; his body was covered with prominent veins; he was toothless, covered with flabby tendons, and grey-haired; he was humped; his mouth was sunken;* he was broken down, diseased, and leaning on a staff. He had long passed his youth; there was a rattling cough in his throat; bent forward by the weight of his body, he was leaning on a staff with the weight of his body and members.

Though knowing what the sight meant, the Bodhisattva thus questioned the charioteer:

"Who is this weak, powerless man, with dried-up flesh, blood and skin, prominent veins, whitened head, scattered teeth, and emaciated body, painfully tottering on, leaning on a staff?"

The charioteer replied[5]:

"Lord, this is a person overpowered by age (decay, *jará*); his organs are feeble; he is in pain, and his strength and vigour are gone. Abandoned by his friends, he is helpless and unfit for work, like wood abandoned in a forest."

The Bodhisattva said:

"Correctly explain, charioteer, if this be the peculiarity of his tribe, or is it the condition of the whole world? Quickly

* Lit. grooved as is the beam on which rests the thatch-frame of a hut. The idea is that the chin and the upper jaw remaining projecting, and the teeth being gone there was a groove or hollow between the upper and the lower jaws.

answer this according to fact, so that I may, on hearing it, enquire about its source."

The charioteer replied:

"Lord, this is not a peculiarity of his race nor of his country. Age wears out youth in the whole creation. Even thou shalt be separated from the society of thy mother and father and kinsmen and relatives. There is no other lot for man."

The Bodhisattva said:

"Condemnable, charioteer, is the sense of the ignorant and the youthful, who, in the pride and intoxication of their youth, do not reflect on decay. Turn back the chariot, I do not wish to see (any thing farther). Of what avail are pleasures and enjoyments to me when I am subject to decay?"

Then the Bodhisattva caused the chariot to be turned back, and entered the palace.

Now, Bhikshus, the Bodhisattva, on another occasion, issuing with a large retinue through the southern gate of the town, proceeded towards the garden. In the way he beheld a diseased person, dried up, overcome with fever, weak, with his body immersed in his own filth, helpless and protectorless, and breathing with difficulty. Beholding this, the Bodhisattva, though knowing it, thus questioned the charioteer:

"Who is this man, charioteer, whose skin has lost its colour, whose organs are all out of order, who is breathing hard, whose whole body is dried up, whose abdomen is swollen, who in his helplessness lies immersed in his own offensive filth?"

The charioteer said:

"He is, lord, a person greatly diseased, overpowered by disease and fear, lying at the point of death; he has no vigour left for recovery, is totally bereft of strength, beyond help and relief, and devoid of support."

The Bodhisattva said:

"Health is as the play of a dream; and so are the dreadful forms of disease and dread. How worthless is he of the name of a sensible man, who, beholding this condition, indulges in pleasures and dalliance, fancying them to be good?"

Thereupon the Bodhisattva caused the chariot to be turned back, and returned to the palace.

Now, Bhikshus, on another occasion the Bodhisattva started, with a large retinue, by the western gate for the garden. He beheld a dead man on the road, with a shroud over him, and followed by his kinsmen, all crying, weeping and moaning with dishevelled hair, their heads bent down, beating their breasts and lamenting. Seeing this he, though aware of its nature, thus questioned the charioteer:

"Charioteer, who is this man being carried on a bier, by men who are casting nails and hair and dust on their heads, and walking while beating their breasts and lamenting in many mournful words?"

The charioteer replied:

"Lord, this man has died in the Jambudvípa. Never more shall he behold his mother and father, his son and wife. Abandoning his house of enjoyment, his mother and father, his relatives and kinsmen, he has attained the next world. He will never again cast a look on his kinsmen."

The Bodhisattva exclaimed:

"Fie on youth surrounded by decay; fie on health besieged by divers ailments; fie on man living a transient life; fie on the enjoyment of men of sense.

"Even were there not decay and disease and death, still there is the great pain to the sustainer of the fivefold senses *(skandhas)*. What good is there in those who are always doomed to decay, disease and death? Turn back, I shall reflect on their deliverance."

Thereupon the Bodhisattva caused the chariot to be turned back, and returned to the palace.[6]

Now, Bhikshus, when the Bodhisattva, on another occasion, started with a large retinue for the garden by the northern gate,[7] there appeared, through the grace of the Bodhisattva and the instrumentality of those Devaputras, a Bhikshu on the road. The Bodhisattva beheld that Bhikshu standing calm, quiet, self-possessed, a perfect Brahmachári; his eyes turned not to this side or that side, but were directed to the junction of the two eyes[8] (the bridge of the nose); cheerfully following his path, cheerful in motion, was cheerfully looking on every side, and cheerfully bearing both his alms-bowl and his vestment. Beholding him, the Bodhisattva, though aware of his nature, thus questioned the charioteer:

"Charioteer, who is this peaceful man of contented mind, whose eyes turn not in restlessness, but are fixed on the junction of the two, who is arrayed in ochre-coloured garment, who is of peaceful action, carrying his alms-bowl, and is neither haughty nor puffed up?"

The charioteer replied:

"Lord, he is a man of the order called Bhikshu. Having abjured all sensuous desires, he is of modest behaviour. Having accepted mendicancy, he beholds his own self and the outside world with the same feeling. Devoid of affection and enmity, he lives by begging."

The Bodhisattva remarked:

"This is well said, and it meets my approbation. Mendicancy has always been held in esteem by the learned. Where there is welfare for self as well as for others there is happy living, and it bears sweet immortal fruit."

Thereupon, Bhikshus, the Bodhisattva caused his chariot to be turned back, and returned to the palace.[9]

Now, Bhikshus, the King S'uddhodana, seeing how the Bodhisattva was thus affected, made arduous exertions for his protection. He caused high walls to be built round the palace, a broad moat to be excavated, heavy doors to be hung, guards to be set up, veterans to be encouraged to do their work of guarding, vehicles to be kept in attendance, and coats of mail to be put on. At the four principal gateways of the town, close by the doors, he caused four large bodies of troops to be stationed for the protection of the Bodhisattva, so that they may be day and night on the watch, and prevent the Bodhisattva from going away. In the inner apartments he issued orders, saying, "Let there be no cessation of music; let all sensuous enjoyments be practised; let all feminine charms be displayed; and let the Prince be so engaged that, his mind being occupied, he may not retire to mendicancy."

On this subject the following Gáthás may be cited:

"At the gate were stationed valiant warriors, armed with swords and other weapons. There were stationed elephants, horses, chariots, and mail-clad veterans mounted on elephants. Moats were excavated, majestic arches and lofty walls were erected, many doors were hung most firmly, and their motion produced a sound which was audible from the distance of two miles (a kros'a.) (1)

"The S'ákyas with downcast mind guarded the gates night and day, and the roar of their mighty vigour reverberated everywhere. The citizens were greatly distressed, and were full of fear lest the beautiful Prince should depart and forsake them, for the departure of this scion of the S'ákya race would destroy the royal line. (2)

"The young ladies had orders not to stop the music; constantly to indulge in sensuous pastimes; to keep the mind enthralled; to display their feminine charms in every possible way, and to make every exertion to put obstruction in the way of the handsome one's departure. (3)

At the time of the departure of the noble charioteer there will be seen these omens: ducks, herons, peacocks, mainas, and parrots will become dumb. In the palace, at the windows, at the gateways, on terraces, and pavilions people will sit sighing in grief, and thinking with their heads bent down. (4)

"In the tanks and lakes the handsomest lotuses will become faded, the trees will be bereft of leaves and blossoms, and none will flower; the strings of the víná, the vallaki and other musical instruments will snap asunder, and trumpets and drums will, without being struck, burst, and produce no music. (5)

"The people were afflicted at heart; the whole town was

immersed in a horrid sleep; no one's mind was turned to dancing, or singing, or pleasure; the king himself was in deep grief, and distracted by the apprehension that the high glory of the S'ákya race would be destroyed. (6)

"Gopá was sleeping in a separate bed, as was the king, and at midnight she dreamt this dream; the whole earth was being shaken, as also the mountains with their stony crests; and trees, torn from their roots by the wind, lay on the ground. (7)

"The moon and the sun did not shine, but were cast on the ground along with the starry host. She saw her hair had been clipt by her right hand, her crown broken, her hands cut off, and so were her feet, and she was denuded. Her pearl necklace was torn, and she saw the shepherd's daughter (a play on the name Gopá) quite mutilated. (8)

She saw her bedstead divested of its four feet and lying on the ground. She beheld the well-decorated and handsome staff of the king's umbrella broken in twain, and all his ornaments lying defaced and scattered in water. Her husband's ornaments and dress and crown she beheld in distress lying on the bed. (9)

"She beheld meteors shooting forth from the town, and the palace immersed in darkness. In her dream she saw the well-decorated jewelled lattices all broken and showy pearl garlands lying scattered; the great ocean was in trouble, and the mountain king Meru torn from its place and trembling. (10)

"These sights saw the S'ákya daughter in her dream, and, waking after the dream, with terror-struck eyes she thus addressed her husband: 'Lord, say what will happen to me; I can remember having seen no such dream before, and my mind is greatly agitated.' (11)

"Hearing this, the prince replied to Gopá in a voice sweet as the twitter of the sparrow, deep as the sound of the drum, and venerable as that of Brahmá, 'Be of good cheer; no evil can happen to you. Only persons who have performed many virtuous deeds can behold a dream like this; none who has gone through many pains can dream such a dream. (12)

"'What you have seen of the quakings of the earth and of broken peaks fallen on the ground, are nothing more than Devas, Nágas, Rákshasas and beings in general, offering you the highest adoration. (13)

"'What you have seen of trees uprooted and of your hair torn with the right hand, mean that you, Gopá, will quickly rend asunder the trammels of pain, and relieve thy purified vision of all objects of longing. (14)

"'What you have seen of the sun and the moon fallen down, and of stars and planets cast down, mean, dear Gopá, that you will, having destroyed all inimical pains, become the adored and admired of the world. (15)

"'What you have seen of discoloured pearl-necklaces, and of nakedness of your entire body, imply that you, Gopá, will soon exchange your feminine body for that of a man for ever. (16)

"'What you have seen of your bedstead dislocated of its feet, and of the staff and ornaments of the umbrella broken, mean that you, Gopá, will, crossing the fourfold sin, behold me the only umbrellaed one in the three regions. (17)

"'What you have seen of ornaments cast about, and my head-dress and apparel heaped on my bedstead, mean that you, Gopá, will soon behold my person with its auspicious marks bepraised in every region. (18)

"'What you have seen of the hundred millions of lights darting out of the town, and of the palace being immersed in darkness, indicate that I shall, dear Gopá, diffuse the light of knowledge in the regions now enveloped in the darkness of delusion. (19)

"'What you have seen of the pearl necklace destroyed and its rich golden thread torn, betoken that I, rending asunder the network of pain, shall soon redeem the thread of understanding after purifying it. (20)

"'Since, Gopá, you picture me in your (mind) with respect and utmost endeavour, during your daily worship, there is no mishap or grief in store for you; soon shall you attain gratification and pleasure. (21)

"'In former times alms were bestowed by me, good behaviour practised, and forbearance always cultivated; therefore, they shall all enjoy gratification and pleasure who attain my grace. (22)

"Endless purifications have been effected by me for ten millions of years (*kalpas*), and the path of the Bodhi purified by my exertions; therefore they shall all rend asunder the threefold sin who attain my grace. (23)

"'Be of good cheer, and grieve not; feel satisfied, and cultivate affection; you will soon be the possessor of gratification and pleasure. Know, dear Gopá, that these signs are auspicious to you.' (24)

"The being who was full of the glory of virtuous deeds, whose head was the fountain of vigour, dreamt the premonitory dreams which become manifest at the time of departure from home of the noblest of beings, full of the merits of former good deeds. (25)

"He beheld immense hands and feet immersed in the waters of the four great oceans, the earth was in deep sleep, and the noble mountain Meru had bent down its head. (26)

"In dream a light was seen which showed that every one on the earth was immersed in dense darkness. An umbrella was uplifted on the earth, and it was resplendent in the three regions, and on whomsoever its light fell he was freed from all distress, and was restored to peace. (27)

"Four beautiful animals of a black colour were scratching (the earth) with their hands and feet; a wonderful bird of four colours changed into one colour was seen walking over a mound of vile, disgusting filth without being in any way soiled. (28)

"Again he saw in his dream a river full of water whereby were many millions of beings, and he was ferrying them over and placing them on firm ground where there was neither fear nor grief. (29)

"Again, he beheld numerous decrepit people, afflicted with disease, devoid of the capacity for recovery, and totally bereft of strength, and he, becoming a physician, was, by the administration of various medicaments, curing them by millions. (30)

"He saw himself seated on a throne on the top of the Sumeru mountain, and disciples with folded hands were humbly saluting him. He saw himself victorious in the midst of a battle, and the immortals in the sky were cheering him with delightful sounds. (31)

"These were the dreams which the Bodhisattva dreamt; they were full of auspicious and charming deeds, and by hearing of them men and gods were filled with delight. It will not be long before this noble being will become the god of gods and men." (32)

NOTES.

1. *The Bodhisattva, having been thus exhorted by the Devaputra, revealed this dream*, p. 255. The southern versions make no reference to the dream. The 'Buddha-charita' is, likewise, silent about it. But the 'Romantic History' amplifies it greatly. According to it the Devaputra T'so-Ping caused seven dreams to appear to the king. In the first the king beheld "a great imperial banner like that of Indra, around which were gathered innumerable crowds of people, who, lifting it and holding it up, proceeded to carry it through Kapilavastu, and finally went from the city by the Eastern gate." The second made the Prince mount a chariot drawn by great elephants and go out by the Southern gate. The third sent out the Prince mounted on a four-horse chaise by the Western gate. The fourth exhibited a discus going out by the Northern gate. The fifth showed the Prince striking a drum with a large mace in the middle of the four great highways of the city. The sixth placed the Prince on a high tower from which he scattered jewels to a large crowd there assembled. The seventh exhibited six men in the suburbs of the city, wailing and plucking their hair in grief.

The king, upon seeing these, was greatly distressed, and convened a council at night, and another the next morning; but the Bráhmaṇ expounders of dreams in his court failed to interpret the dreams. The Devaputra who had caused the dreams then appeared in court in disguise, and expounded the dreams, the exposition in substance being that the Prince would renounce the world. Beal's 'Romantic Legend,' pp. 111*f.*

2. *Then three palaces fitted for use in different seasons were erected*, p. 255. The 'Romantic Legend' interpolates the palaces in its account of the Prince's attaining his majority. See *ante*, Note 1, p. 217. So does the Siamese text, which describes the palaces and their decorations in some detail. Alabaster's 'Wheel of the Law,' pp. 119 *et seq.*

3. *The Bodhisattva ordered the charioteer, "quickly get the chariot ready; I propose to go to the garden,"* p. 256. The 'Romantic Legend' accounts for the desire to go to the garden by saying that the Devaputra T'so-Ping so influenced the songs of the ladies in the palace that they all related to the charms of the garden in mid-spring, and they created a longing for outdoor recreation. Beal's 'Romantic Legend,' pp. 107, 115. The dream is spontaneous according to Bigandet.

4. *Now on the seventh day the whole town was decorated*, p. 256.

This is a repetition of the preparations made for the tournament, (*ante*, p. 203).

5. *Lord, this is a person overpowered by age*, p. 257. The reply of the charioteer, according to the 'Buddha-charita,' in this, as in the subsequent cases, was inspired by the Devaputra. (Beal's version, p. 33.) It would also have it that the sights seen were visible only to the Prince and his charioteer, but not to the retinue of the Prince (p. 36).

6. 7. *The Bodhisattva caused the chariot to be turned back, and returned to the palace*, p. 559. The *Bodhisattva on another* occasion, started *with a large retinue for the garden, by the northern gate*, p. 559. The return and departure, according to the 'Buddhacharita,' did not take place as stated here. "The charioteer, remembering the king's exhortation, feared much nor dared go back; straight forward then he pressed his panting steeds, passed onward to the gardens, (came to) the groves and babbling streams of crystal water, the pleasant trees, spread out with gaudy verdure." The ladies in

the garden surrounded the Prince and tried their utmost, by the display of their amorous arts and other fascinations, to entertain the Prince, but failed. The Prince remained unmoved. Udáyi, the minister's son, then came to him, and argued with him at great length in order to divert him from his mournful mood. He specially adverted to the instances of Viśvámitra, Agastya, Gautama, S'ankha, Indra, Vṛihaspati, Paráśara, Kavanga and other great Bráhmaṇic saints who had succumbed to the charms of the fair sex. The Prince, however, was greatly superior to him in dialectics, and completely defeated him. The ladies, failing to entertain the Prince, returned to the city in shame and sorrow, and when the garden was deserted by all others, the Prince himself came back, deeply immersed in painful thoughts. Beal's 'Buddha-charita,' pp. 37—46.

8. *Directed to the junction of the two eyes*, p. 260. According to the Yogís, the best way to prevent the mind from wandering during meditation is to keep the eyes directed towards the tip of the nose; but here the bridge of the nose is preferred, though it is not always visible. See my translation of Patañjali, p. 22.

9. *The Bodhisattva caused his chariot to be turned back, and returned to the palace*, p. 260. The 'Buddha-charita' has given quite a different version. According to it the occasion is that of the ploughing match (*ante*, p. 190), when the Prince, after seeing the exercises of the husbandmen, retired to a corner and took his seat under a jambu tree. A Devaputra came to him in the disguise of a Bhikshu, and lectured him on the vanity of the world. On his way back from the garden the Prince met his kinsmen and friends "all of whom, joined in relationship, dreaded the pain of separation." Hearing the words "separation and association" his mind turned towards hermitage, and he repaired to his father, to obtain his permission to retire from the world. (Beal's version, pp. 47 to 52.) The Burmese version gives a different turn to the story. According to it the Prince was returning from the ploughing match in great pomp and state, and when he entered the city, a princess, "named Keissa Gautami, was contemplating from her apartments the triumphant entrance of Phralaong into the city. She admired the noble and graceful deportment of Prince Meiddat, and exclaimed with feelings of inexpressible delight, 'Happy the father and mother who have

such an incomparable son! happy the wife who is blest with such an accomplished husband!' On hearing those words, Phralaong desired to understand their meaning and know their bearing. 'By what means,' said he to himself, 'can a heart find peace and happiness?' And he set about ardently for the happy state of Nirvana." (Bigandet's Legend I, pp. 58 *f.*) The 'Romantic Legend' [p. 21] relegates the visit to the king for his permission after the interview with the Bhikshu.

CHAPTER XV.

THE RENUNCIATION.

The Bodhisattva thinks of leave-taking. Appears before his father's palace. Leave obtained. Arrangements to prevent the Prince's departure. Gautamí's arrangements. The four resolves of the Bodhisattva. Distorted and disgusting condition of the ladies of the palace. The Bodhisattva's 32 reflections. His vision of the celestial hosts worshipping him. His conversation with Chhandaka. Celestial hosts come to worship him. Poetical description of the departure. Grief of the guardian divinity of the city. The Bodhisattva's progress. He parts with his horse and ornaments, cuts off his top-knot and puts on a hermit's garb. Grief in the palace on the Prince's departure. Return of Chhandaka to the palace. Gopá's grief. Chhandaka's description of the departure.

Now, Bhikshus, the Bodhisattva thus reflected; "it would be unbecoming and ungrateful on my part if I should go away without informing the great king S'uddhodana and obtaining the permission of my father." Accordingly, in the depth of the night, descending from the palace in which he was dwelling, he went and stood before the palace of the great king S'uddhodana. As he stood, the whole of the palace became ablaze by the light of his person. The king was thereby awakened, and seeing the light, he called the warder, and asked, "Warder, has the sun arisen from which comes this light?"

The warder replied: "Lord, the first half of the night has scarcely yet transpired.

"'The light of the sun produces shadows of trees and walls; it heats the body and produces perspiration; and ducks, peacocks, parrots, koels, and brahmaṇi-geese raise their respective voices at break of day. (1)

"'This light, however, lord of men, is pleasant and gratifying; it is an exciter of gladness and beneficial; it produces no burning sensations; of walls and trees there is no shadow: it is doubtless due to (our) attaining this day some merit.' (2)

"He, the king, from his seat, cast his eyes on the ten sides; he beheld near him the pure being of faultless eyes. He wished to arise from his bedstead, but did not, the owner of might and knowledge showed his respect for his father (by advancing towards him). (3)

"The Prince, standing in front, thus addressed the king: 'Do not interrupt me any more, nor should you grieve. Lord, the time and moment for my departure having arrived, pardon me, king, on your part and on the part of your kin and people for my act.' (4)

"The king, with tearful eyes, thus replied to him: 'what advantage will there be by thy departure? Ask whatever you require, and I shall grant it. Be merciful to the royal race, to me, and to the kingdom.' (5)

"The sweet-voiced Bodhisattva thus responded: 'Lord, I desire that you should give me four blessings, should you be able to grant them, and with them I shall abide here, and you will always see me in the house, for I shall not depart. (6)

"'I desire, lord, that decay shall never assail me, and I shall continue in my youthful radiance all along. I should always remain in health, and no disease shall attack me. I should be of unmeasured life, and never be subject to death. (7)

"'I should always be abundantly wealthy, and no misfortune shall assail me.' The king was overpowered with deep grief on hearing these words. 'Son, you want what I have no power to grant. The fear of decay, disease, and death as also of misfortune, (8)

Sages, even after living for eons (kalpas), have not been able to overcome.'

"Hearing these words of his father, the Prince said, 'Lord, if you cannot now grant me the four blessings,—freedom from the fear of decay, disease, death and misfortune,—(9)

"'Then listen, king, to my prayer for another gift; it is departure; offer me no obstruction.' On hearing these words of the noble being, the king suppressed his love and rent asunder the bonds of filial affection. (10)

"'Your desire for the emancipation of the world is worthy of encouragement, as it will be beneficial. May your wishes be fulfilled.'"[1] (11)

Now, Bhikshus, the Bodhisattva, returning to his palace, sat on his couch. None could know anything of his going and coming.

Now, Bhikshus, when the night had ended, king S'uddhodana assembled the S'ákyas, and, relating all the facts, asked them: "The Prince is sure to depart. What should we do?"

The S'ákyas said, "Lord, we shall protect him."

"How?"

The S'ákyas said, "We are a host of S'ákyas, and he is alone. What power has he to defeat us by force?"

Thereupon five hundred scions of the S'ákya race, well-armed, highly proficient, well taught in the use of the arrow and other arms, and of mighty power in gymnastics, were, by order of the king, posted at the Eastern gate of the town for the protection of the Bodhisattva. Each of these scions had under him five chariots and a hundred retainers, and each chariot had five fighting men and a hundred followers, and these were posted for the protection of the Prince. Similar bodies of guards were placed at the Southern, Western and the Northern gates (the details are repeated in the text). Elderly S'ákyas, both male and female, placed themselves at every square, at every cross-road and highway, to protect the Prince. King S'uddhodana, attended by a retinue of five hundred chiefs mounted on horseback or on elephants, kept watch all night at the gate of his own palace.

"The Gautama lady Mahláprajápatí sent for her attendants (and ordered them), 'Do ye place bright lights at the door, and set up beacon lights bright as the maṇi jewel on staffs;[2] hang up strings of lights and make this house refulgent. (1)

"'Engage yourselves in music; keep yourselves awake without winking all night; and watch the Prince, so that he may not depart without any one knowing it. (2)

"'Attired in mail, holding quivers, and armed with swords, bows, arrows, iron spears, iron clubs, let every one exert for the protection of my dear son. (3)

"'Close all the gateways with their massive doors, mounted on machines and chains;[3] open them not at improper times, nor allow a single soul to go out of this place. (4)

"'Decorate yourselves with jewelled necklaces, with pearl necklaces, with face ornaments, with crescents, with chains, zones, earrings, chaplets of coins[4] and anklets.

"'Should he suddenly start for the good of men and gods, like a mad elephant, do you so exert your power as not to hurt him. (6)

"'Those of you women holding lances, who protect the bedstead of the Prince,[5] be not drowsy, but keep your eyes open like birds. (7)

"'For the protection of the king cover this room with jewelled net-work. Recite sweet letters and sounds all the night through, and protect the defectless. (8)

"'Let each awake the next; be not remiss; watch all through the night, so that he may not depart, forsaking his kingdom and his royalty. (9)

"'On his departure everything in the royal race will be grievous, and this royal line of long standing will be cut off.'" (10)

Now, Bhikshus, twenty-eight great Yaksha generals led by Paṇchika, the Yaksha generalissimo, and five hundred sons of Hárití (a Yakshiṇí) assembled and held this consultation: "This day, venerable sirs, the Bodhisattva will make his departure; it is meet, therefore, that we should exert ourselves for his worship."

The four great kings (of the quarters), entering the metropolis named Aḍakavatí, invited a large concourse of Yakshas; "this day, venerable sirs, the Bodhisattva will make his departure, and it is meet that he should issue with the feet of his horse sustained by you."[6]

The Yaksha assemblage said; "His nature is as hard as the thunderbolt; that noblest of beings is infrangible, Náráyaṇa himself, endowed with immense power and vigour, and never to be shaken. One may pluck the great Meru as easily as if it were a common hillock, and hold it aloft in the sky; but none can support him who is weighted with the Meru mountain of Jina merits and endowed with virtue and knowledge."

Vais'ravana said: "He, the ruler, is heavy to those men who are inflated with vanity; but know that he is light to those who are weighted with love. With exertion and earnestness apply yourself, and you will find him as light as a floss of cotton flying in the air. I shall march in front; do you bear the horse. In the departure of the Bodhisattva there is a large fund of virtue and respectability."

Now, Bhikshus, S'akra, the king of the gods, addressed the Devas of Trayastriñśa: "this day the Bodhisattva will make his departure, therefore you all should earnestly apply yourselves to his worship."

A Devaputra of the name of Lalitavyúha said, "I shall in the meanwhile put to sleep all men, women, boys and girls in the great city of Kapilavastu."

S'ántasumati, another Devaputra, said, "I shall at the same time make the sound of all the horses, elephants, donkeys, camels, buffaloes, women, men, boys and girls to melt away and be inaudible."

Vyúhamati, a Devaputra, said, "I shall prepare the road through which the Bodhisattva will make his exit by erecting under the sky a line of benches measuring in length seven cars, and resplendent as the diamond and the Maṇí jewel; by setting up along the line parasols, flags, and pennons; by strewing on it various kinds of flowers; and by making it redolent with the aroma of diverse incenses, pills and pastilles."

The Núga king, Airávata, said, "I shall hold up on my trunk a pavilion thirty-two yojanas in extent. Ascending on it the Apsarasas may engage in concert, and by music and songs offer due homage to the progress of the Bodhisattva."

S'akra himself, the king of the Devas, said, "I shall throw open the doors and point out the way."

Dharmachárí, a Devaputra, said, "I shall make the palace to appear repulsive."

Sanchodaka, a Devaputra, said, "I shall make the Bodhisattva arise from his bed."

Then the Nága kings Varuṇa, Manasví, Ságara, Anavatapta, Nanda, and Upananda, thus remarked: "We too shall engage ourselves in the worship of the Bodhisattva; we shall produce a cloud befitting the season, and shower therefrom powdered Uragasára sandal-wood."

Thus, Bhikshus, did the Devas, Nágas, Yakshas, and Gandharvas deliberate and settle their resolves.

When the Bodhisattva was reclining on his bedstead in the female apartments of the palace of music, and cogitating about religion, and thinking of the careers of former Buddhas and the good of the whole creation, four of his former desires presented themselves prominently before his mind. What were these four? "Desiring the supremacy of Sayambhu and the faculty of omniscience I had fortified myself with this resolve. Beholding living beings in pain, I had said, Ah, yes, rending asunder the wheel of the world, I shall proclaim the sound of redemption to those people who have fallen bound on the great wheel of the world; I shall redeem the beings who are loaded with the heavy fetters of desires." This was the first former desire which became prominent.

"Ah, yes, I had said, I shall spread the light of religion, the destroyer of the darkness of ignorance, for the people who have been lost in the wilderness of the world's ignorance and darkness, and whose eyes are enveloped in the case of the darkness of ignorance, and who are devoid of the eye of wisdom. Showing the lamp of knowledge, by administering the medicine of the threefold emancipatory knowledge, with the adjunct of means (*upáya*) and wisdom (*prajñá*) I shall cure the eye of knowledge of those who are blinded by all engrossing ignorance, darkness and dense mass of impervious obscurity." This was the second former desire which became prominent.

"Ah, yes, I had said, for those who have uplifted the standard of vanity, who have immured themselves in pride and selfishness, who are in the grasp of the shark of selfishness (*lit.* me and mine,) I shall rectify the power of cognition, and, by pointing out the true path to those who are in the quest of self, knock down the flag of vanity." This was the third former desire which became prominent.

"Ah, yes, I had said, for those who are of peaceless mind, who are drowsy, who are covered with the veil of quality, who have a velocity which is no velocity, who are whirling about from this region to another, and from that to this, who are not retired from the world, who are mounted on the wheel of fire, I shall unfold a peaceful and sense-satisfying religion." This was the fourth former desire that became prominent.

At this moment the inner apartments were made to appear distorted and repulsive by Dharmachárí, the Devaputra, through certain Devaputras of the class S'uddhávásakáyika. Having made everything appear in a disordered and inauspicious form, the celestials, from under the sky, thus addressed the Bodhisattva in Gáthás:

They said, "the great sages, sons of gods, know that thy eyes are wide open like a full-blown lotus; how can you feel any pleasure in dwelling on this cremation ground?"

Thus exhorted by the chief gods, the Bodhisattva for a moment cast his eyes on the inner apartments; he saw, in short, the ladies lying naked on a cremation ground.

He, the Bodhisattva, cast his eyes on the ladies; he looked at them with attention, (he found) some of them had their dresses in disorder; some of them had their tresses dishevelled; some of them had their ornaments scattered about; some had their tiaras knocked off; some had their chins resting on their shoulders; some had their mouths distorted; some had their eyes staring; some had saliva flowing down their mouths; some were groaning; some were laughing; some were talking wildly; some were grinding their teeth; some had their faces discoloured; some had their beauty disfigured; some had their arms extended; some had their faces distorted; some had their heads uncovered; some had their heads veiled; some had their faces twisted on one side; some had their bodies mutilated; some had their members broken; some were humped; some were troubled with a racking cough; some were reclining on drums (mṛidañgas) with their bodies and heads twisted; some were lying unconsciously while holding in their hands víná, vallaki and other musical instruments; some were making a noise with their teeth by biting their flutes; some were knocking on the kimpala, nakula, sampa, táḍava,[7] and other musical instruments; some were winking and opening their eyes; some were gaping wide. Beholding this repulsive scene of the ladies lying on the ground, the Bodhisattva realised in his mind the idea of the cremation ground.

On this subject this may be said:

"Beholding these, that lord of beings, drawing a merciful sigh, thus spoke in distress: "Alas! how can I associate with the beings here assembled; I must retire to asceticism. Those who associate with worldly persons, immersed in the darkness of delusion and indulging in evil disposition and sensuality, are like birds in a cage; they never acquire their freedom."

Now, the Bodhisattva, having again examined with the opening light of religion the inner apartments and the beings there, and aggrieved by the sense of profound sorrow, thus gave vent to his lamentation:

(1) These stupid beings are being slaughtered, even as the condemned are by hangmen,

(2) These stupid beings are taking delight, even as the ignorant do, in well-painted vases filled with offal,

(3) These stupid beings are sinking, even as elephants do in water,

(4) These stupid beings are being fettered, as are thieves in a prison,

(5) These stupid beings are disposed, as are pigs, to rush into filth,

(6) These stupid beings are attached, as are dogs, to hollow bones,

(7) These stupid beings are dropping, like moths, into the flame of a lamp,

(8) These stupid beings are being destroyed, as are monkeys in a trap, (*valaya* means both a trap or enclosure as also bracelets),

(9) These stupid beings are being tortured, as fishes caught in a net,

(10) These stupid beings are being vexed, as are serpents by sticks,*

(11) These stupid beings are being impaled, as are malefactors on spikes,

(12) These stupid beings are rotting, even as weak elephants do in a morass,

(13) These stupid beings are in distress, as are those whose ships are wrecked in mid-ocean,

(14) These stupid beings are precipitating themselves, as the born-blind do in a large waterfall,

(15) These stupid beings are progressing, like water in a crevice, downwards to the nether regions,

(16) These stupid beings are being smashed, as is the great earth at the end of an eon,

(17) These stupid beings are whirling like a potter's wheel turning on its pivot,

(18) These stupid beings are kept roaming about like the born-blind on a mountain,

(19) These stupid beings are pulling at different sides like leashed dogs,

(20) These stupid beings are being dried up like grass and trees in summer,

(21) These stupid beings are wasting like the moon in the wane,

(22) These stupid beings are being eaten up, as are serpents by Garuḍa,[8]

(23) These stupid beings are being devoured like boats by a great whale, (makara).

* Not given in M. Foucaux's translation.

(24) These stupid beings are being despoiled like caravans by robbers,

(25) These stupid beings are being broken down like sála trees by a storm,

(26) These stupid beings are being killed like animals by fierce poison,

(27) These stupid beings, full of desires, are being cut up, like children, by razors dipped in honey,

(28) These stupid beings are being carried away like wood on a strong current of water,

(29) These stupid beings are playing, like infants, with their own excrement,

(30) These stupid beings are being struck, like elephants, with the goad (*añkuśa*),

(31) These stupid beings are being destroyed like little children by rogues,

(32) These stupid beings are throwing away the root of all good, like wealth by gamblers,

(33) These stupid beings are being eaten up like the merchants by the Rákshasís.[9]

Having by (the sound of) these thirty-two remarks[10] filled the inner apartments, the Bodhisattva conceived the improprieties of the corporeal form, suppressed the idea of repulsion, produced the idea of abhorrence, reflected on his own age, beheld the wretched condition of the body, perceived that one body proceeded from another, reflected on the idea of welfare, suppressed the idea of misfortune, and from the sole of his foot to the top of his head he examined his body; he found it had arisen from impurity, it consisted of impurity, and it continually discharged impurity. At this juncture the following verses were recited:—

"The crop of the field of works is nurtured by the water of desire, and is called body. It is disfigured by tears, perspiration, and exudation of urine; pervaded by molecules of blood; full of the secretions of the pelvis and the head, of pus, fat, and sanies; daily watered by disease; it is replete with filth, and redolent with repulsive odours of various kinds. (1)

"It is a composition of bones, teeth, hair, and fibres; it is encased in an envelope of skin, and covered with hair; within it there are spleen, liver, serum, saliva; it is weak; it is bound by marrow, and tendons, like a (musical) instrument, and shaped with flesh; it is environed by diverse diseases; it has griefs, and is oppressed by hunger and thirst. (2)

"It is, to living beings, a hell with many portals, an abode of death and decay. Who is the sensible person, who, beholding all this, can call his body, the domain of enemies, his own?" (3)

Thus did the Bodhisattva reflect on the body while abiding in his body.

The Devaputras, assembled under the sky, thus addressed Dharmachárí, a Devaputra.

"How is it, sir, that the Bodhisattva is still tarrying? He is looking at the female apartments, he is examining them, and exciting the mind; he is repeatedly closing his eyes. Is it, that this being, profound as the ocean, is unable to fathom the depth; or is his mind not able to renounce his companions? Let him not, invoked by the pure ones, forget his former resolve."

Dharmachárí replied: "Say not so; knowing that, even before this (sight), he had, by the practice of Bodhi, become free. For one who has, by the renunciation of work, already arrived at the last stage, how doubt you that he will be free ?' '

Now, Bhikshus, the Bodhisattva, with firm resolve, unfaltering mind, and determined understanding, descended from the bedstead, with ease proceeded to the Palace of Music, and, standing, facing the east, lowered the jewelled lattice with his right hand.[11] Then entering the chamber, he folded his hands so as to make all his ten nails meet; he invited all the Buddhas of former times, and, saluting them, cast a look towards the sky. He there beheld the sovereign of the immortals, he of a thousand eyes, surrounded by a hundred thousand Devas, holding flowers, incenses, aromatics, flower-garlands, unguents, powders, dresses, parasols, flags, pennons, earrings, jewelled necklaces, and strings, and, with bended body, saluting him.

He beheld, likewise, the four guardians of regions, all attired in armour and mail-coats, armed with swords, bows, arrows, iron clubs, lances, tridents, beautifully decorated with crowns and crests of jewels, and attended by Rakshas, Rákshasas, Gandharvas, and Nágas saluting him.

He beheld, also, the sun and the moon, the two sons of gods, standing on his two sides, and Pushya, the prince of constellations, had arisen.

Seeing that midnight had arrived, the Bodhisattva addressed Chhandaka:

"Tarry not, Chhandaka; bring me the noble horse duly caparisoned. All my blessings have attained maturity; verily my object will this day be accomplished."

On hearing this, Chhandaka, with afflicted heart, thus replied: "Whereto wilt thou proceed, O thou of expanded brow, of eyes rivalling the petals of the lotus; O thou lion among kings, (beautiful as) the fullmoon of autumn, as the white lily full blown by the moon; thou of a face like the fresh-blown lotus, of refulgence like purified gold, or the sun, or the moon without a mark; radiant as the sacrificial fire enlivened by clarified butter; brilliant as the Maṇi jewel, or the lightning; awe-inspiring like the maddened elephant; and of majestic motion like the cow, the bull, the lion, or the swan?"

The Bodhisattva said,

"For that for which I sacrificed my hands, feet, eyes, handsome and dear wives, kingdom, wealth, gold, apparel, (1)

"Richly bejewelled elephants, and horses of mighty power and valour, swift as the wind; for which I cultivated good conduct,[13] cherished forbearance, and assiduously applied myself to vigour, power, meditation, and knowledge, (2)

"For innumerable millions of eons; for coming into contact with the auspicious and peaceful Bodhi. The time has arrived for my redeeming mankind having bodies always subject to decay and death." (3)

Chhandaka observed: "I did hear, honoured sir, that immediately on thy birth thou wast presented to astrologer Bráhmans for examination, and they addressed king S'uddhodana, saying, 'Lord, prosperity will attend thy royal race.' The king asked, 'How so?' They replied, 'This prince of a hundred auspicious marks has taken birth as your son; he is full of the splendour of virtue. He will be a universal sovereign, the lord of the four continents, and master of the seven treasures. Should he, however, cast his eye on the afflicted world and, forsaking the inner apartments, go forth, he will obtain the condition of the decayless and deathless Bodhi, and soothe mankind with the water of religion.'* But, listen, sir, to my wishes and desires."

The Bodhisattva asked, "What are they?"

He replied, "Lord, people undergo divers kinds of fasts and austerities, putting on skins on their body, matted hair on their crowns, and rags and bark for their apparel; they allow their nails and hair and beard to grow long in different styles; they torture the flesh in their body in a variety of ways; they carry on rigorous fasts and austerities. And why so? (In the hope) 'we shall obtain the wealth of men and gods.' Lord, thou hast already attained that wealth. [Thou art the master of] this wealthy, delightful, flourishing, peaceful kingdom, abounding in food and thickly populated; these most excellent gardens, rich in various kinds of fruits and flowers, resonant with the voice of innumerable birds, having tanks decorated with blue, red and white lotuses and water-lilies, and resounding with the cry of geese, peacocks, koels, herons, sárasas, blooming in mangoes, as'okas, champakas, kuvalakas, sessamums, and saffron, planted along their banks,—gardens decorated with numerous jewelled arbours, with flower-beds formed like dice-boards, with jewelled seats interspersed, with jewelled networks hung above, and adapted for enjoyment in every season, replete with the pleasures of the summer, the rainy season, the autumn, and the winter. These lofty palaces are like the cloud

* In some MSS. a line occurs here, the purport of which is not clear, and so it has not been translated.

of autumn, like the lofty Kailás'a mountain, like Vaijayanta,[13] or like the pure court of the gods; they are devoid of grief and annoyances; they are set off with covered courtyards, doors, gates, windows, chambers, pavilions, and turrets covered with networks set with jewelled bells. Such, lord, are the inner apartments; they are resonant with the music of the tunava, panava, vína, flute, sampwara, táḍava, chará, kimpala, nakula, the sweet-sounding mṛidanga, and the drum,—with dancing, singing, joyous and charming concerts, with laughter, gestures, plays, and other enticing accomplishments. And thou, son of a god, art youthful; thou hast neither exceeded juvenescence, nor art considered young; with a soft body, fresh black hair, by no means passed the age of enjoyment. Therefore, do thou enjoy, like Indra of the thousand eyes, the lord of the immortals. After that we can retire."

At that time this Gáthá was recited :—

"O, thou, proficient in amorous enjoyments, enjoy even as does the lord of the immortals in the region of the three-times-ten; thereafter, having attained maturity, we shall commence fasts and penances."

The Bodhisattva said, "Verily, all these objects of enjoyment, Chhandaka, are transitory, fleeting, inconstant, and naturally changing; passing away with the rapidity of a mountain torrent; transient as dewdrops; sorrowful; hollow as an empty fist; weak as the trunk of the plantain tree; painful like unwholesome food; like the autumn cloud now produced and now gone; transient as the lightning in the sky; producing ultimate mischief like poisonous food; pain-producing as the máru-creeper; [worthless] as the scribblings of persons of infantile sense; comparable to bubbles on water; naturally quickly changing; like the illusion of a mirage; arising from a perversion of cognizance; comparable to illusions; proceeding from perverseness of the mind; comparable to dreams; derivable by acceptance through the perversion of vision; full of suffering like the sea; exciter of thirst like salt water; difficult of touch like the head of a serpent; fit to be avoided by sages like a great precipice; full of dangers, quarrels, faults and vices. Known as such they are avoided by the wise, condemned by the learned, censured by the respectable, shunned by the sensible, accepted by the senseless, and indulged in by the ignorant."

At that time this Gáthá stanza was recited:

"To be shunned by the sensible as the head of a serpent; condemnable as an impure pot of urine; knowing sensuous desires to be the destroyers of all (true) enjoyment, Chhandaka, I feel no sympathy for them."

Then Chhandaka, like one pierced with a dart, crying with tearful eyes, full of sorrow, thus remarked:

"Lord, for that for which some undergo manifold and rigorous fasts, have hairy skin, matted hair, long hair, long nails, long beard, and beggar's garb; or, wearing bark, many with emaciated body betake to fasts, live upon herbs, coarse grains, nettles *(Ovidea verticellata)*, holding their heads upwards, observe the penance of the cow[14], (1)

"Cherishing the hope 'we shall hereby be the noblest, the pre-eminent, in this world, the highest emperors, the guardians of quarters, or S'akra, the wielder of the thunderbolt, or Yama, or the lords of the Devas, or of the Nirmitas, or dwell in the region of Brahmá, the deviser of the felicity of meditation.' (2)

"All that, thou, the noblest of men, hast at thy command. Thy kingdom is vast, rich, prosperous; thy gardens and pleasure-grounds and palaces are lofty as the Vaijayanta (palace of Indra). Thy female apartments are resounding with the sounds of the flute and the lute, with songs and music, with dancing and concerts, in well-trained harmony;—enjoy these desirable objects, and depart not, O thou compassionate lord!"

The Bodhisattva said:

"Chhandaka, listen; hundreds of sufferings have been endured by me in my former existences,—fetters, imprisonments, beatings, menaces,—for sensuous objects, but they have not produced peace of mind. (1)

"Formerly, my pure mind was overcome by sensuous desires, bewildered by delusion; my vision was blinded by film; these desires are the suppressors of the cognition of self, and the leaders to the path of pain. (2)

"They are produced by the want of knowledge of religion; they are fickle, changing constantly like the cloud; they are like the lightning; they may be compared to dewdrops; they are hollow, worthless, and unsubstantial; they have no soul; they are naturally void. (3)

"My mind takes no delight in such objects. Bring me, Chhandaka, my noble charger, Kaṇṭhaka, duly caparisoned. Thereby may be accomplished my former aspirations. I shall now be the noblest of all, the lord of all religion, the sovereign of religion, the sage." (4)

Chhandaka said:

"Forsake not these resplendent sleeping ladies, with eyes beautiful as the petals of a full-blown lotus; these decorated with magnificent necklaces and jewels and precious stones; these (beings) brilliant as the lightning detached from the cloud in the sky. (1)

"How do you think of abandoning concerts of the sweet-toned flute, the *paṇava*, the *mṛidaṅga* and the *vaṅśa*,—these sounding like the voice of the *chakora* and the *kalaviṅka* as in the homes of the Kinnarís? (2)

"The pleasing utpala, the autumnal champakas, the sweet-scented garlands of threaded flowers, the odorous incense and the excellent black frankincense; reject them not, nor the unguents and the vestments. (3)

"These viands, well dressed and of excellent flavour and taste, these beverages well mixed with sugar,—do not reject them. Lord, whereto are you going? (4)

"These excellent unguents, warm in winter and soothing in the summer, made of the uragasára sandal-wood, these vestments of Benares, these excellent and charming clothings—reject them not. Lord, whereto are you going? (5)

"These are the five (classes of) objects of desire (dear) even to the greatest of the gods; enjoy them, O master of the power of enjoyment! Afterwards you can retire to the forest, O noble S'ákya!" (6)

The Bodhisattva replied:

"For uncountable and endless eons have I, Chhandaka, enjoyed these sensuous objects of beauty, sound, odour, flavour, and taction, of all the various kinds known to man; but I have not been gratified thereby. (1)

"By me, son of a noble king, sovereignty has been exercised over an empire comprising the four continents,—an emperor lording over the seven jewels. I have had the fullest share of the pleasures of the female apartments. I have reigned over the lords of the three-times-ten, and of the Yámas. (2)

"Forsaking them, when I retired from here to the region of the Nirmitas, I enjoyed the proudest and the noblest of beauty; I exercised sovereignty over the lord of the Súras, and revelled in the richest objects of desire; but I have not been gratified thereby. (3

"What satisfaction can I then this day derive by indulging in these worthless objects? I shall therefore, Chhandaka, abjure this painful world immersed in a wilderness of grief, (4)

"Always burning in the wild fire of pain, without shelter, without a future, in the dense darkness of delusion and ignorance, always oppressed by the fear of decay, disease and death, overcome by the pain of birth, and overpowered by enemies. (5)

"Knowing this I shall embark on board the barque of religion, which is firm as adamant, and loaded with the cargo of penance, good behaviour, complaisance, vigour, (occult) power, benevolence; stout of back, which is made of the adamant of exertion, and stoutly bound together. (6)

"Going on board that vessel I shall first ferry myself over, and then shall I rescue countless beings from all worldly sins, and carry them across the ocean of grief, swelling with the billows of anger, infested by the sharks of passions and enemies, and difficult to pass over. This is my wish. (7)

"After ferrying me across this worldly ocean with its sharks of inimical desires and the cannibals of pain, I shall place the countless beings in the sky of peace, in decaylessness, and immortality." (8)

On hearing this, Chhandaka wept bitterly, and then asked, "Is this your unalterable resolve?"

The Boddhisattva replied, "Listen to me, Chhandaka, for the emancipation of beings, for their welfare, my resolve is fixed, unalterable, changeless, firm, and as immovable as the noble Meru mountain."

Chhandaka enquired, "Lord, what may be your resolution?"

The Boddhisattva replied: "Were the adamantine thunderbolt, the battle-axe, the iron club, arrows and stones to fall in showers, were the lightning to lose its brightness, iron to melt into a fluid, were the crest of the mountain burning aglow to fall on my head, still the desire for home would not revive in me."

At this moment the immortals, assembled in the sky, cast showers of flowers, and raised the joyous cry, "Glory be to the Lord, the supreme owner of intelligence, who grants security to the world! Nothing can tinge the mind of the noble being, no more than can darkness, dust or meteors stain the sky; it can no more imbibe a desire for worldly pleasures than the new-blown lotus the clear water."

Now, Bhikshus, the Devaputras S'ántamati and Lalitavyúha,[15] having heard the firm resolve of the Bodhisattva, put to sleep the whole of the men, women, boys and girls of Kapilavastu, and suppressed every sound.

Now, Bhikshus, the Bodhisattva, perceiving that the inhabitants of the town were all asleep, that midnight had arrived, and that the lord of the stellar heaven was in the constellation Pushya,[16] knowing, too, that the time for departure had arrived, thus addressed Chhandaka, "Grieve not, Chhandaka; bring me Kaṇṭhaka duly caparisoned, and tarry not."

No sooner was this speech delivered, than the four guardians of the quarters heard it, and forthwith they retired to their respective homes, and, performing the worship of the Bodhisattva in their chamber, quickly returned to the great city of Kapilavastu.

There, too, came from the east Máhárájá Dhṛitaráshṭra, the lord of the Gandharvas, attended by innumerable hundreds of thousands of millions of followers, playing on various musical instruments. Arriving there, he circumambulated the great city of Kapilavastu, and, taking his position on the east side, stood saluting the Bodhisattva.

From the south came the great king Virúḍhaka, attended by tens of millions of hundreds of thousands of Kumbháṇḍakas, carrying in their hands many necklaces of pearls, and bringing jewels of various kinds, and pitchers full of scented waters of different descriptions. Arriving there, he circumambulated the great city of Kapilavastu, and at the southern spot from which he had started on his circumambulation took his position, and stood saluting the Bodhisattva.

In the same way from the west quarter came the great king Virúpáksha, attended by many tens of millions of hundreds of thousands of Nágas with numerous pearl necklaces, various kinds of jewels and aromatic powders, produced in the rainy season, and blowing zephyrs loaded with perfumè. Arriving there, he circumambulated the great city of Kapilavastu, and at the spot on the west from which he had started on his circumambulation, took his position, and stood saluting the Bodhisattva.

From the northern quarter came the great king Kuvera, attended by ten millions of hundreds of thousands of Yakshas bringing diamonds, jewels, and precious stones, and holding lamps and flambeaus in their hands, and armed with bows, swords, arrows, iron clubs, tomaras, tridents, discuses, kanayas,[17] darts, and other offensive instruments, and protected by stout armour and mail-coats. Having arrived there, he circumambulated the great city of Kapilavastu, and, coming to the spot from which he had started on his circumambulation, took his position on the north, and stood saluting the Bodhisattva.

S'akra, the king of the gods, also came, accompanied by the gods of the class Tráyastriñs'at, bringing excellent flowers, pastilles, essences, flower garlands, unguents in powder, apparel, parasols, standards, pennants, and ornaments. Having arrived, he circumambulated the great city of Kapilavastu, and, coming to the spot from which he had started on his circumambulation, took his position with his companions in the sky, and remained saluting the Bodhisattva.

Now, Bhikshus, Chhandaka, having heard the words of the Bodhisattva with tear-bedimmed eyes, thus addressed him; "Venerable sir, thou knowest well the time, the moment, the opportunity; this is not a fit time for departure. Now, what dost thou ordain?"

The Bodhisattva replied, "Chhandaka, this is the time."

Chhandaka enquired, "for what purpose is this the time?"

The Bodhisattva answered: "For that for which I longed for ages,—for the salvation of mankind. I desired and longed that, after attaining the decayless and deathless rank of the Bodhi, I may rescue the world; the moment for that has arrived."

This is the law of religion.

On this subject it may be said:

"The gods of the earth and of the sky, as also the guardians, S'akra, the sovereign of the gods, and his suite, the Devas of the class Yáma, as also the Tushitas, Nirmitas, Paranirmitas and Devas of other classes, (1)

"Varuṇa, also Manasví, the king of the Nágas, Anavattapta, Ságara,—they all assembled to worship the noble being at the time of his departure. (2)

"Such of the Devas of the Rúpávachara region, as were of peaceful conduct, and always devoted to meditation, also came in a body for the worship of the adored of the three regions, the noblest of men. (3)

"From the ten quarters came Bodhisattvas with their respective suites who had formerly followed the (three) jewels, impelled by the desire—'we shall behold the departure of the Jina, and perform due worship.' (4)

Pariśishṭaparvan (Sans.) Fasc. I—III @ /6/ each ..	Rs. 1	2
Pingala Chhandaḥ Sútra, (Sans.) Fasc. I—III @ /6/ each	1	2
Prithiráj Rásau, (Sans.) Fasc. I—VI @ /6/ each	2	4
Ditto (English) Fasc. I	0	12
Páli Grammar, (English) Fasc. I and II @ /6/ each	0	12
Prákṛita Lakshaṇam, (Sans.) Fasc. I	1	8
Parásara Smṛiti (Sans.) Fasc. I—V @ /6/ each	1	14
Śrauta Sútra of Ápastamba, (Sans.) Fasc. I—XII @ /6/ each ..	4	8
Ditto Áśvaláyana, (Sans.) Fasc. I—XI @ /6/ each ..	4	2
Ditto Láṭyáyana (Sans.) Fasc. I—IX @ /6/ each ..	3	6
Ditto Śánkháyana (Sans.) Fasc. I—II @ /6/ each ..	0	12
Sáma Veda Saṃhitá, (Sans.) Vols. I, Fasc. 1—10; II, 1—6; III, 1—7; IV, 1—6; V, 1—8, @ /6/ each Fasc.	18	14
Sáhitya Darpaṇa, (English) Fasc. I—IV @ /6/ each	1	8
Sánkhya Aphorisms of Kapila, (English) Fasc. I and II @ /6/ each ..	0	12
Sarva Darśana Sangraha, (Sans.) Fasc. II	0	6
Śankara Vijaya, (Sans.) Fasc. II and III @ /6/ each	0	12
Sánkhya Pravachana Bháshya, (English) Fasc. III	0	6
Sánkhya Sára, (Sans.) Fasc. I	0	6
Suśruta Saṃhitá, (Eng.) Fasc. I and II @ /12/ each	1	8
Taittiríya Áraṇya Fasc. I—XI @ /6/ each	4	2
Ditto Bráhmaṇa (Sans.) Fasc I—XXIV @ /6/ each	9	0
Ditto Saṃhitá, (Sans.) Fasc I—XXXIII @ /6/ each	12	6
Ditto Prátiśákhya, (Sans.) Fasc. I—III @ /6/ each	1	2
Ditto and Aitareya Upanishads, (Sans.) Fasc. II and III @ /6/ each	0	12
Ditto Aitareya Svetáśvatara Kena Íśá Upanishads, (English) Fasc. I and II @ /6/ each	0	12
Táṇḍyá Bráhmaṇa, (Sans.) Fasc. I—XIX @ /6/ each	7	2
Tattva Chintámaṇi, Fasc. I—IV (Sans.) @ /6/ each	1	8
Uttara Naishadha, (Sans.) Fasc. III—XII @ /6/ each	3	12
Uvásagadasáo, Fasc. I and II @ /12/	1	8
Váyu Puráṇa, (Sans.) Vol. I, Fasc. 1—6; Vol. II, Fasc. 1—6, @ /6/ each Fasc.	4	8
Vishṇu Smṛiti, (Sans.) Fasc. I—II @ /6/ each	0	12
Vivádáratnákar, Fasc. I and II @ /6/	0	12
Vrihannáradiya Purána, Fasc. I	0	6
Yoga Sútra of Patanjali, (Sans. & English) Fasc. I—V @ /14/ each ..	4	6
The same, bound in cloth	5	2

Arabic and Persian Series.

'Álamgírnámah, with Index, (Text) Fasc. I—XIII @ /6/ each ..	4	14
Áín-i-Akbarí, (Text) Fasc. I—XXII @ 1/ each	22	0
Ditto (English) Vol. I (Fasc. I—VII)	12	4
Akbarnámah, with Index, (Text) Fasc. I—XXXVI @ 1/ each ..	36	0
Bádsháhnámah with Index, (Text) Fasc. I—XIX @ /6/ each ..	7	2
Beale's Oriental Biographical Dictionary, pp. 291, 4to., thick paper, @ 4/12; thin paper	4	8
Dictionary of Arabic Technical Terms and Appendix, Fasc. I—XXI @ 1/ each	21	0
Farhang-i-Rashídí (Text), Fasc. I—XIV @ 1/ each	14	0
Fihrist-i-Ṭúsí, or, Ṭúsy's list of Shy'ah Books, (Text) Fasc. I—IV @ /12/ each	3	0
Futúḥ-ul-Shám Waqidí, (Text) Fasc. I—IX @ /6/ each	3	0
Ditto Azádí, (Text) Fasc. I—IV @ /6/ each	1	8
Haft Ásmán, History of the Persian Mansawi (Text) Fasc I ..	1	18
History of the Caliphs, (English) Fasc. I—VI @ /12/ each ..	4	2
Iqbálnámah-i-Jahángírí, (Text) Fasc. I—III @ /6/ each ..	1	8
Iṣabáh, with Supplement, (Text) 40 Fasc. @ /12/ each	30	2
Maghází of Wáqidí, (Text) Fasc. I—V @ /6/ each	1	10
Muntakhab-ul-Tawáríkh, (Text) Fasc. I—XV @ /6/ each ..	5	14
Muntakhab-ul-Tawáríkh (English) Vol. II, Fasc. I—IV @ /12/ each ..	3	0
Muntakhab-ul-Lubáb, (Text) Fasc. I—XVIII @ /6/ each	7	2

(Turn over.)

Mu'áṣir-i-'Álamgírí (Text), Fasc. I—VI @ /6/ each .. Rs.	2	4
Nukhbat-ul-Fikr, (Text) Fasc. I	0	6
Niẓámí's Khiradnámah-i-Iskandarí. (Text) Fasc. I and II @ /12/ each ..	1	8
Suyúṭy's Itqán, on the Exegetic Sciences of the Koran, with Supplement, (Text) Fasc. II—IV, VII—X @ 1/ each	7	0
Ṭabaqát-i-Náṣirí, (Text) Fasc. I—V @ /6/ each	1	14
Ditto (English) Fasc. I—XIV @ /12/ each	10	8
Táríkh-i-Fírúz Sháhi, (Text) Fasc. I—VII @ /6/ each	2	10
Táríkh-i-Baihaqí, (Text) Fasc. I—IX @ /6/ each	3	6
Wís o Rámín, (Text) Fasc. I—V @ /6/ each	1	14
Zafarnámah, Fasc. I—V @ /6/ each	1	14

ASIATIC SOCIETY'S PUBLICATIONS.

1.	ASIATIC RESEARCHES. Vols. VII, IX to XI; Vols. XIII and XVII, and Vols. XIX and XX @ /10/ each .. Rs.	80	0
	Ditto Index to Vols. I—XVIII	5	0
2.	PROCEEDINGS of the Asiatic Society from 1865 to 1869 (incl.) @ /4/ per No.; and from 1870 to date @ /6/ per No.		
3.	JOURNAL of the Asiatic Society for 1843 (12), 1844 (12), 1845 (12), 1846 (5), 1847 (12), 1848 (12), 1850 (7), @ 1/ per No. to Subscribers and @ 1/8 per No. to Non-Subscribers; and for 1851 (7), 1857 (6). 1858 (5), 1861 (4), 1864 (5), 1865 (8), 1866 (7), 1867 (6), 1868 (6). 1869 (8), 1870 (8), 1871 (7), 1872 (8), 1873 (8), 1874 (8), 1875 (7), 1876 (7), 1877 (8), 1878 (8), 1879 (7), 1880 (8), 1881 (7), 1882 (6), 1883 (5), 1884 (6), @ 1/ per No. to Subscribers and @ 1/8 per No. to Non-Subscribers.		
	N. B. The figures enclosed in brackets give the number of Nos. in each Volume.		
	Centenary Review of the Researches of the Society from 1784—1883 ..	3	0
	General Cunningham's Archæological Survey Report for 1863-64 (Extra No., J. A. S. B., 1864)	1	8
	Theobald's Catalogue of Reptiles in the Museum of the Asiatic Society (Extra No., J. A. S. B., 1868)	1	8
	Catalogue of Mammals and Birds of Burmah, by E. Blyth (Extra No., J. A. S. B., 1875)	3	0
	Sketch of the Turki Language as spoken in Eastern Turkestan, Part II, Vocabulary, by R. B. Shaw (Extra No., J. A. S. B., 1878) ..	3	0
	A Grammar and Vocabulary of the Northern Balochí Language, by M. L. Dames (Extra No., J. A. S. B., 1880)	3	0
	Introduction to the Maithili Language of North Bihár, by G. A. Grierson, Part I, Grammar (Extra No., J. A. S. B., 1880)	1	8
	Part II, Chrestomathy and Vocabulary (Extra No., J. A. S. B., 1882) ..	3	0
5.	Anis-ul-Musharrahin	3	0
6	Catalogue of Fossil Vertebrata	2	0
8.	Catalogue of the Library of the Asiatic Society, Bengal	3	8
9.	Examination and Analysis of the Mackenzie Manuscripts by the Rev. W. Taylor	2	0
10.	Han Koong Tsew, or the Sorrows of Han, by J. Francis Davis ..	1	8
11.	Iṣṭiláhát-uṣ-Ṣúfíyah, edited by Dr. A. Sprenger, 8vo.	1	0
12.	Ináyah, a Commentary on the Hidayah, Vols. II and IV, @ 16/ each ..	32	0
13.	Jawámi-ul-'ilm ir-riyáẓí, 168 pages with 17 plates, 4to. Part I ..	2	0
14.	Khizánat-ul-'ilm	4	0
15.	Mahábhárata, Vols. III and IV, @ 20/ each	40	0
16.	Moore and Hewitson's Descriptions of New Indian Lepidoptera, Parts I—II, with 5 coloured Plates, 4to. @ 6/ each	12	0
17.	Puraṇa Sangraha, I (Markandeya Purana), Sanskrit	1	0
18.	Sharaya-ool-Islám	4	0
19.	Tibetan Dictionary by Csoma de Körös	10	0
20.	Ditto Grammar " "	8	0
21.	Vuttodaya, edited by Lt.-Col. G. E. Fryer	2	0

Notices of Sanskrit Manuscripts, Fasc. I—XX @ 1/ each	20	0
Nepalese Buddhist Sanskrit Literature, by Dr. R. L. Mitra	5	0

N.B. All Cheques, Money Orders &c. must be made payable to the "Treasurer Asiatic Society" only.

CPSIA information can be obtained
at www.ICGtesting.com
Printed in the USA
BVOW06s1157011117
499155BV00019BA/1014/P